# Immigrants in Industrial America

## 1850-1920

Edited by Richard L. Ehrlich

Published for the Eleutherian Mills–Hagley Foundation
and the Balch Institute
by the University Press of Virginia
Charlottesville

THE UNIVERSITY PRESS OF VIRGINIA


*First published 1977*

Proceedings of a Conference Sponsored by the Balch Institute and the Eleutherian Mills–Hagley Foundation November 1–3, 1973



Frontispiece: Rear of Stark Mills, Amoskeag (Mills) nos. 4, 5, and 8, circa 1890. (Courtesy Manchester Historic Association.)

Library of Congress Cataloging in Publication Data
Main Entry under title:

Immigrants in industrial America, 1850–1920.

1. Alien labor–United States–History–Congresses. 2. United States–Foreign population–History–Congresses. 3. Ethnicity–Congresses. I. Ehrlich, Richard L., 1943– II. Balch Institute. III. Eleutherian Mills–Hagley Foundation, Greenville, Del.
HD8081.A5I48 331.6′2′0973 76-56376
ISBN 0-8139-0678-4



Printed in the United States of America

# Contents

# Tables

Immigrants in Industrial America

# Figures

# Introduction

## *Richard L. Ehrlich*

In late 1972 discussions began among members of the Eleutherian Mills–Hagley Foundation staff regarding the sponsorship of a conference designed to explore the relationship between immigration and industrialization. Since one of the Foundation's goals is the encouragement of the study, knowledge, and appreciation of industrial history, the choice of topics for a number of Foundation symposia has been a reflection of these concerns. After giving careful consideration to the scope and relative importance of this particular topic, the Conference committee concluded that the immigrants-in-industry proposal had considerable merit.

Further enhancing the appeal of this particular project was an awareness that ethnic studies in general had recently begun to attract the attention of a number of able young scholars. Since most of these investigators were not economic historians, and since, as a consequence, their work transcended the normal scope of the Foundation's endeavors, it was decided to attempt to obtain outside guidance and support for this undertaking. To this end, contact was made with the Balch Institute of Philadelphia, an organization specializing in immigration, ethnic, racial, and minority group history, and with Professor Herbert Gutman of the City College of New York. After several exploratory meetings, the Balch Institute agreed to sponsor jointly the Conference and the publication of the proceedings. A steering committee composed of staff members representing both institutions was established, and subsequently discussions were held with Professor Gutman, who provided invaluable assistance in shaping the Conference's focus and in choosing participants.

Collectively, the papers presented ably illustrate an emerging consensus among a sizable group of historians regarding the significance of ethnicity as a factor in the interaction between immigrants and the urban-industrial environment encountered in the United States. Thus, the most pervasive and certainly the most significant theme of the Conference is encompassed in the argument that the behavior of immigrants in America was very much a function of their respective ethnic backgrounds rather than being exclusively a reflection of external circumstances, such as class membership. This, of course, implies that, ultimately, behavioral patterns defined in the New World can be explained only with reference to the specific experience of different groups in the Old.

This point of view runs counter to the melting pot thesis which, until very recently, dominated the historiography of ethnic history. Rejecting the proposition that the encounter with industrial America was overwhelmingly disorienting and destructive of traditional life-styles, the authors assert that the immigrant peoples who flocked to the United States in such great numbers brought with them highly resilient cultures that were able to survive in their new environment. Because of this resilience, the immigrants are seen not as passive agents upon whom a new and alien culture was quickly imposed but rather as individuals able to maintain their customs and, to some extent, to influence the institutional forms they encountered in the United States.

Four of the papers presented arrived at these conclusions by focusing on the immigrant family and its relationship to the industrial environment of the nineteenth and early twentieth centuries. For example, in an analysis of the Polish experience in Philadelphia, Caroline Golab finds that in spite of the vicissitudes encountered in America, these newcomers were able to maintain their traditional family relationships in the United States. In formulating this proposition, Professor Golab relies heavily on approximately four hundred oral interviews conducted with persons who provided personal statements of their own experiences. These interviews document the strenuous and, in the author's view, largely successful efforts of Polish women to secure employment compatible with their cultural heritage as well as the vigor in the United States of the same pattern of familial solidarity that was a hallmark of the Polish family in the Old World.

Similar findings are reported for Irish and German women in New York City's Sixth Ward by Carol Groneman. Based largely on data drawn from the 1855 New York State manuscript census schedules, this study establishes that among the Irish, unmarried women commonly worked outside the home; however, once married, they sought work that allowed them to remain at home and shoulder the traditional responsibilities of motherhood. Coupling this observation with evidence indicating that immigrant households in the Sixth Ward exhibited a stable structural pattern, Professor Groneman concludes that "even when forced by necessity to work, [immigrants] did so in ways that would reinforce, rather than disrupt, their traditional familial values" (p. 40).

Tamara Hareven also rejects the view that immigrants were simply passive agents in the process of industrialization. Relying heavily on a very rich collection of business records of the Amoskeag Mills of Manchester, N.H., Hareven details a fascinating pattern of interaction between the transplanted culture of the French Canadians who worked in Manchester's textile industry and the realities of work in the mills. She concludes that the immigrant laborers were in fact able to recreate certain patterns of kin relationships indigenous to their homeland. But a note of caution is also introduced against carrying the revision of the stereotype of family passivity and disintegration to the other extreme, which, in the author's opinion, is "as removed from historical reality as the earlier image of social breakdown" (p. 49).

Virginia Yans-McLaughlin in her study of Buffalo, N.Y., Italians documents their efforts to preserve traditional family relationships in the face of economic pressures that obliged married women to seek employment. Rather than risk undermining the customary role of the mother in the home by allowing her to work within the context of the urban-factory setting, Italian families opted instead for cannery and field work for the women and children. According to Professor Yans-McLaughlin, the canneries "provided a unique work opportunity where laboring and living spaces existed in close proximity." Under these circumstances, mothers could supervise their own offspring in the sheds and be paid for the efforts of both, or, in the case of children too young to be useful, they could work assured that "in the living quarters, ever-present parents and kin kept a watchful eye on all community members" (p. 72). The adaptation which these arrangements represent is presented as evidence of the validity of stressing in ethnic history a reciprocal and dynamic relationship between the immigrant's culture and the conditions encountered in his new environment.

Instead of concentrating on the family in demonstrating the resilience of immigrant cultures, three papers look at the relationship between immigrants and politics in Jersey City, the organization and management of American industry, and the use of the boycott by certain members of the working class in the United States. In the essay dealing with Jersey City, Douglas Shaw shows clearly the expression in politics of both native and Irish cultures during the nineteenth century. Before 1860 politics in this city were firmly under the control of its native-born citizens, who, according to the author, "attempted to use the city's institutions to coerce the Irish into new cultural and behavioral norms" (p. 88). The decade of the sixties marked the triumph of the Irish in Jersey City politics and, as a consequence, was a period during which the Irish were able to adjust the operations of city government in order to sustain their culture. However, this success was short-lived as nativist elements in the city were able during the early 1870s to thwart Irish gains. This was accomplished in collaboration with the largely native-born state legislature through charter revisions that had the effect of stripping the Irish of political power in the city for a period of at least fifteen years.

Managerial reform is the focus of David Montgomery, who asserts that the propensity of immigrants to behave according to norms that were at variance with the expectations of industrial employers was a primary causal factor in the interest shown during the early twentieth century in corporate welfare programs, professional personnel management, and scientific management. Collectively, these programs were designed to improve productivity, but, according to Montgomery, immigrants were frequently able to thwart the intent of employers. Their success during the first quarter of the twentieth century is largely attributed to the strength of what are referred to as "preindustrial cultures" in the United States as well as the adoption of American working-class mores.

Michael Gordon also chronicles the transfer of culture in his study of boycotting by Irish immigrants in New York City during the 1880s. Gordon traces the origin of the boycott from roots in Ireland, where it emerged in the context of a struggle with English landlords. In Ireland the boycott represented an effort to bring to bear family and community pressures on offending parties through social ostracism. This tactic was brought to the United States by immigrants who broadened the weapon's scope to include economic sanctions imposed against businesses which, for various reasons, incurred the ire of Irish-Americans. Therefore, it is argued that "the boycott represented an assertion of Irish cultural identity in Ireland *and* New York" (p. 114), and that modification in the United States of this Old World behavior should be seen as part of an ongoing process of acculturation.

The Laurie, Hershberg, Alter paper and the papers of Laurence Glasco and Clyde Griffen rely heavily on quantitative data—manuscript population censuses, manuscript manufacturing censuses, city directories, tax lists, and techniques that have only recently attracted the attention of scholars concerned with occupational mobility. These essays demonstrate the shortcomings of models of occupational stratification that do not adequately take into account the rapid changes that occurred in the nature of work during the nineteenth century. Furthermore, by focusing on the hierarchy of nineteenth-century industrial employment and the manner in which immigrants fit into this picture, the authors raise a note of caution not, for the most part, strongly in evidence in the other contributions to this volume regarding the great emphasis placed on ethnicity in explaining the experience of immigrants in the United States.

The Laurie, Hershberg, Alter study is an outgrowth of the data collected by the Philadelphia Social History Project, which Hershberg heads. It seeks to document alterations in the occupational hierarchy within the city's fourteen largest industries between 1850 and 1880, and also develop a profile of the ethnic composition and occupational distribution of the male labor force during the same period. The findings document the weakness of analyses of occupational status tied to static contemporary models of stratification. The authors also discover that while the generally accepted conclusion that Irish immigrants were heavily represented at the bottom of the economic ladder, Germans in between, and native-born at the top held true in Philadelphia, the occupational distribution for sons of immigrants and native-born indicates a degree of convergence that undermines the credibility of ethnicity as a factor in predicting the kind of career the offspring of immigrants would pursue.

Using the Irish, Germans, and native-born whites of mid–nineteenth century Buffalo as a case study, Laurence Glasco also investigates the relationship between ethnicity and occupations. Quantitative data for this analysis are drawn from the New York State manuscript census for 1855, which is employed to construct a profile of occupational stratification as well as to determine the correlation between skill and two demographic variables, age and persistence. Also investigated is the degree to which variations in patterns of property ownership, family structure, and fertility rates were attributable simply to variations in employment and resultant socioeconomic status rather than underlying ethnocultural differences. The findings lead to the conclusion that except for the Germans, age and persistence did not have a major impact on occupations and that adjusting for variables such as level of skill reduced, but by no means eliminated, the differences in property ownership, household structure, and fertility noted among the ethnic groups studied.

Clyde Griffen's scrutiny of the careers of Poughkeepsie, N.Y. German, Irish, and native-born workers between the 1830s and the turn of the century is, like the Laurie, Hershberg, Alter and Glasco papers, important both for its innovative methodology as well as its findings. Griffen's research relies heavily on tracing the careers of working-class residents of Poughkeepsie through successive census enumerations in order to determine the role played by factory employment in mobility as well as the significance of self-employment for status and economic well-being. His findings are essentially the same as those of the Laurie study, which found that for many, factory work represented a step up the economic ladder and that self-employment after the Civil War increasingly became a liability rather than a manifestation of economic well-being and independence.

The meeting concluded with a summation by John Modell, who complained that the importance of ethnicity in understanding the interaction between American society and the immigrant was at least an underlying assumption of all papers presented at the conference. This point of view, Modell argued, is not shared by all scholars in the field, and hence it would have been useful to have some representation from the opposing camp on the program. Professor Modell then proceeded to step into the breach he perceived by asking whether what he called the "sophisticated filiopietism" of the revisionists who dominated the conference does not in fact distort the old assimilation-acculturation paradigm which they purport to be testing. He suggested that the so-called classical synthesis which is under fire has not necessarily been discredited by the new ethnic history because these studies have characteristically focused on relatively short time periods. Only after broadening the chronological scope of such investigations will it be possible to determine "whether in fact the hypothesized linear trends—assimilation, acculturation, mobility-to-white-collar, family nuclearization, and rationalization of life in general have taken place" (p. 208).

*Greenville, Delaware*
*November 1975*

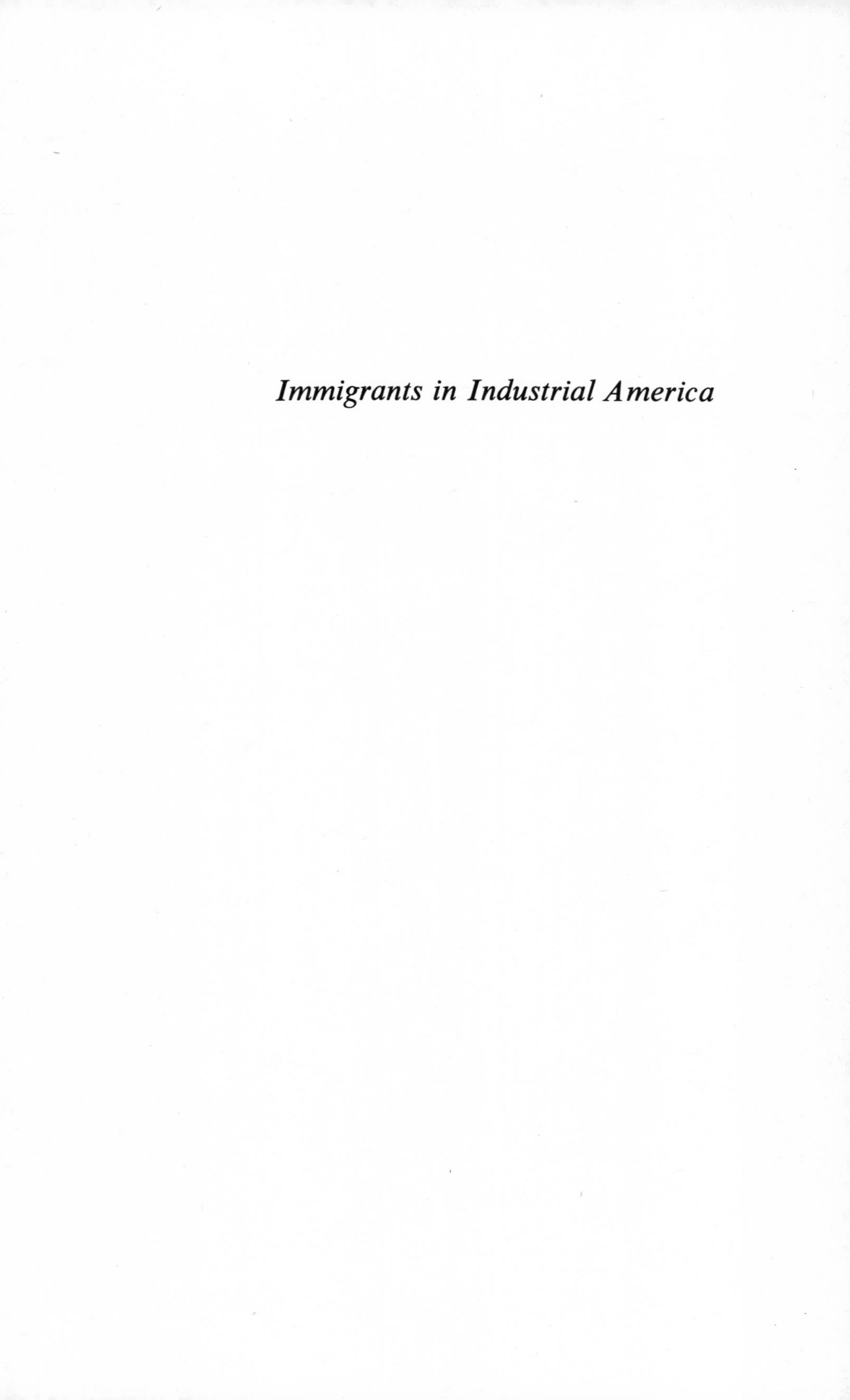

*Immigrants in Industrial America*

# I The Impact of the Industrial Experience on the Immigrant Family: The Huddled Masses Reconsidered

*Caroline Golab*

IN ORDER TO evaluate properly the impact of the industrial experience on the immigrant family, the researcher must first examine his or her biases and preconceptions. Which industrial experience? America's? What part of America? When? the textile mills of Lowell in 1880? the anthracite mines of Wilkes-Barre in 1910? the steel mills of Pittsburgh in 1900? the railroad camps in Denver in 1865? What about Europe's industrial experience? or Russia's? or Italy's? or England's? or Poland's? or Sweden's? Weren't the immigrants affected by these experiences? Which immigrant family? Poles? Poles in Chicago or Poles in Shamokin, Pennsylvania? Northern Italians? Sicilians? Sicilians in South Philadelphia or Sicilians in Reading Railroad camps? Greeks? Jews? Armenians? Irish? Chinese? What immigrant family? the family left behind in the Old Country? the family that emigrated together or the family established in America after marriage there? The family as defined in American (WASP) terms, or the family as defined by the immigrants? the nuclear family of husband and wife with children? the extended family of parents, grandparents, brothers, sisters, aunts, uncles, and cousins? or the multi-nucleated family group with brothers and their wives, sisters and their husbands, aunts and aunts-in-law, uncles and uncles-in-law, cousins and cousins-in-law?

The simple sweep of the phrase "the impact of the industrial experience on the immigrant family" does not allow for differences: differences in time, place, and definition; differences in peoples; differences in motives and expectations; differences in perception and perspective. An approach is needed which tempers the usual American-centered, or one-sided, interpretation of immigration and which presents immiration as it really was: one continuous process of "coming from," "bringing with," and "going to,"–the process of the adaptation of a stranger to a new environment. What is needed is a framework that allows for inputs from both sides of the Atlantic or Pacific, for only within such a framework can we begin to assess the impact of the industrial experience on the immigrant family.

In keeping with this need for proper perspective, I offer a framework that has as its clue the following rule: when encountering new situations, people can react or adapt to them only in terms of what they bring with them to that encounter. Accordingly, Europeans who came to America between 1870 and 1920 confronted an environment with preestablished physical, political, social, ideological, and economic structures (the last of which, at least initially, was the most important). How they reacted or adapted to this structured environment depended in great measure upon (1) the idiosyncracies of their particular culture (such as their urban or rural orientation; their preferences or dislikes for certain forms of work; the construct and depth of their family systems); (2) the stage of development of the society which they were leaving (preindustrial, industrializing, or industrialized) and their experiences in this society before emigration; and (3) the particular nature of their emigration (voluntary or involuntary; permanent or temporary).

By using this framework to establish guideposts and by selecting a particular group, the Poles, to place within it and to serve as a reference point, we can explore some of the more salient aspects and implications of the impact of the industrial experience on the immigrant family. At the very least we can put the topic into a more meaningful perspective for the understanding of American immigration in general.

Among other things, our explorations will reveal that

1. Long before they touched the shores of the New World, the immigrants had already felt the impact of an industrializing society. Indeed, the very act of emigration was a response to the vast social and economic changes that were gradually transforming European society throughout the nineteenth century; more particularly, it was a response to changes that were affecting the basic social structures of societies.

2. The nature of a group's immigration (voluntary or involuntary, temporary or permanent) greatly affected family formation, initial adjustment, and even location of settlement in the New World. Not all groups came to America as families; for many, marriage and the formation of a family were an American and not a European experience.

3. In order to survive and to form permanent communities in America, the immigrants had to adjust to, or neutralize, certain features of the United States economy of 1870-1920 (periodic unemployment, irregular employment, low wages). The primary mode of adaptation was to turn the family into a working, or economic, unit. As it was impossible to live solely on the income of the male breadwinner, it was necessary for other members of the family, primarily the wife, to earn additional income.

4. Because it was essential that women work, immigrant communities would take root and persist primarily in those areas where sources of

female employment were available; the symbiotic relationship of male and female employment was crucial to the formation of strong immigrant, or ethnic communities and neighborhoods.

5. Preindustrial or peasant values of the family persisted into contemporary industrial society; industrialization does not necessarily entail the eradication of preindustrial cultural values.[1]

> A man without land is like a man without legs: he crawls about but cannot get anywhere.
>
> —Polish proverb

During the four decades preceding World War I, Poland, in all its varieties—Austrian, Russian, and Prussian[2]—experienced vast demographic, social, and economic changes, all of which were part of the laborious process of passing from an old agrarian order to a new, industrial one.[3] While no one at that time fully understood these changes, the peasant farmer was very much aware of what was happening. That the population was increasing was undeniable: sons and daughters were not only living to maturity but were also living longer; so was the peasant himself. Towns were crowded with people. Cities were expanding, or, like Częstochowa and Lódź, appeared to spring up from nowhere. Land, in contrast, was becoming less and less available—"too little land for too many sons." Furthermore, try as he would, the peasant farmer, operating increasingly in a market economy, could not make ends meet. To be self-reliant was impossible: outside goods and services were increasingly needed—and desired. Debts mounted. Properties were mortgaged or sold. The need to earn money, to find work elsewhere, became constant and acute. Migration in search of work was inevitable under these circumstances, and emigration became the ultimate solution. Thus it was this changing, industrializing, transitional society that created a "peasant proletariat roaming the countryside, indeed the world, for employment in agriculture and industry."[4] For the Pole the creation of

[1] These revelations are the results of interviews conducted by the author between 1967 and 1972 with approximately four hundred Polish immigrants in Pennsylvania and Illinois. Thus, the evidence used to substantiate most of the findings contained in this paper is the statements and experiences of the immigrants themselves.

[2] Poland, it must be recalled, did not exist at this time. It had been wiped from the map of Europe in 1795, divided between Austria, Russia, and Prussia and not put back together again until Versailles, 1919.

[3] For more detailed discussion of this point, see my "The Polish Experience in Philadelphia: The Migrant Laborers Who Didn't Come," in *The Ethnic Experience in Pennsylvania*, ed. John Bodnar (Lewisburg, Pa., 1973), pp. 39-73.

[4] Victor Greene, *The Slavic Community on Strike: Immigrant Labor in Pennsylvania Anthracite* (Notre Dame, Ind., 1968), p. 26.

this peasant proletariat represented the final response to all those inscrutable forces which were threatening to devour his way of life, a way of life that was organized, first and foremost, around the family as defined in special Polish terms.

In traditional Polish nomenclature the concept of family entailed much more than the whittled-down version of Anglo-Saxon America. The family as seen through Polish eyes was not the nuclear arrangement of husband, wife, and children (better referred to as the "marriage group") nor was it the extended family of mother, father, children, grandparents, aunts, and uncles. Rather, it was, for all intents and purposes, a small clan, a multicentered social group that included all blood and law relatives, without distinction and exception, usually up to the fourth degree. To quote the experts, William I. Thomas and Florian Znaniecki: "The adequate scheme would represent the family as a plurality of nuclei, each of them constituted by a marriage-group, and relations radiating from each of them toward other marriage-groups and single members, up, down, and on both sides, and toward older, younger, and collateral generations of both husband and wife." This construct provided no room for personal relationships between individuals. One was first, last, and always, a member of a family group, so much so that one had no identity or security outside of the family. The principle of familial solidarity dominated, manifesting itself "both in assistance rendered to, and in control exerted over, any member of the group by any other member representing the group as a whole." The assistance rendered and the control exerted did "not depend on the personal character of the members, but only upon the kind and degree of their relationship; the familial relation between two members admits no gradation, as does love or friendship."[5] Familial solidarity was reinforced by the opinion of the community, especially the village and the parish. Thus the control of the group, and loyalty to it, were strong, if not compelling. In exchange for what may seem to contemporary eyes to be undue social control, rigidity, stagnancy, and even oppression, the individual received identity, security, stability, warmth, and intimacy.

All other relationships, that of husband and wife, parents and children, and even the tie to the land, were determined by the principle of familial solidarity. Husband and wife were not two individuals coming together for personal, sentimental, or romantic reasons; rather, each was a representative of his or her family group. Parents were repositories of great authority because they not only represented the rest of the group but were also backed "by every other member in their

[5] *The Polish Peasant in Europe and America,* vol. 1, *Primary-Group Organization* (Boston, 1918), pp. 88, 89, 96, 90.

exertion of their authority" and were "responsible before the group for their actions."[6]

Children were expected to contribute to the family's upkeep before and after marriage. If a son or daughter was employed before marriage, it was precisely so that the money could be used to support the entire family. In this simple form of familial communism there was no concept of keeping earnings for oneself; these were automatically turned over to one's father for management and disposition. After marriage the child continued to contribute to the support of the family (both blood and law relatives) according to his or her ability. When parents were very old, sick, or retired, the necessity of aiding them financially was accepted without question: "it is now a consciously moral duty powerfully reinforced by the opinions of the familial group." Because the family group had many nuclei and was not patriarchal, the principle of familial solidarity was not weakened by the death of the parents. The relationship between brothers and sisters remained intact and even intensified.[7]

Marriage was essential to the principle of familial solidarity. An individual could not achieve importance unless he were married, because one needed a family in order to be important; an individual could not manage money and property unless he were married, because money, property, and land were controlled only by families. Furthermore, it was believed that men who did not marry would waste themselves in a life of disorder and profligacy, whereas marriage forced a man to economize, to save, and to put some order into his life. Accordingly, married persons possessed higher status. Finally, as sex outside of marriage was socially unacceptable and was technically unheard of (premarital sex must ultimately culminate in marriage), marriage, sanctioned by God through the church, was the only sexual outlet. In short, to remain unmarried was almost sinful. The pressure exerted by the group became irresistible; "it is better to make a bad marriage than not marry at all."[8]

The concrete manifestation of familial solidarity was property—more specifically, land. Land was essentially a social unit that determined the status and position of the family within the community.[9] The peasant's intention was always to improve the position of his family. This could best be accomplished by improving or increasing landholdings, principally through marriage, but by purchase if necessary. If at all possible, land was not to be divided but was to be passed on in its

[6] Ibid., 1:91-92; see also 2:184-85.

[7] Ibid., 1:94, 95.

[8] Ibid., 1:108, 123 ff., and 113-34. These attitudes continue to be expressed by the immigrants interviewed between 1967 and 1972. Second- and third-generation Polish-Americans interviewed during this same period also supported most of these views; the concept of a formal wedding as the sign of social approval of the group was repeatedly expressed.

[9] Ibid., 1:159.

entirety to one son (not necessarily the eldest), who was obligated to make settlement (usually in cash) with his brothers and sisters. "Sale, division, or mortgaging of the farm means a lowering of the social standing of the family"; it was, therefore, to be avoided at all costs.[10]

Because land was so vital in determining family standing (that is, social status in the community) and because by the mid-nineteenth century it was becoming increasingly difficult to hold on to it, in order to support a wife and children by means of it or to buy more, the peasant farmer became most willing to exchange his unskilled labor for wages. Money earned would enable him (1) to contribute to the support of his parents—an obligation inherent in the social system and one he could not escape; (2) to support his wife and children; (3) to rescue family property from debt; or (4) to buy land in order to reinstate himself within the solidarity of the familial community.

To earn money, the peasant farmer would seek work. First he went to the village or to another farm; then to the city or to another province; next to the big agricultural estates of Prussia, Russia, and Denmark or the growing industrial centers of Silesia, Moravia, and the Ukraine. In the course of these migrations he was exposed to new people, places, and things; he saw towns and even cities; he encountered machines and factories. He carried these experiences home with him to his family and passed information on to others in his village. At some point in his sojourn he most likely worked in industrial or related activities: mining; street, road, railroad, and bridge construction; steel and iron manufacturing; oil and sugar refining; tanning; slaughtering and meat packing; painting, chopping, digging, dredging, hauling, loading, unloading—the countless fundamental tasks associated with industrialization and urbanization that required little or no skill and training, only muscle and effort.

Finally, the peasant farmer's migrations brought him to America (or Canada, Brazil, Argentina, or Australia). America was merely another alternative, perhaps the final and most profitable one, available to someone desperately in need of work to preserve a way of life that was slipping through his fingers. Nonetheless, before he ever sailed for America, the Pole had become accustomed to migrating throughout an industrializing Europe; indeed, it is rare today to find a Polish immigrant who had not migrated to some other part of Europe and who had not performed some industrial or nonagricultural task before coming to America.[11]

[10] Ibid., 1:118.

[11] To date, interviews with male Polish immigrants have yet to produce one who had not migrated in search of work in Europe (or North Africa, or South America) before settlement in America; most often the migrations were to the more industrialized portions of Russian Poland and Germany or to the big agricultural estates of Prussia and Denmark.

Migration in search of work, especially long-distance migration, was confined mainly to the younger male segments of the Polish population. Always their intention, at least initially, was to return home; they viewed their futures not in America but in Poland. At least 40 percent, perhaps 60 percent, of the Poles who migrated to America returned to Poland. More would have done so had not World War I and economic opportunity intervened. The Poles who went to America, therefore, were not immigrants. They were temporary workers, peasant-farmers turned migrant-laborers.[12] Accordingly, they traveled alone. Usually they were not married and hence were unencumbered with wives and children. Moreover, they were not poverty-stricken but had paid for their own passage or had received help from their families. Because of their motives in coming and because they were alone, they were also very mobile. They were free and willing to go wherever unskilled work was available—Chicago, Detroit, Saint Louis, Chicopee, Wilmington, Nanticoke, Shamokin, or South Hadley. Conversely, when times took a turn for the worse, they were the first to move elsewhere in search of work or the first to return home.[13] The constant migrating, both in Europe and America, posed a threat to the Pole's sense of familial solidarity. It separated him from the personal supervision and control of his family and thereby initiated his "personal individualization." He was learning, slowly and painfully, that "now he counts by himself." He supported himself and had the companionship of newly acquired friends; he no longer seemed to require the family to fill his economic, social, and emotional needs. This process of personal individualization, begun in Europe by the stimulus of migration, continued even more rapidly in America. There the peasant found himself even further removed from the physical interference and control of his usually omnipresent and dominating family; only the letter and the photograph would be left to exert any influence. Eventually, too, the strictures of marriage would be altered; instead of two families joining together, there would be only two brave people, alone against the world—or so it seemed.

[12] Approximately two-thirds of the immigrants interviewed knew of relatives or friends who had returned to Poland before 1917, and virtually all knew of relatives or friends (themselves included) who were planning to return but were unable to because of the war. See also Paul Fox, *The Poles in America* (New York, 1922), p. 64; Thomas and Znaniecki, 1:192; H. J. Habakkuk, "Family Structure and Economic Change in Nineteenth Century Europe," *Journal of Economic History* 15 (1955): 1-12.

[13] Young, male, unskilled, unmarried, unencumbered, mobile, intending to return, migrant-laborers, not immigrants; these terms can also be applied to the Italians, Greeks, Slovaks, Ukranians, and other Slavic peoples. The true immigrants were the Irish and the Jews, peoples whose emigration was involuntary and permanent. They left their homelands with no prospects or intentions of returning. They fled as families (migrant laborers, in contrast, did not come with families), and oftentimes arrived with little or no money, having

> As to work, I haven't worked for four weeks. There is no work. Brother still works, but is not doing well, because almost all factories are closed. Times are so good in America that people are going begging. (Adam Racskowski to his family in Poland, March 2, 1908)
>
> —Thomas and Znaniecki, *The Polish Peasant*

Industrial capitalism in the United States around the turn of the century operated in an environment virtually free of the mechanisms which, after Franklin D. Roosevelt, increasingly came to add greater stability as well as a measure of humanity to the American economy. This early industrial economy, therefore, possessed many distinguishing characteristics that made it very different from the industrial economy we know today. Hallmarks of this Old Economy were chronic unemployment for large numbers of workers; partial or irregular employment for still larger numbers; wage rates for most workers at, or very near, the subsistence level; regular recurrences of recessions and depressions; nonexistence of health, old age, unemployment, and death benefits (that is, no retirement pensions, Blue Cross / Blue Shield, Social Security, severance pay, unemployment compensation, aid to families with dependent children); a general lack of a sense of responsibility of employers toward employees, especially in unskilled industries; and bad to horrendous working conditions that produced many accidents, injuries, disabilities, and deaths. The name of the game was survival, a game which was like Russian roulette in that one never knew when he would lose his job, break a leg, contract tuberculosis, etc., etc. To survive, it was essential to work. But work was that aspect of his life over which the worker had the least control. Nevertheless, it remained his constant preoccupation.[14]

The most abhorrent aspects of the Old Economy were unemployment, irregular or partial employment, and low wages. Although these ailments picked no favorites, foreign laborers suffered the most since they constituted the bulk of the unskilled and were the most economically impotent members of the labor force. A study undertaken in 1914 by the Pennsylvania Department of Labor and Industry's Division of Immigration and Unemployment (even the name of the division is indicative of how

sold the last of their belongings to finance the crossing. Because there were wives and children to think of—to feed and to house almost immediately—these groups were not so free to move about in search of work; mobility for them was a luxury. Thus, the initial port of disembarkation and its environs became the final home for the vast majority of them, even well into the eighth decade of the twentieth century. See my "Polish Communities of Philadelphia, 1870–1920: Immigrant Distribution and Adaptation in Urban America," Diss. Pennsylvania 1970, chap. 1.

[14] The letters of immigrants compiled by Thomas and Znaniecki (vols. 1 and 2) talk constantly about work, especially the lack or irregularity of it.

closely linked these two conditions were) revealed that between June 1913 and June 1914 "practically one-fourth of the men who ought normally to be employed have been compelled to shift their occupation, or have been thrown out of employment."[15] The industries most responsible for this predicament were metal and metal products, textiles and mining—the very industries that relied so heavily on foreign labor.[16]

In 1915 the Metropolitan Life Insurance Company surveyed 78,058 families in Philadelphia who had policies with the company.[17] These families contained 137,244 wage earners (or 18 percent of all wage earners in the city). More than 10 percent of these wage earners were unemployed at the time of the survey, and 19.7 percent were working part-time. Based on these findings, Metropolitan Life concluded that in Philadelphia in March 1915, 79,000 persons were unemployed and 150,000 were working part-time. The textile, clothing, building, and metal industries (electric and steam railway equipment and ships) were the chief culprits: one-fifth of their workers had been out of work for more than six months. Once again, foreigners were heavily represented in these industries.[18] In reporting its findings to the mayor, the insurance company concluded that "unemployment is permanent, if not steadily increasing," and went on to warn that "when we ordinarily assume that men and women who are willing and able to work are minus a job only in times of unusual and widespread industrial depression, such as we experienced during the last winter—we lose sight of the fact that there is always, even in the most prosperous times, a large amount of unemployment and part-time employment for these same workers."[19]

Table 1 shows the average number of foreigners employed in Pennsylvania and certain selected counties (those employing the most foreigners) for the years 1915–20. In 1916, for example, Pennsylvania employed 612,144 foreigners; in 1920, 449,034, a decrease of 163,110 persons. The impact is greater if we look at the situation in the counties on a yearly basis. In some cases the fluctuation in foreign employment is staggering. Philadelphia, for example, employed 72,923 foreign laborers in 1916; 93,670 in 1918; but only 59,537 in 1920 (this was due

[15] Pennsylvania, Department of Labor and Industry, "Report of Division of Immigration and Unemployment," *First Annual Report of the Commissioner of Labor and Industry, 1913* (Harrisburg, Pa., 1914), pp. 277-78.

[16] *Third Annual Report of the Commissioner of Labor and Industry of the Commonwealth of Pennsylvania, 1915*, pt. 1, "Statistics of Production, Wages, Employees for the year 1915" (Harrisburg, Pa., 1918).

[17] Joseph H. Willits, *Philadelphia Unemployment* (Philadelphia, 1916), p. 15.

[18] *Third Annual Report of the Commissioner of Labor and Industry of the Commonwealth of Pennsylvania, 1915*, pt. 1, "Statistics of Production, Wages, Employees for the year 1915" (Harrisburg, 1918).

[19] Willits, p. 15.

*Table 1.* Average number of foreigners employed in Pennsylvania and selected counties, 1915–20

| | 1915 | 1916 | 1917 | 1918 | 1919 | 1920 |
|---|---|---|---|---|---|---|
| Pennsylvania | 516,481 | 612,144 | 545,154 | 546,609 | 451,011 | 449,034 |
| Selected counties | | | | | | |
| Allegheny | 103,973 | 96,668 | 98,631 | 109,070 | 85,630 | 89,738 |
| Beaver | 5,815 | 12,836 | 12,692 | 9,505 | 9,852 | 11,387 |
| Bucks | 1,567 | 1,271 | 1,157 | 4,657 | 3,034 | 1,277 |
| Cambria | 21,331 | 20,615 | 21,676 | 19,008 | 17,332 | 17,783 |
| Chester | 2,492 | 4,018 | 4,427 | 4,204 | 2,368 | 3,127 |
| Dauphin | 7,112 | 4,130 | 4,945 | 4,182 | 3,696 | 3,632 |
| Delaware | 4,150 | 6,735 | 6,640 | 10,157 | 11,032 | 9,546 |
| Fayette | 23,124 | 22,345 | 22,680 | 22,687 | 20,503 | 17,263 |
| Indiana | 3,596 | 10,557 | 11,482 | 8,359 | 7,026 | 7,204 |
| Jefferson | 3,244 | 7,126 | 3,145 | 3,329 | 3,019 | 2,849 |
| Lackawanna | 32,834 | 29,903 | 23,228 | 29,598 | 27,676 | 25,785 |
| Lehigh | 6,776 | 7,935 | 6,948 | 6,248 | 5,255 | 5,562 |
| Luzerne | 48,039 | 48,781 | 41,486 | 42,235 | 39,849 | 37,195 |
| Mercer | 5,676 | 7,587 | 6,762 | 8,980 | 5,510 | 5,953 |
| Northampton | 16,740 | 20,056 | 14,638 | 23,392 | 14,001 | 11,723 |
| Northumberland | 8,955 | 8,543 | 5,930 | 5,696 | 6,275 | 5,775 |
| Philadelphia | 80,208 | 72,923 | 72,739 | 93,670 | 59,197 | 59,537 |
| Schuylkill | 20,140 | 24,124 | 17,240 | 15,822 | 16,154 | 13,852 |
| Westmoreland | 30,983 | 31,353 | 30,008 | 26,812 | 25,801 | 26,287 |

SOURCES: Pennsylvania, Dept. of Labor and Industry, *Third Annual Report of the Commissioner of Labor and Industry of the Commonwealth of Pennsylvania, 1915*, pt. 1, Statistics of Production, Wages, Employees for the Year 1915 (Harrisburg, 1918); idem, Bureau of Statistics and Information, *Report on Productive Industries, Railways, Taxes and Assessments, Waterways & Miscellaneous Statistics of the Commonwealth of Pennsylvania for the Year 1920* (Harrisburg, 1921), pp. 13–50.

mainly to a boom and then a reversal in the textile industries). Luzerne County employed 48,781 foreigners in 1916, but the number steadily declined to 37,195 by 1920 (a decline in the anthracite industry was responsible). Schuylkill County employed 24,124 foreigners in 1916 and only 13,852 in 1920–again reflecting the hard times in the anthracite industry. In 1916 Northampton County employed 20,056 foreign laborers, 23,392 in 1918, but only 11,723 in 1920—one-half the number employed in 1918; this was due to the rising and falling fortunes of steam railroads.

In 1916 Allegheny County offered work to 96,668 foreigners, 109,070 in 1918, 85,630 in 1919, and 89,738 in 1920, another reflection of the steel and mining industries. And so on county by county.

One can only wonder what became of all these people—the 163,110 foreign men and women, for example, who lived and worked in Pennsylvania in 1916 but who are unaccounted for by 1920. Since it is highly unlikely that they all died, most either migrated to another state or country in search of work or were unemployed. Thus industry in Pennsylvania, typical of the rest of the nation, was erratic, irregular, and unpredictable, in its demand for labor and was thereby contributing both to the mobility of the population and its unemployment. The constant fluctuations elicited this comment from the Metropolitan Life Insurance Company: "In industrial concerns employees are continuously coming and going. The number hired and fired is out of all proportion to the number employed. The average concern hires as many new persons during a year as it employs regularly. Such an excessive hiring and firing is costly to employers, has a degenerate effect on employees, and is one of the basic causes of unemployment."[20]

Partial or irregular employment was equally prevalent and debilitating. Before World War I the normal workweek was six days. A few places and industries were introducing the half-holiday on Saturday, but this practice was still in its infancy. Thus, if fully employed, the worker expected to work at least 312 days a year (granting him a holiday for Christmas). To work less than this number meant an unanticipated reduction in income that the worker could ill-afford. As Table 2 shows, in the period 1914–20 employment in Pennsylvania's industries did not once average more than 287 days (in 1916). Once again, the impact is more revealing when viewed at the local level, county by county, or industry by industry (see Table 3).

Low or inadequate wages were another aspect of the Old Economy that greatly influenced immigrant behavior. Even if the worker was gainfully employed for 312 days a year—which was most unlikely—his earnings were not adequate to support him and his family. For example, in 1917 the street railway workers of Seattle, in the course of a dispute over wages, submitted a minimum budget of living expenses to their employer.[21] The total budget of $1,917.88 for a family of five allowed $12.00 for children's education, $30.00 for reading matter of all kinds, including the newspaper, $120.00 for life insurance, and $120.00 for old age savings. The company reduced the budget to $1,505.60 by eliminating all reading matter, reducing education expenses from $12.00 to $11.00, old-age savings from $120.00 to $100.00, and life insurance from $120.00 to

[20] Ibid., p. 2.
[21] James T. Adams, *Our Business Civilization* (New York, 1929), pp. 50-52.

*Table 2.* Average days in operation in Pennsylvania industries, 1915–20

| Industry | 1915 | 1916 | 1917 | 1918 | 1919 | 1920 |
|---|---|---|---|---|---|---|
| Building and contracting | 265 | 269 | 265 | 270 | 269 | 268 |
| Chemicals and allied products | 303 | 297 | 292 | 304 | 290 | 290 |
| Clay, glass, and stone | 278 | 279 | 270 | 255 | 245 | 252 |
| Clothing manufacture | 283 | 283 | 282 | 290 | 267 | 253 |
| Food and kindred products | 281 | 280 | 284 | 302 | 295 | 292 |
| Leather and rubber | 292 | 290 | 294 | 297 | 284 | 278 |
| Liquors and beverages | 261 | 279 | 283 | 290 | 276 | 278 |
| Lumber and its remanufacture | 276 | 282 | 282 | 284 | 280 | 278 |
| Paper and printing industries | 289 | 296 | 292 | 297 | 296 | 294 |
| Textiles | 275 | 290 | 287 | 284 | 273 | 253 |
| Laundries | 281 | 284 | 286 | 280 | 281 | 252 |
| Metals and metal products | 287 | 296 | 290 | 300 | 263 | 290 |
| Mines and quarries | 232 | 262 | 255 | 240 | 205 | 230 |
| Public service | 324 | 344 | 326 | 358 | 351 | 352 |
| Tobacco and tobacco products | 276 | 261 | 278 | 278 | 265 | 253 |
| Miscellaneous | 286 | 292 | 291 | 260 | 289 | 292 |
| All industries | 281 | 287 | 285 | 285 | 275 | 278 |

SOURCES: *Third Annual Report*, p. 3; *Report on the Productive Industries of the Commonwealth of Pennsylvania for 1916–1917–1918–1919* (Harrisburg, 1920); *Report on Productive Industries, 1920*, p. 53.

$30.00. Five dollars per person was allowed for recreation (including tobacco) and $4.00 for all miscellaneous expenses. The workers insisted that they could not survive on anything less than $1,917.88 but nevertheless had to settle for much less. As workers in Pennsylvania's mines, steel mills, and textile mills earned much less than $1,505.60 per year, it is difficult to understand how they survived. The average daily wage in Pennsylvania in 1915 was $2.22; in 1916, $2.76. If a man worked 300 days a year, he would not earn more than $825.00 per year. Pennsylvania's Department of Labor and Industry considered $900.00 a year per family to be the poverty line. It would seem that virtually all wage earners and their families in Pennsylvania lived in poverty; at least such is the case if the family was supported solely by a wage earner employed full time in one of Pennsylvania's industries (see Table 4).

*Table 3.* Average number of days worked, all industries, in Pennsylvania and selected counties, 1914–20

| | 1914* | 1915 | 1916 | 1917 | 1918 | 1919 | 1920 |
|---|---|---|---|---|---|---|---|
| Pennsylvania | — | 281 | 287 | 285 | 285 | 275 | 278 |
| Selected counties | | | | | | | |
| Allegheny | 279 | 287 | 297 | 291 | 294 | 281 | 280 |
| Bucks | 268 | 279 | 287 | 276 | 230 | 285 | 287 |
| Cambria | 293 | 289 | 305 | 306 | 302 | 253 | 257 |
| Carbon | 273 | 290 | 288 | 307 | 286 | 300 | 278 |
| Chester | 283 | 292 | 300 | 285 | 287 | 295 | 291 |
| Clarion | 289 | 285 | 288 | 268 | 278 | 254 | 273 |
| Clearfield | 272 | 285 | 288 | 283 | 290 | 230 | 252 |
| Dauphin | 283 | 295 | 293 | 300 | 292 | 288 | 282 |
| Delaware | 275 | 292 | 292 | 293 | 291 | 287 | 282 |
| Fayette | 277 | 276 | 287 | 277 | 287 | 246 | 266 |
| Huntington | 265 | 278 | 284 | 272 | 258 | 232 | 256 |
| Indiana | 260 | 264 | 281 | 280 | 281 | 252 | 272 |
| Jefferson | 273 | 286 | 293 | 286 | 293 | 240 | 267 |
| Lackawanna | 281 | 286 | 295 | 284 | 293 | 282 | 271 |
| Lehigh | 279 | 285 | 285 | 291 | 286 | 284 | 280 |
| Luzerne | 268 | 277 | 285 | 283 | 278 | 268 | 272 |
| Mercer | 250 | 287 | 300 | 285 | 288 | 280 | 279 |
| Northampton | 275 | 288 | 287 | 286 | 295 | 288 | 284 |
| Northumberland | 260 | 281 | 289 | 272 | 283 | 278 | 269 |
| Philadelphia | 286 | 289 | 295 | 291 | 293 | 289 | 282 |
| Schuylkill | 266 | 285 | 289 | 293 | 286 | 277 | 255 |
| Washington | 284 | 291 | 293 | 290 | 285 | 264 | 273 |
| Westmoreland | 276 | 288 | 314 | 288 | 278 | 261 | 272 |

SOURCES: *Second Annual Report of the Commissioner of Labor & Industries of the Commonwealth of Pennsylvania, 1914*, pt. 1, Production, Wages, Employees, Welfare and Educational Work (Harrisburg, 1915); *Third Annual Report; Report on Productive Industries, 1916–1919; Report on Productive Industries, 1920.*

* Figures for 1914 do not include mining industries.

*Table 4.* Average daily wage in Pennsylvania industries, 1916–19

| Industry | 1916 | | 1917 | | 1918 | | 1919 | |
|---|---|---|---|---|---|---|---|---|
| | Male | Female | Male | Female | Male | Female | Male | Female |
| Building and contracting | $2.39 | $1.23 | $2.75 | $1.45 | $3.64 | $1.75 | $3.76 | $0.77 (?) |
| Chemicals and allied products | 2.67 | 1.18 | 3.07 | 1.32 | 3.92 | 1.65 | 4.58 | 2.13 |
| Clay, glass, and stone products | 2.52 | 1.25 | 3.05 | 1.54 | 4.06 | 1.82 | 4.64 | 2.10 |
| Clothing manufacture | 2.39 | 1.30 | 2.80 | 1.45 | 3.41 | 1.75 | 4.19 | 2.11 |
| Food and kindred products | 2.44 | 1.23 | 2.74 | 1.28 | 3.33 | 1.46 | 3.89 | 1.82 |
| Leather and rubber goods | 2.27 | 1.30 | 2.61 | 1.46 | 3.27 | 1.72 | 4.09 | 2.15 |
| Liquors and beverages | 3.27 | 1.06 | 3.47 | 1.09 | 4.14 | 1.49 | 4.51 | 1.88 |
| Lumber and its remanufacture | 2.11 | 1.17 | 2.52 | 1.29 | 3.09 | 1.59 | 3.55 | 1.95 |
| Paper and printing industries | 2.53 | 1.19 | 3.01 | 1.37 | 3.57 | 1.69 | 4.23 | 2.01 |
| Textiles | 2.15 | 1.30 | 2.55 | 1.46 | 3.31 | 1.87 | 4.02 | 2.36 |
| Laundries | 2.61 | 1.13 | 2.86 | 1.26 | 3.64 | 1.53 | 4.01 | 1.79 |
| Metal and metal products | 2.94 | 1.33 | 3.66 | 1.74 | 4.67 | 2.20 | 5.61 | 2.55 |
| Mines and quarries | 2.79 | 1.73 | 3.97 | 1.75 | 5.78 | 1.49 | 6.44 | 2.81 |
| Public service | 2.56 | 0.96 | 3.07 | 1.44 | 3.97 | 1.71 | 4.08 | 3.31 |
| Tobacco and its products | 1.81 | 1.41 | 2.26 | 1.71 | 2.55 | 1.89 | 3.00 | 2.26 |
| Miscellaneous industries | 2.37 | 1.13 | 3.10 | 1.37 | 5.41 | 1.84 | 4.83 | 2.10 |
| AVERAGE | 2.76 | 1.27 | 3.40 | 1.48 | 4.59 | 1.85 | 4.84 | 2.19 |

SOURCE: *Report on Productive Industries for 1916–1917–1918–1919*, pp. 66, 106, 146, 186.

> If Konstanty wrote you to send him a girl, answer him that he may send a ship-ticket either to the one from Popow or the one from Grajewo. . . . For if he does not marry, he will never make a fortune and will never have anything; he wastes his work and has nothing. And if he married he will sooner put something aside. For he won't come back any more. In America it is so: Whoever does not intend to return to his country, it is best for him to marry young; then he will sooner have something, for a bachelor in America will never have anything, unless he is particularly self-controlled. (Antoni Butkowski to his parents in Poland, Dec. 31, 1902)
>
> —Thomas and Znaniecki, *The Polish Peasant*

The usual response of the worker to unemployment, irregular employment, and low wages was to find another job or to hold down several jobs at once. In periods of permanent or prolonged unemployment, this often meant that the worker had to move in order to find work. Obviously, this was much easier for the single or unattached foreign migrant-laborer than it was for the immigrant or native-born American worker with wife and children. Indeed, the geographic mobility of the foreign-born worker, especially the migrant-laborer, was tremendous. Just as he had migrated from place to place in his homeland, so too, did he migrate from place to place in America—always in search of work. Parish records, city directories, and interviews with immigrants testify to this intense mobility. In some Polish settlements in Philadelphia, less than 20 percent of those living in the city in 1905 are present in 1910 or 1914. Some Polish settlements added thousands of members every year—only to lose twice as many at a later date; these departees would show up next in the smaller cities and towns of northeastern Pennsylvania, New York, New Jersey, Delaware, and even Chicago or Milwaukee. Referring again to Table 1, one continues to wonder what happened to the 11,586 foreign workers, most of them Slavic and Italian, who worked in Luzerne County in 1916 but who are not employed there in 1920; or the 19,332 who were employed in Allegheny County in 1918 but who were gone by 1920; or the 5,861 in Fayette County in 1915 who are not there in 1920; or the 7,049 in Lackawanna County in 1915 who are unaccounted for by 1920; or the 11,669 in Northampton County in 1918, but not employed there in 1920; or the 34,133 working in Philadelphia in 1918 but not working there in 1920. Since not all of these persons could have died, disappeared, or been content to remain unemployed for very long, they must have sought work elsewhere; they migrated.[22]

The impact of this hypermobility on the formation of ethnic communities and community-creation in general remains largely unstudied. It could be argued that with so much turnover in the population it would be almost impossible for immigrants to form stable communities, and yet they did. Even so, there could be no community-creation if America had to rely on the migrant laborer. He was not the stuff of which communities were made. He had no attachment to this country, let alone to the locality in which he was temporarily employed. Here today, he would be gone tomorrow. He would be the first to move on or to return to his homeland should the economy experience one of its ever-recurring downturns.

Communities could be formed only by true immigrants, by persons who saw their futures in America. Toward this end, it was marriage, with the prospect of children, that became the most decisive factor converting the Pole from a migrant-laborer to a permanent resident; it forced him to view his future as being here, and not in Poland. Marriage was also responsible for diminishing or curtailing his peripatetic existence: arrangements other than workmen's camps and boardinghouses had to be made; steady, settled work was to be preferred because there were now others to think about. In short, marriage and family were essential prerequisites for the establishment and persistence of communities.

[22] In his study of nineteenth-century Newburyport, Mass., Stephan Thernstrom also found "exceptional mobility of unskilled laborers." In a section entitled "Men on the Move: The Problem of Geographical Mobility," he stresses the prevalence of geographic mobility as a natural part of life for the unskilled laborer. "Slightly less than 40 percent of all the unskilled laborers and children living in the community at mid-century were still there in the Census of 1860. . . ." The "typical" Newburyport laborer did "not live in Newburyport very long. Contemporary observers were correct in characterizing the new working class as floating. For a majority of these permanent transients, Newburyport provided no soil in which to sink roots. It was only one more place in which to carry on the struggle for existence for a few years until driven onward again" (*Poverty and Progress: Social Mobility in a Nineteenth Century City* [Cambridge, Mass., 1964], pp. 84-85, 87, 90, 199, 31, 113, 134).

> As to the girl, although I don't know her, my companion who knows her, says that she is stately and pretty. I believe him, as well as you, my parents. For although I don't know her, I ask you . . . Shall I send her a ship-ticket, or how else shall I do? (Konstanty Butkowski to his parents in Poland, Dec. 21, 1902)
>
> Tell me who has been married among the young people, because one girl wrote two letters to me and I have the wish to bring her to me. She lives near the manor. . . . (Adam Raczkowski to his sister in Poland, Jan. 30, 1909)
>
> And now, dear parents,. . . I have an opportunity to be married. I have a fine boy, because uncle and auntie have known him for three years. . . . He is boarding with them. (Aleksandra Rembienska to her family in Poland, Oct. 14, 1911)
>
> —Thomas and Znaniecki, *The Polish Peasant*

Unlike the Jews or the Irish, the Italians, Poles, and other Slavic groups did not emigrate as families. A study of records of eight Polish parishes in Philadelphia reveals that the vast majority of Poles in this city were single men between the ages of nineteen and thirty. The records also show, however, that marriage was very popular with these men and that they did, in fact, marry young Polish women between the ages of seventeen and twenty-three. If the vast majority of Poles in America were men, where did they find these young Polish women? Obviously, there could be no marriage, no family, no conversion to immigrant status, and no community-creation without them.

Since a large portion (40 percent to 60 percent) of all Polish migrants returned to Poland, not all Polish men in America were looking for wives. For those who remained, there were, in general, two ways of finding a wife. Each predominated in certain areas, depending upon local conditions and the extent to which the individual was still controlled by, or under the influence of, his family. The young man could acquire a wife directly from Poland or he could meet his future wife after she had immigrated to America.[23] In the first situation, the parents of the son would select the girl, or the son would have known of her previously or learned about her from friends; he would then write to her, and after a period of correspondence, would ask her to join him in America. In this arrangement the couple knew each other slightly or not at all; the opinion of the group, be it family or the new friends that temporarily replaced the

[23] By 1915 there was also a pool of young Polish women born in America and of marriage-able age.

family in America, was a determining factor, not only in the decision to marry but in the final selection of a wife.

Not all women came from Poland at the invitation of prospective husbands. There was a substantial pool of young women who came as migrant-laborers; the institution of migration was by no means reserved only for men. After 1910 the number of single women-migrants appears to increase. Lured by prospects of work (the chance to earn money for a dowry) and marriage (it was generally believed that it was easy to get married in America and that Polish-American husbands were better), most of these girls joined relatives, usually brothers (or young uncles) who had been in America for some time. They found work in textile and garment factories or, more often, in service—cleaning, ironing, and cooking. Since the idea of a single girl working in a factory was never fully accepted by the Polish community, and given the revered place of marriage in the Polish social system, unmarried Polish girls in America did not remain unmarried for very long.[24]

In general, marriage tended to increase the propensity of the migrant-laborer to remain in America. Family-creation led to community-and institution-creation. The more an individual embedded himself within this growing network, the harder it became for him to extricate himself. Thus with the establishment of social bonds and structures to rival those of the Old Country, no longer was it easy for the laborer and his family to pack up and move back to Poland. Nevertheless, although it changed the Pole's horizons from the far side of the Atlantic to this one and although it was the essential ingredient for the establishment of permanent communities in America, marriage was in large part a response to the peculiarities of the Old Economy—the unemployment, the partial employment, and the low wages. Despite all statements to the contrary, it was easier for the Polish workingman to survive in America if he were married than if he were single.[25] To survive in America, the workingman could not depend upon his wages alone. It was safer to rely on the added earnings of a wife and children. These earnings would keep him fed and sheltered in times of unemployment, sickness, or injury. The family was an economic necessity for anyone opting to remain permanently in America.

During hard times the Polish family responded to the crisis as a unit so that each of its members could survive—the principle of familial solidarity allowed no distinctions and provided for no exception. Moreover, the Pole had another incentive to seek additional earnings; the need to

[24] Thomas and Znaniecki, 1:127.

[25] This was buttressed by the Polish cultural value which held that men without marriage could not and would not save, economize, etc., but would waste their time and money on drink, women, and other nasty pursuits.

send money to family and relatives in Poland. Even when he became an immigrant he did not forsake this practice. It was a legacy of his former status as migrant-laborer, but it was a practice that was firmly rooted in the construct of the traditional Polish family. Once again, the principle of familial solidarity prevailed, if not triumphed.

> Now, dear parents, for girls there is work in America, but not for men. (Aleksandra Rembienska to her parents in Poland, Oct. 14, 1911)
>
> —Thomas and Znaniecki, *The Polish Peasant*

Employment for women, no matter how poor the remuneration, was crucial to the formation of strong ethnic communities and neighborhoods. This was especially true for immigrants such as the Poles and Italians, whose members were mainly unskilled laborers, but it applied to all poor immigrants in general. Thus the families of Italian street laborers in Philadelphia who were employed for only part of the year, families of Polish and Slovak coal miners in Northeastern Pennsylvania, families of Italian and Polish railroad workers, and families of Jewish peddlers and aspiring merchants—all managed to survive because wives and daughters were able to find work in garment, textile, and tobacco manufacture or by cleaning, cooking, and ironing for others. The only alternative to a working wife was a husband who earned much money. This meant a husband who possessed a skill or a very steady job which paid well. But these were the very things the unskilled Polish, Slavic, and Italian worker did not have; and despite higher wages the skilled or semiskilled worker was also subjected to the vicissitudes of the business cycle.

A working wife brought additional income to the family in several ways: by participating directly in industry, either in the factory or at home; by self-employment; and by performing a miscellany of needed services that rarely appeared in published statistical reports. Moreover, each group had its unique pattern. Italian women, for example, avoided factories before, as well as after, marriage, preferring industrial homework in the garment trades of self-employment. Polish women tended to avoid factory work after marriage and, in general, preferred domestic service and the servicing of lodgers and boarders. Jewish women, in contrast, were rarely found in domestic service but were prominent in industry, both at home and in the factory, and, more than any other group, were self-employed shopkeepers. In 1915 approximately 14 percent of Pennsylvania's industrial workers were women employed in the manufacture of clothing, textiles, food products, leather and rubber goods, paper, tobacco, and metal products. Immigrant women constituted from one-tenth to three-quarters of all women employed in various branches of these industries. If American-born children are included, the percentages are even higher. Irish women predominated in textiles, Jewish and Italian women in the needle trades. The tobacco industry relied primarily on Jewish women, but in the smaller cities and towns of the state Polish and Italian women were also utilized. All groups participated in food processing, paper, rubber, leather, and metal manufacture. Indeed, the entrance of women into the industrial work force, especially the factory, coincided with the arrival of the immigrant woman and her children:

> Prior to the coming of immigrants from eastern and southern Europe, women in Pennsylvania industry did not play a great part. Women of English, Welsh, Scotch, and German descent did not find industrial employment particularly attractive. Upon the coming of the recent immigrants, however, many of them with large families and small means, female members of the family sought employment to eke out a living. Pursuits presenting the most immediate opportunities naturally were the manufacturing and mechanical occupations. Comparatively few women are engaged in agricultural and allied occupations, but the number engaged in cigar and tobacco manufacturing, in textile manufacturing and as dressmakers, sewers and sewing machine operators is great. We find no less than 3,858 engaged in cigar and tobacco factories, over 1,300 in knitting mills and over 6,600 as sewers and sewing-machine operators in factories. Approximately 4,800 are engaged as dressmakers and seamstresses not in factory employment. It is interesting to note that several hundred women of foreign origin are engaged as laborers in blast furnaces and rolling mills, shoe factories, and other industries where employment is unpleasant and very heavy. About 4,000 native-born of foreign or mixed parentage are also engaged in manufacturing and mechanical pursuits. A striking proportion of the women of foreign origin engaged in industrial pursuits are semi-skilled operatives. On the whole, the woman of foreign birth is willing to accept employment at a lesser wage than the man.[26]

The exact number employed in Pennsylvania in industrial homework—a hybrid situation that enabled the worker to earn money in industry while working at home—cannot be determined with certainty.[27] A survey

[26] *Third Annual Report, 1915,* p. 249.

[27] The employment of women in homework was sporadic and inconsistent. Not all women so employed worked at it every day, every week, all year long. Thus, while the average number employed at any one time might have been 12,000, twice that number of women could have done some homework for some part of the year without affecting the average number employed at any one time; this would mean that 24,000 families, not 12,000, received additional income from homework. Moreover, certain forms of homework were seasonal—assembling valentines, Christmas and Halloween decorations, sewing baseballs, etc.—thereby concealing the fact that more women were engaged in homework for some parts of the year than the average figure would indicate. Finally, the statistics do not include

conducted by Agnes Mary Hadden Byrnes in cooperation with the Pennsylvania Department of Labor and Industry reported an average of 12,394 industrial homeworkers for 1916, not including 5,000 persons making army clothes.[28] Ninety-six percent of these homeworkers were women; 71 percent were married and 19 percent were widowed, divorced, or deserted; 25 percent were foreign-born, more than half of whom were Italian, the remainder being Jewish, Polish, other Slavic groups, Irish, English, and so on. The overwhelming majority of homeworkers resided in Philadelphia, Berks, Lancaster, Luzerne, Lackawanna, Lehigh, York, Northampton, Montgomery, Dauphin, Delaware, Schuylkill, and Allegheny Counties. Although Philadelphia contained the largest concentration, smaller cities and towns, all located in the heavy industrial areas of the state, were well represented. The textile, garment, and tobacco industries employed the bulk of the homeworkers, but to her surprise Byrnes found homeworkers manufacturing everything from "soup to nuts": bags, bolts, books, brushes, chairs, cough drops, candy eggs, curtains, embroidered and lace goods, flags, banners, gas mantles, gas meters, leather gloves, gloves other than leather, hair goods, handkerchiefs, hats with artificial flowers, hooks, eyes, patent fasteners (safety pins), jewelry, silverware, lampshades, leather goods, metal novelties, neckware, dress and hat trimmings, novelty goods, paper goods, razor blades, sanitary rubber goods and corsets, sheets, pillow cases, trimmings for shoes, silk goods, spectacle cases, suspenders, garters, toilet preparations, toys, sporting goods (baseballs), dolls' dresses, umbrellas, parasols, and woolen goods.[29]

The types of homework activity associated with these products usually required little or no skill; never did the homeworker actually manufacture an entire shirt, flag, sheet, or toy. Basic work was completed in the shop. Women performed subsequent functions, such as stringing and wiring tags; assembling valentines, Christmas bells, Halloween decorations, and paper party hats; sewing rags together for carpets; knotting fringes of rugs; covering baseballs; closing the thumbs of gloves and inverting the gloves; knitting and twisting shawl fringes; mending machine-made laces and curtains; finishing goggles by sewing

---

large chunks of homeworkers who were deliberately unreported. It was a common practice for large garment and textile firms in New York, Philadelphia, Baltimore, and Wilmington to set up ad hoc operations in the smaller towns and cities of Pennsylvania where female labor was plentiful in order to pay the cheapest rates possible and at the same time "avoid the demands of labor organizations in cities." This practice was very common in the industrial centers of northeastern Pennsylvania—Luzerne and Lackawanna counties, for example.

[28] Agnes Mary Hadden Byrnes, *Industrial Homework in Pennsylvania* (Harrisburg, Pa., 1923).

[29] Ibid., p. 18.

silk nosepieces onto metal and shell frames and putting velvet braid on side shields and plastic headbands on masks; sewing safety pins, needles, hooks, and eyes to cards; removing bastings from cotton dresses; pressing seams; taping underwear; sorting scraps of leather; and removing paper patterns from embroidered blouses.

The supply of labor available to perform these routine and endless tasks was totally elastic—there was never a shortage of willing workers. Quite the contrary, Italian women in Philadelphia, for example, complained that there was never enough work to keep willing hands busy. Because the labor supply was so plentiful, and hence cheap, it appears that its very presence often delayed the introduction of machines and factory methods. Instead of moving toward mechanization, certain industries could afford to remain labor-intensive. Byrnes reports that "the manufacturers both of tags and of hooks and eyes have machines in the factory to perform the process done by hand in the homes, yet the cheap labor supply makes handwork profitable."[30] Moreover, the presence of a ready labor supply was undoubtedly a major factor behind the establishment of such industries in any given area.[31]

Because homework was so routine and the labor supply so abundant, wages were notoriously low. Women who sewed rags together for carpets, finished men's clothing, taped underwear, mended hosiery, strung tags and carded hooks, eyes, and patent fasteners earned nine cents an hour. "An hourly rate of pay of nine cents, a working week of 54 hours, would yield to the wage earner $4.86—an income far below that which is necessary for subsistence." Homework that required a modicum of skill or experience would pay slightly more, but even if a woman worked full time, fifty to sixty hours a week, rarely would she earn more than $200.00 in one year—and what woman with children could afford to spend fifty-four hours a week, fifty-two weeks a year sewing safety pins to cards? Industrial homework, consequently, was never the main source of income for the family; it was always supplemental.[32]

[30] Ibid., p. 7.

[31] "The postmaster of one small village declared that the 'women of the town like to help out the men,' that all of them assist in the manufacture of cigars and cigar boxes, either in the factory or in the home. He said that the town had been a tumbled-down village, until firms from outside the state came and built two cigar factories. All the women then went to work and transformed a village of old shacks into a model town" (Ibid., p. 26).

[32] Ibid. The earnings of the homeworker were actually *less* than presented; she had overhead expenses which must be deducted—scissors, knives, scrapers, needles; electricity or gas expenses since she usually worked in the evenings or at night. Her employer, on the other hand received additional benefits: "When work is slack, he does not incur the loss of the employer of inside workers whose factory hands seek other jobs, nor does he bear the expense of the upkeep of a factory running at part capacity. In the case of a rush order he is not obligated to pay the increase of wages for overtime work" (Ibid., p. 44).

Despite the low wages, homework was very popular because it provided a convenient way to earn additional income. Women could remain at home with their children, sick husbands, or aging parents; they could perform the tasks at their own pace and could fit them into the lulls of household routine. Since Italian women avoided factories before, as well as after, marriage, and since Polish women tended to avoid factories after marriage, these women made their chief contributions to the textile and garment industries while working at home. Moreover, homework, especially in the textile and garment industries, provided employment for "helpers," usually husbands, children, and even the physically handicapped and crippled—people "unfit to carry the burden of steady industrial employment."[33] Persons who used helpers earned more money because they could produce more work.

That the prevalence of, and demand for, homework was due to the nature of the Old Economy is undeniable. Byrnes found that the total yearly incomes of the families of home workers was very low: "one sees a correlation between the low salaries of these husbands of home workers and the industrial work of the wife at home." The result was that "poverty in the great proportion of cases makes homework necessary." Most of the husbands of home workers were laborers. Some were employed in manufacturing and mechanical industries; others, chiefly Italians, were "day laborers shoveling dirt in the street or for the railroad." As the work of the common laborer was often seasonal, "the burden of support may fall upon the wife during the months of her husband's idleness." Even when husbands were employed regularly, or possessed a skill, it was often necessary for the wife to seek homework because the "underpayment of the husband with regular employment makes the contribution of the wife a necessity." Finally, "it is not only low wages of the husband, irregular or seasonal work, uncertain returns from industry or agriculture which lead women to become industrial workers at home, but the varied catastrophies of life associated with disease and industrial accidents."[34]

In addition to industrial work, a small percentage of immigrant women was self-employed. These women operated groceries, bakeries, confectionaries, dry goods, variety, and tobacco stores, restaurants, saloons and laundries; they peddled wares, from old shoes to lace trimmings; hawked fruits and vegetables and sold newspapers; some manufactured calendars, canvas shopping bags, and pretzels; crocheted bootees, scarves, and hats; canned homegrown fruits and vegetables for sale, etc., etc. Self-employment was especially popular among Jewish women, but Italian and Polish women would occasionally become shopkeepers; in all of

[33] Ibid., pp. 47, 46.
[34] Ibid., pp. 50-52.

Philadelphia's Polish settlements women ran groceries, bakeries, confectionaries, laundries, or restaurants. Italian and Jewish women were more likely to be peddlers and hawkers than were Polish women. In all groups commercial proceeds usually were used to supplement the husband's income; however, if the woman were widowed, divorced, or deserted, or if her husband were incapacitated, these incomes constituted the primary means of support of the family (and there were many widows and women with incapacitated husbands). Where shops were fully functioning family enterprises, women and children served as clerks, salespeople, stock boys, delivery boys, cashiers, busboys, dishwashers, waiters, waitresses.

Among migrant workers such as Poles and Italians, the presence of shops and stores, whether male- or female-operated, was an important indicator of the level of development and stability of the immigrant community. Shopkeepers were invariably immigrants, persons who not only were staking their futures in America but in a precise piece of it. Accordingly, it was this self-employed group that was the least mobile. It was also the group that provided the leadership for the incipient immigrant community, giving support to the church and synogogue and other institutionalized forms of community life—schools, newspapers, fraternal and social organizations.[35]

Besides self-employment and employment in industry, immigrant women performed a host of essential services for pay. Among Polish women domestic service and the servicing of lodgers and boarders were the most popular. Before they were married, Polish women would work in textile, clothing, tobacco, boot, shoe, and paper box factories; or they would hire themselves out as domestics. After they were married, or after the birth of the first child, they were less likely to work in factories because of family and household responsibilities, but often would return to the factories when children were older or when one child was old enough to look after the others. It was domestic service that continued to be the mainstay of Polish women after marriage.[36]

Domestic service tended to be universal wherever Polish women were found. Indeed, the stereotype of the Polish cleaning lady was formed quite early, but with good justification, since Polish women preferred this

[35] See Golab, *Polish Communities,* chap. 4. This study of Polish settlements in Philadelphia indicates that horizontal (industrial) and vertical (occupational) stratification was vital to the generation and stability of permanent communities. Certain occupational roles (self-employment, service, skilled, etc.) had to be filled if a community were to form, grow, and prosper. In the age of the Old Economy a minimal amount of industrial diversification was also required so that communities would not risk annihilation simply because one factory or one industry closed down or was hit hard by recession.

[36] Thomas and Znaniecki, 2:251, 254.

type of work above all others and were very proficient at it. It is difficult, however, to estimate the numbers of immigrant women, Polish and otherwise, employed in domestic services because of the nature of the work: it was irregular, unregulated, and exploitative; private arrangements between the women and their employers (usually families and individuals as well as offices, hotels, businesses, hospitals, schools, churches, and department stores). If the worker did not go out to clean someone's office or home, she took in laundry and ironing. This latter arrangement was most prevalent in settlements where there were large numbers of migrant-laborers without wives. In either situation—going out to work or bringing it in—hours were usually adjustable and compatible with family routine; one could work in the late evening, early morning, and all night. Slavic women were assured of employment because of their reliability and because of their willingness to work for whatever pay they could get, thereby offering stiff competition to their black and Irish counterparts. During the hard times of the Old Economy, especially its final breakdown, the Great Depression, entire families were known to have survived because of women's earnings from domestic work.

> He said that the town had been a tumbled-down village until firms from outside the state came and built two cigar factories. All the women then went to work and transformed a village of old shacks into a model town. (The postmaster of a small town, c. 1916)
> —Mary Hadden Agnes Byrnes, *Industrial Homework in Pennsylvania*

Because of the peculiarities of the Old Economy to which the immigrants had to adjust and because a working wife was essential for this adjustment, immigrants would most often settle and form communities only in those areas that provided (or created) employment for women. Employment opportunities for women were essential for the creation of permanent and cohesive communities. Additional income reduced the need to move about in search of work and hence enabled the family to remain in one place for a considerable length of time. Unless families were allowed to stay put for some time, there could be no formation, let alone sense, of community. It can be argued, therefore, that strong ethnic communities and neighborhoods took root only in areas where it was possible to establish a symbiotic relationship between male and female employment (and even "male" and "female" industries).

The prevalence of homework among immigrant women in Philadelphia is one example of this symbiotic relationship. While husbands and fathers were digging ditches, building subways, paving streets, unloading ships, loading railroad cars, refining oil and sugar (and also while they were unemployed), Italian, Jewish, and Slavic women were gainfully busy with their needles. Strong ethnic communities formed and prospered in Philadelphia because both men and women could find employment there. Indeed, the immigrants themselves were very much aware of this fact and often gave up chances of better-paying employment elsewhere if it would be difficult for women to find work. The Polish women of the Fairmount section of Philadelphia have been cleaning the offices, hotels, hospitals, and department stores of the adjacent downtown area since 1905. The community remained in Fairmount only because of the nearby employment resources for women.

In the smaller industrial cities and towns of Pennsylvania, similar symbiotic relationships are found. While men were employed in coal mines and steel mills, women were working in the textile and tobacco industries or cleaning buildings and washing clothes.[37] One of the industries most irregular in its employment was the mining industry. In fact, of all industries in Pennsylvania it had the worst record of total number of days in operation: 232 in 1915, 262 in 1916, 255 in 1917, 240 in 1918, 205 in 1919 (see Table 2). Foreigners, primarily Poles, Slovaks, "Magyars," and Italians, constituted the majority of workers in the mines. With such constant and extreme fluctuations, prolonged periods of unemployment, low wages, horrid working conditions, and high accident potential, it is remarkable that any communities were able to form at all. And yet Polish and Italian communities did take root, quite successfully, in towns such a Archibald, Dickson City, Dunmore, Jermyn, Jessup, Moosic, Moscow, Old Forge, Olyphant, Taylor, and Throop in Lackawanna County; Ashley, Dallas, Dupont, Duryea, Edwardsville, Hanover Township, Hazleton, Nanticoke, Pittston, Plains, Plymouth, Shickshinny, Swoyersville, and Wilkes-Barre in Luzerne County; Coal Township, Kulpmont, Mount Carmel, and Shamokin in Northumberland County. Most of these remain strong Polish and Italian centers to the present day. Closer examination reveals that from the outset the survival of these immigrant communities depended upon the ability of the women to find

[37] The symbiotic relationship which existed in these areas between mining and textile and garment manufacture becomes even more evident in the years after World War II when the coal industry declined and miners lost their jobs. As male unemployment soared, it was soon apparent that the reason so many families stayed in the area was that the women were employed, or were able to be employed, in textile and garment factories. The women kept the families fed and clothed until the former miners could find other work or until industries could be coaxed into moving into the area. It was a repeat of the pattern of fifty years earlier when immigrant families survived on the earnings of women during "hard times." Also, like their predecessors, the younger unmarried segments of the population, primarily the men, left the area in order to find work elsewhere.

work (see Table 5). Northeastern Pennsylvania may have been the anthracite stronghold of the nation, but what is often overlooked is the presence of other industries, "women's" industries, primarily textile and garment manufacture, but also food products and paper box, boot, shoe, and tobacco manufacture. In fact, northeastern Pennsylvania was a national center for the production of silks, silk goods, and silk throwsters. Lackawanna and Luzerne Counties employed more women in silk manufacture than did Philadelphia, traditionally considered to be the great textile center.[38]

> Our suspicion . . . is that the core of these differences has to do with different expectations about close relatives; that is, in one ethnic group the expectations of how a husband, or a wife, a father or a mother, a brother or a sister, a cousin, an aunt, or an uncle should behave are likely to be quite different than in another ethnic group.
>
> —Andrew M. Greely, *Why Can't They Be like Us?*

Despite the change in cultures and language, despite the hard times, the uncertain future, the constant moving about, and the living in cities under the least favorable of circumstances, the Poles who chose to remain in America managed to survive. They established families, sank roots, and formed communities. Perhaps it is precisely because their sense of family was so strong and so fundamental to their lives that they were able to succeed. Thomas and Znaniecki, however, in their classic study of the subject, would have us believe that the Polish family disappeared in America, never to be seen again. For them, the Polish family became "merely a natural organization based on personal connections between its members, and these connections are sufficient only to keep together a marriage group, including perhaps, occasionally, a few near relatives."[39] Thomas and Znaniecki, unfortunately, spoke too soon. They ended their study in 1918 in the very midst of the Polish family's attempts to adjust to its new environment, an adjustment which, before anything else, had to be an economic one. Like Thomas and Znaniecki, contemporary historians and sociologists have also stopped too soon. The final adjustments were made after 1920. It was in these years that the bulk of the children were born or raised and communities solidified. To understand fully the impact of the industrial experience on the immigrant family, we need to study

[38] *Second Annual Report of the Commissioner of Labor and Industry of the Commonwealth of Pennsylvania, 1914,* pt. 1, "Production, Wages, Employees, Welfare and Educational Work" (Harrisburg, 1915).

[39] Thomas and Znaniecki, 1:98.

*Table 5.* Average number of total employees and female employees employed in Pennsylvania and selected counties, 1914–20

| | | 1914* | 1915 | 1916 | 1917 | 1918 | 1919 | 1920 |
|---|---|---|---|---|---|---|---|---|
| Pennsylvania | T † | — | 1,503,881 | 1,735,543 | 1,802,813 | 1,827,101 | 1,523,609 | 1,614,099 |
| | F‡ | — | 208,310 | 213,972 | 229,518 | 240,757 | 222,763 | 240,450 |
| Selected counties | | | | | | | | |
| Allegheny | T | — | 262,159 | 220,060 | 235,647 | 282,458 | 221,621 | 243,235 |
| | F | — | 16,333 | 14,632 | 15,362 | 17,127 | 14,747 | 16,066 |
| Carbon | T | 6,147 | 11,360 | 10,619 | 11,228 | 12,628 | 12,173 | 13,000 |
| | F | 1,263 | 1,129 | 918 | 1,284 | 1,183 | 1,243 | 1,371 |
| Delaware | T | 14,610 | 19,115 | 32,418 | 33,267 | 49,582 | 70,363 | 50,953 |
| | F | 3,942 | 4,766 | 3,985 | 5,022 | 6,435 | 5,735 | 5,403 |
| Lackawanna | T | 20,025 | 60,375 | 55,030 | 49,993 | 63,355 | 63,214 | 62,718 |
| | F | 6,846 | 6,742 | 7,205 | 9,027 | 9,415 | 9,964 | 11,705 |
| Lehigh | T | 27,993 | 25,039 | 25,816 | 24,760 | 24,475 | 24,254 | 26,386 |
| | F | 8,157 | 7,719 | 6,855 | 6,879 | 6,598 | 6,668 | 7,732 |
| Luzerne | T | 25,439 | 84,524 | 86,591 | 78,160 | 89,508 | 86,601 | 85,965 |
| | F | 8,828 | 8,915 | 10,408 | 11,320 | 13,066 | 11,988 | 12,501 |
| Northampton | T | 33,934 | 76,810 | 44,783 | 46,789 | 54,513 | 34,711 | 37,703 |
| | F | 8,078 | 9,104 | 8,273 | 7,243 | 7,061 | 6,580 | 7,815 |
| Northumberland | T | 8,033 | 24,248 | 23,715 | 23,620 | 25,779 | 25,923 | 26,676 |
| | F | 2,959 | 3,785 | 4,130 | 4,698 | 4,685 | 4,690 | 4,977 |
| Philadelphia | T | 308,710 | 313,783 | 314,068 | 332,340 | 492,819 | 297,436 | 317,601 |
| | F | 92,302 | 89,682 | 87,452 | 90,878 | 93,980 | 80,591 | 83,747 |
| Schuylkill | T | 8,964 | 44,805 | 53,305 | 42,716 | 43,238 | 47,681 | 47,197 |
| | F | 3,217 | 3,678 | 4,494 | 4,986 | 4,682 | 5,655 | 5,571 |

SOURCE: *Second Annual Report.*
* Mining industries not included in the totals.
† Total
‡ Female

the results of the past fifty years. In a sense, the final returns of the impact are just now coming in. We have to bridge the gap from immigrant to ethnic, from foreigner to that special American creation that is the very product of the process of adaptation.

A detailed study of immigrants and their children after 1920 would reveal that preindustrial or preimmigration values of the family still persist in modern industrial America. Industrialization did not necessarily entail the total eradiction of preindustrial or peasant values, and, more important, it did not imply that there could be one and only one form of adaptation to industrial society. There is nothing in the process of industrialization and nothing in the nature of industry per se which dictates that there can be only one type of adaptation. We have been blinded for too long by the model of the Anglo-Saxon nuclear family. If adaptation is looked at only from the perspective of the Anglo-Saxon experience in America, then of course there can be only one form of adaptation; anyone who deviates from it can be said never to have adapted—or assimilated.

Thus, with all due respect to Thomas and Znaniecki, the Polish family, slightly modified to be sure, did survive the industrial experience—European as well as American. It was impossible for the Poles immediately to recreate their special sense of familial solidarity in America because the family members necessary for it were not physically present at the time; one needed brothers, sisters, mothers, fathers, grandparents, aunts, uncles, cousins—in addition to husband, wife, and children. Because they were migrant-laborers, the Poles did not emigrate as families; those that stayed, married and had their children in America. It was only during the past fifty years that the Polish family was able to reconstitute itself in America, to produce once again a clan of relatives, up and down, sideways, without distinction or exception.

There is such a thing as a Polish family among the second and third generations which differentiates it in values, expectations, and even structure from a Jewish, Italian, black, or Anglo-American family. For many the fundamentals of familial solidarity remain; the concept and recognition of a clan exists. Among second- and third-generation Polish-Americans an aunt, uncle, cousin, or grandparent has just as much right to be concerned about one's affairs as one's parents, brothers, or sisters. The relationship between siblings is strong and becomes stronger after the death of the parents; a parent (patriarch or matriarch) is not necessary for the family's survival. The Polish family remains multi-nucleated; one marriage-group, usually the most prosperous, tends to assume leadership of the clan. In-laws are still co-opted by the family they marry into; little distinction is made between blood and law relatives in terms of treatment and attitudes. Once accepted into the family, in-laws are offered the same support, moral and financial, as would be given to blood relatives and are, of course, expected to acquiesce in the control of the family group. The in-law remains solidly within the family (because they *are* the family) even after the death of the blood relative who brought the two families together. It is still common for Polish parents to counsel their son or daughter about marriage: "Remember, you don't just marry the person, you marry a family."

The socialization of children tends to remain hierarchical, authoritarian, and intergenerational rather than horizontal. That is, the role played by the peer group among Polish children is weak when compared to Italians, Irish, and blacks. Consequently, Polish and Slavic youth in general (unlike their Irish, Italian, or black counterparts) have always been less likely to form gangs. Moreover, the Poles have a very low (or nonexistent) rate of juvenile delinquency.[40] Respect for grandparents is real and is expressed even in the absence of parents or grandparents. Herbert Gan's *Urban Villagers* describes certain aspects of Italian working-class family attitudes that are exactly the opposite of those of the Polish family, a finding that throws further doubt on the validity of equating family patterns solely with class:

> The extended family system is limited generationally, for relationships between adults and their parents—the immigrant generation—are fewer and less intimate than those between adults of the same generation. Visits with parents are exchanged, but parents are generally not part of the continuing social life of the family circle. Widowed parents do not live with their children if other alternatives are available. While old people are allowed to function as grandparents, they are freely criticized for spoiling their grandchildren, or for insisting on outmoded ideas. Compared with the middle class, in fact, the older generation receives little respect or care. . . . The lack of respect toward the older generation is especially noticeable among children, who tease and insult old people behind their backs, including their own grandparents.[41]

The Polish extended family is not limited generationally; parents and grandparents are always part of the continuing social life of the family circle; in fact, they are fundamental to it. There is no more revered person in the Polish family than the grandparent—"busia" (*babka*) and "dziadzia" (*dziadek*). Children are taught to respect the older generations of

[40] Statements on gangs and juvenile delinquency are based on a study of crime statistics in Polish sections of Philadelphia, Baltimore, Chicago, Scranton, and Wilkes-Barre, and interviews of parish priests, school principals, civic leaders, social workers, and police captains in predominantly Polish wards of these cities.

[41] Herbert J. Gans, *Urban Villagers: Group and Class in the Life of Italian-Americans* (New York, 1962), pp. 46-47.

parents and grandparents (and they are taught to internalize, not just verbalize, this respect). Thus, the Polish child takes other generations in addition to his own as his reference point, in contrast to the peer group orientation of Gans's Italians, Whyte's street corner kids, or Liebow's youngsters on Tally's corner.[42] Finally, there are indications that Slavic peoples remain the most unwilling of all groups to place their aged parents in retirement homes; whenever possible, parents will live with the married son or daughter most able to provide for them.

Helping other members of the family is still accepted and practiced. More affluent aunts and uncles will help less fortunate nieces and nephews; more fortunate brothers and sisters will help less affluent brothers and sisters; children help parents, and vice versa—to make the down payment on a house, to start a business, or to put the children through college. During the Great Depression, the Poles in Philadelphia very rarely showed up on the relief rolls or sought public assistance—to the great astonishment of state and city officials, since the unemployment rate among male members of the group was very high. The Poles preferred to help each other (or to send the womenfolk out to work) rather than depend on the government; in this situation the help extended beyond the family to include any member of the ethnic group. There is also evidence that this attitude prevailed during the depression wherever Poles were found in the country. The depression differed in degree, but not in kind, from all other recessions and depressions they had experienced since arrival in America; they survived the others without charity and government help, they reasoned, so why shouldn't they survive this one?

After fifty years Poles continue to send money to relatives in Poland—to relatives they have never seen (except in photographs). Millions of dollars are sent each year by Chicago Poles alone. It is estimated that the total amount sent "home" annually by Polish-Americans is so great that it constitutes a substantial—and vital—part of Poland's economy.[43] Tens of thousands of second- and third-generation Polish-Americans return to Poland every year to visit the relatives they have never seen; the Polish-American travel business, consequently, is a multi-million-dollar enterprise.[44] Because the sending of money to Poland is still common (and persisted even during the depression), it would seem that the Poles have been super faithful to their legacy; they came as migrant-laborers with the intention of earning money to send home, all in accordance with the rules and regulations of familial solidarity.

[42] William Foote Whyte, *Street Corner Society: The Social Structure of an Italian Slum* (Chicago, 1943); Elliot Liebow, *Tally's Corner* (Boston, 1967).

[43] See, for example, "Polonia Come Home," *Time,* Aug. 21, 1972, pp. 33-34.

[44] Interviews with Polish-American travel agents in New York, Chicago, and Philadelphia reveal that, as Polish-Americans become more affluent, they travel more—to Poland.

Wherever found, Slavic groups have traditionally had one of the highest (if not the highest) percentages of home ownership.[45] Once the decision had been made to remain in America, the first goal was to buy a house—the ultimate in social as well as economic security. Just as in his traditional culture the Pole could not be a full member of his community without land, so, too, he could have no social standing within his group in America unless he also owned land, here, a house. The names and the places may have changed, but the rules and regulations stayed the same. If he could not improve the position of his family by owning land in Poland, at least he could reproduce the familial group and its values in America by owning a home of his own. This was the true attraction of America. America allowed him to achieve here what he couldn't do in Poland.

Thus the family as an organization of primary relationships, the values placed on these relationships, and the expectations arising out of them may be at the very heart of ethnic persistence in America today. The material or tangible attributes of immigrant culture (language, dress, customs, foods) may have disappeared, but such aspects of immaterial culture as family values remain. And they remain within groups that are becoming increasingly middle class in terms of income and education. Ethnicity, then, is not necessarily a function of class, as is maintained by some, but evolves into new forms within the American class structure; and the family is the key to its persistence.[46]

This paper has questioned our whole concept of the impact of the industrial experience on the immigrant family. As is apparent, the need for proper perspective is paramount. Unless the immigrant's adaptation to American industrial society is viewed as a total process—the "coming from" (the reasons for leaving), the "bringing with" (his cultural values and experiences), and the "going to" (the structured environment he encountered in America)—we can never fully understand how any group of people rearranges and reconstructs itself when challenged by a new set of circumstances. Finally, we must realize that the process has not ended (nor may it ever) but is still continuing. Indeed, rather than obliterating or homogenizing the immigrant family, the industrial experience, at least in America, enabled new forms and responses to evolve. And these new forms and responses constitute the essence of ethnic persistence in the United States today.

[45] Other groups, Italians, for example, have high ownership rates today, but this is more a post–World War II phenomenon for these groups. Among Poles home ownership was strong from the very beginning—from the minute they made the decision to stay in America. See U.S. Census figures on home ownership for Polish, Italian, and Jewish sections of Philadelphia, Chicago, and Baltimore, 1920–1970.

[46] Herbert J. Gans and Milton Gordon, *Assimilation in American Life: The Role of Race, Religion, and National Origins* (New York, 1964).

# II "She Earns as a Child—She Pays as a Man": Women Workers in a Mid-Nineteenth-Century New York City Community

*Carol Groneman*

LITTLE IS REALLY known about the mid-nineteenth-century urban immigrant poor. The image of a disorganized and brutalized lower class portrayed by contemporary middle- and upper-class observers, essentially a reflection of their own ethnic, class, and religious prejudices, colors present-day accounts of the period. Immigration, labor, and urban historians continue to posit this distorted picture either because they accept the stereotype or because sources leading to any other view have been ignored.[1] Based primarily on an invaluable and hitherto neglected resource, the 1855 New York state census manuscript schedules, this paper begins to reexamine this unknown world by focusing on a brief moment in time and on a single subgroup within this large and heterogeneous population: the Irish immigrants living in New York City's Sixth Ward in the 1850s.[2]

Several questions must be asked. Since contemporary evidence indicates that a single income was often insufficient to support a working-class family in the mid-nineteenth century, how did these immigrants cope with the daily struggle for survival? Traditional historical sources, which provide information only on individual incomes, cannot adequately answer this question and in fact obscure the real patterns of work in a poor

[1] Oscar Handlin, *The Uprooted* (New York, 1951), pp. 154–57; idem., *Boston Immigrants,* 2d ed. (Cambridge, Mass., 1959), p. 120; Nathan Glazer and Daniel Patrick Moynihan, *Beyond the Melting Pot,* 2d ed. (Cambridge, Mass., 1970), p. 239; Douglas T. Miller, *Jacksonian Aristocracy: Class and Democracy in New York, 1830–1860* (New York, 1967), p. 184; Robert Bremner, *From the Depths* (New York, 1956), p. 58; James Richardson, *The New York Police: From Colonial Times to 1901* (New York, 1970), p. 27; Alexander Callow, Jr., *The Tweed Ring* (New York, 1966), pp. 55–62.

[2] The manuscript schedules of the 1855 New York State census are located at the county clerk's office, New York City. The 1855 state census was chosen rather than the 1850 federal census for two reasons: the 1850 census did not enumerate women's occupations and did not include the major German and Irish immigration of the early 1850s. Historians, such as Robert Ernst in *Immigrant Life in New York City, 1825–1863* (New York, 1949), have previously used the manuscripts to enumerate, for example, carpenters, or Italians, or shopkeepers, but the wealth of material on household and family relationships provided by the manuscripts has been entirely neglected.

immigrant community. Evidence from the census manuscripts indicates that in almost one-half of Irish households in the Sixth Ward, at least two members of each household, most often the husband and working wife, contributed to the family income. Because women assumed the major burden of supplementing family income, it is important to establish not only how many women worked but what effect Irishwomen's economic function had on traditional family patterns and relationships. Did the profound changes these preindustrial peasants faced in industrializing America bring about, as most American social historians have concluded, the breakdown, disruption, and disorganization of immigrant families, values, and culture? Finally, was the work pattern we find in the Sixth Ward unique to the Irish, or did it cut across ethnic lines to include other working-class groups? An examination of the relationship between family and work roles discussed in this paper can shed some light on this larger issue of immigrant adaptation to new work processes and life-styles in America's urban centers.

The neighborhood chosen for study was New York City's Sixth Ward, a traditional Irish working-class area. Bounded by fashionable Broadway and the colorful Bowery, the Sixth Ward was itself home to the notorious Five Points slum. While predominantly Irish, a heterogeneous mixture of nationalities, races, and religions mingled on the streets of the ward. Native-born whites and blacks and earlier Irish immigrants shared the neighborhood by the late 1840s and 1850s with recently arrived Irish famine emigrants, Germans, Italians, and Dutch, and Polish and Russian Jews. Over 25,000 people crowded into this small ward. Availability of work in the factories, foundries, shops, markets, docks, hotels, the publishing industry, and building, transportation, and clothing trades attracted immigrants to this and other lower Manhattan wards. For working-class families faced with the problem of irregular and seasonal male employment, areas like the Sixth Ward offered a solution to this dilemma by providing work for wives and children.

We have a general, though inadequate, picture of mid-nineteenth-century wages, prices, and rents in New York City's immigrant neighborhoods from contemporary newspapers, government reports, and compiled census statistics.[3] For example John Mitchell, the editor of the New York

[3] See, for example, J. D. B. DeBow, *Statistical View of the United States . . . a Compendium of the Seventh Census of 1850* (1854; reprint ed., New York, 1969); Eighth Census, *Statistics of the United States in 1860* (Washington, D.C., 1893); N. W. Aldrich, *Wholesale Prices, Wages, and Transportation,* U.S., Report no. 1394, 52d Cong., 2d sess. (Washington, D.C., 1893); U.S., Department of Labor, Bureau of Labor Statistics, Bull. no. 499, "The History of Wages in the United States from Colonial Times to 1928" (Washington, D. C., 1929); U.S. Industrial Commission on Immigration, *Reports,* vol. 15 (Washington, D.C., 1901); Edith Abbott, "Wages of Unskilled Labor in the United States, 1850–1900," *Journal of Political*

*Citizen,* estimated in 1854 that rent took one-half of a poor man's income and that food and fuel prices had risen over 30 percent that year.[4] Both the *New York Daily Times* and the *New York Tribune* suggested that a moderate income for a family of four required approximately eleven dollars per week in the early 1850s.[5] But many men and women earned far less: factory operatives and common laborers averaged less than five dollars per week, and the lowest-paid seamstresses earned only about two dollars per week. Although some unionized workers increased their wages by periodic strikes in the early fifties, even these wages hardly kept pace with the rising cost of living. Women's wages, consistently lower than those of their male counterparts, rose little during the 1840s and fifties and, in some trades, actually declined. The depressions of 1854-55 and 1857, combined with seasonal and irregular employment throughout the period, generally left the individual worker's income far below the minimum standard suggested by the *Times* and the *Tribune.*[6]

Sixth Ward Irish families responded to these economic conditions by supplementing the income of the head of the household through the earnings of other family members, usually the wife. But more than economic need affected both a woman's decision to work and the type of work she performed. Age, family relationship, and availability of work influenced Sixth Ward Irishwomen in a variety of ways that require careful analysis. We can begin by examining the numbers of workingwomen in relation to their age and the kinds of work they performed.

No less than 44 percent of the 4,200 Sixth Ward Irishwomen aged fifteen to forty-nine were gainfully employed. As might be expected, the percentage of employed women decreased with age, but the decrease was not marked since 35 percent of all women over forty years of age still worked. The most common employment for young Irishwomen in the area was domestic and personal service—including working as hotel maids, waitresses, and cooks, as well as personal servants, housekeepers, and laundresses. Half of the women between the ages fifteen to nineteen and 40 percent of those twenty to twenty-nine were employed in these occupations (see Table 6). Servants in private households worked as many

*Economy* 13 (1905): 321–67. For contemporary newspaper accounts, see the investigations reported in the *New York Tribune,* Aug. 14, 19, 29 and Sept. 3, 5, 9, 11, 17, 1845; May 27, June 8, 17, 29, July 20, 28, 1853; *America's Own* (New York), Apr. 14, July 7, Sept. 1, 1849.

[4] *The Citizen* (New York), Feb. 25, Mar. 18, 1854; also *New York Tribune,* Feb. 21, 1854. Greeley estimated an increase of 50 percent in the cost of provisions in New York City between 1843 and 1850 (*New York Tribune,* Nov. 14, 1850).

[5] *New York Daily Times,* Nov. 8, 1853; *New York Tribune,* May 27, 1851.

[6] Stanley Lebergott, *Manpower in Economic Growth: The American Record since 1800* (New York, 1964), p. 150; Norman Ware, *The Industrial Worker, 1840–1860,* 2d ed. (Chicago, 1964), p. 31; John R. Commons et al., *The History of Labour in the United States* (New York, 1919), 1:488; Carl Degler, "Labor in the Economy and Politics of New York City: A Study of the Impact of Early Industrialism," Diss. Columbia 1952, pp. 175–76.

*Table 6.* Occupations of Irishwomen in the Sixth Ward by age, 1855

| Occupation | % of Irishwomen aged 15–19 | 20–29 | 30–39 | 40–49 | 50+ |
|---|---|---|---|---|---|
| Sewing trades | 40.5 | 29.3 | 16.9 | 16.4 | 14.1 |
| Domestic service | 50.6 | 39.9 | 26.4 | 27.3 | 28.5 |
| Taking boarders | 0.9 | 25.5 | 49.9 | 47.9 | 47.5 |
| Petty enterprises | 0.3 | 0.5 | 1.8 | 3.1 | 3.5 |
| Store keeping | 0 | 0.8 | 2.8 | 3.1 | 4.4 |
| Other manufacturing industries * | 7.5 | 3.0 | 0.9 | 1.0 | 1.9 |
| Professions | 0 | 1.0 | 0.9 | 1.0 | 0 |
| Total | 99.8 | 99.9 | 99.9 | 99.8 | 99.9 |
| Number | 333 | 828 | 435 | 242 | 160 |

SOURCE: Data compiled from the 1855 New York State Census manuscript schedules.
*Upholsterers, type-polishers and cutters, printers, bookbinders and folders, confectioners, makers of ink, pianos, cigars, cards, and boxes.

as fifteen hours a day, oftentimes seven days a week, in dark unventilated kitchens. They occupied cramped, overcrowded sleeping quarters and received between four and eight dollars a month in addition to room and board. Although living conditions might be crowded and food often the leftovers from the family table, servants' physical needs were probably better filled than those of other workingwomen who had to pay rent and buy food out of their meager salaries. Servants complained mostly about the long hours, lack of free time, and the disdainful and haughty attitude of certain employers.[7]

Besides domestic servants in individual households, numerous women worked as chambermaids, waitresses, cooks, and laundresses for the many hotels in the Sixth Ward. Twenty-five Irishwomen, for example, worked at the Carlton House on Broadway and thirteen at Pat Garrick's Sixth Ward Hotel. In an investigation conducted in 1857, a New York state committee found that four-fifths of the servants, even in first-class hotels, slept in overcrowded garrets, receiving compensation roughly comparable to domestic workers in private households. Unlike private domestics, however, hotel workers had more time to escape the drudgery

[7] *New York Tribune,* Nov. 6, 1845, Sept. 16, 1846; William Burns, *Life in New York* (New York, 1851), n.p.; U.S. Congress, Senate, *Report on the Condition of Woman and Child Wage-Earners in the United States,* vol. 9, Document no. 645, 61st Cong., 2d sess.; Helen Sumner, "History of Women in Industry in the United States" (Washington, D.C., 1910), pp. 177–85; Virginia Penny, *The Employments of Women: A Cyclopedia of Women's Work* (New York, 1863), pp. 423–33; Lebergott, pp. 278–84.

of housework because they were not expected to be available beyond required working hours.[8]

The next largest occupation for young Irishwomen, the sewing trades, including dressmaking, tailoring, cap and vest production, millinery, and artificial flower manufacture, accounted for 40 percent of the jobs held by women aged fifteen to nineteen and 30 percent of those aged twenty to twenty-nine. Many Sixth Ward needle trades workers shared the conditions described by the 1853 *New York Tribune* investigation of the needlewomen of New York. Shops located in the lower wards gave out piecework to seamstresses who were paid $0.08 and often as little as $0.04, per shirt. Since finishing three shirts was a hard day's work, the *Tribune* estimated that some needlewomen, taking into consideration the time expended to obtain and return the goods as well as journeys to secure their pay, could conceivably have earned $0.50 for an entire week's labor. Though most milliners, dressmakers, and other needle trades workers earned between $3.50 and $6.00 per week, according to the *Tribune,* there were hundreds of tailoresses and seamstresses who, due to irregular and seasonal employment, earned an average of less than $2.00 per week. "A woman," the *Tribune* commented, "may be defined to be a creature that receives half price for all she does, and pays full price for all she needs. . . . She earns as a child—she pays as a man."[9]

Young Irishwomen also worked in other areas of manufacture, such as type cutting, printing, bookbinding, and making ink, cigars, cards, and boxes. Women in these industries were concentrated at the lowest levels of skill and received about one-half to one-third the wages of men doing comparable work. Apprenticeships for women in most industrial occupations lasted from a few days to a few months, and most of the work required, above all, manual dexterity and stamina. Conditions varied greatly: from the light and airy workshop of the Bible House and Tract Society Publishing Company, to the dangerous, chemical-filled factories of the ink makers. Wages were usually paid by the piece, and a contemporary study, Virginia Penny's *Employments of Women*, suggests an average wage of $3.50 to $6.50 per week.[10]

Peddling was not an important source of employment for young women, but this activity became increasingly common in each succeeding

[8] New York, State Assembly, Document no. 205, "Report of the Select Committee to Examine into the Condition of Tenant Houses in New York and Brooklyn" (Albany, 1857), 3:87. See also Sumner, p. 179; Penny, *Employments of Women,* pp. 428–33; Burns.

[9] *New York Tribune,* June 8, 1853. The statement from the *Tribune* was quoted in Virginia Penny, *Think and Act* (Philadelphia, 1869), p. 84.

[10] Virginia Penny sent out questionnaires to employers and visited many establishments, particularly in New York City, between 1859 and 1861. See also Sumner, pp. 195–230; Edith Abbott, *Women in Industry* (New York, 1924), pp. 246–61.

age category. The older woman who sold fruits, vegetables, or candies was a familiar and sometimes colorful figure in the immigrant neighborhoods. For example, when the City Hall Park apple woman was threatened in July 1845 by a policeman and told to move on, "being a full-blooded Sixth Warder, and consequently somewhat accustomed to little scenes of tumult," she pummeled him unmercifully, much to the amusement of the passing crowd. Throughout the city about 1,300 huckster women, mostly older Irishwomen, sold fruits and vegetables on the fringes of the New York markets. Around the City Hall Park, Printing House Square, and near the Bowery, women and some young girls peddled flowers, newspapers, candy, and fruit to the hundreds of passersby.[11]

Storekeeping was also the province of a relatively few older women: Mary Cavanagh ran a dry goods store on Pearl Street; in an adjacent shop Ann Welsh sold fancy goods; the gold balls of the pawnbroker hung outside Bridget Costello's shop on the Bowery; and Catherine Sweeney sold candy in a rear shop on Baxter Street. A few women were involved in large-scale enterprises. For example, Ann Furgus, a thirty-five-year-old widow ran a boardinghouse on Center Street housing over fifty boarders and employing a staff of six domestics. Most women classified here as storekeepers, however, managed small grocery-liquor stores. Up by 4:00 A.M. to buy the fruits and vegetables brought by the farmers to market, one proprietress in the late 1850s described how she opened her store at 5:00 A.M. and did not close until 10:00 at night. Even with those long hours she could not make more than three or four dollars per week after deducting the weekly rent of six or seven dollars and the cost of fuel and candles.[12]

We have seen that age was an important factor in determining the kinds of work in which Sixth Ward Irishwomen were employed, but in order to understand the larger issue of the effects of women's work on the family, we must discuss workingwomen in relation to their position within the household. How did a woman's role within the family, as wife, daughter, or widowed head of the household, affect both her decision to work and the type of work she would perform? The great majority of women working outside the home in domestic service, factories, and some sewing trades were young, single women whose role within the

[11] *Subterranean* (New York), July 19, 1845; Penny, *Employments of Women,* p. 159; *New York Tribune,* Sept. 14, 1845; *Young America* (New York), Nov. 1, 1845; James MacCabe, *Secrets of the Great City* (Philadelphia, 1868), p. 504; Burns.

[12] All individuals are taken from the manuscript schedules of the New York State census. See also, Penny, *Employments of Women,* pp. 121–22. Women who ran stores, boardinghouses, or family businesses jointly with their husbands were not listed as gainfully employed in the 1855 census. They are enumerated in present-day censuses, however, in a category called "unpaid family worker."

household as daughter, relative, or boarder, did not depend on remaining at home throughout the workday. This was not the case with married women. When forced by economic necessity to provide supplementary income for their families, they did so by working within their homes, thereby minimizing the strains on family life.

The major occupation of these married women was one that has been ignored by historians relying exclusively on the compiled census statistics: taking in boarders (see Table 7). While "boardinghouse keeper" was an occupational classification in the census, it encompassed only a small proportion of the many households renting space to one or more boarders. Women taking a few boarders into their homes were simply not counted by census takers as gainfully employed, although they received an average $1.25 per week for each boarder.[13] Since this work was carried on in the home, it was looked upon as an extension of women's traditional work-role, even though it was a money-making occupation. The arbitrary application of the definition of gainful employment by census takers, and the dependence on the compiled statistics by later historians, has resulted in the exclusion of fully 25 percent of the Sixth Ward married women from the statistics of the gainfully employed.

*Table 7.* Irish working wives by age, 1855

| Age | All Irish working wives % | All Irish working wives No. | Irish working wives other than those taking boarders % | Irish working wives other than those taking boarders No. |
|---|---|---|---|---|
| 20–29 | 28.4 | 258 | 6.3 | 16 |
| 30–39 | 30.8 | 227 | 3.0 | 7 |
| 40–49 | 25.5 | 95 | 2.4 | 3 |
| 50–59 | 25.4 | 43 | 3.6 | 2 |

SOURCE: 1855 N.Y. State Census manuscript schedules.

It is interesting to speculate on the amount of possible income these women sacrificed by working in the home. The Sixth Ward factories, for example, paid an average of $5.50 per week to women workers.[14] Since most industrial trades were easily learned with a few week's apprenticeship, skill probably had little influence on the limited number of married women working outside the home. The lower wards also offered other

[13] *New York Tribune,* Mar. 7, 1845.

[14] The average wage is based on the wages given in the 1855 New York State Census Manuscript, Manufacturing Statistics, Sixth Ward.

employment opportunities outside the home, and many single women worked in the local hotels, department stores, and laundries. Therefore, it is reasonable to hypothesize that Sixth Ward married-women's work in the home reflected more than limited opportunities, namely, an element of conscious choice. Women who chose this particular occupation very likely did so because it allowed them to continue to function in their role as housewife and mother while also contributing to the family's support.

This is not an insignificant suggestion. A considerable body of historical literature insists that immigration and the alienation of the large city led to disruption and breakdown of the family. The evidence presented here concerning married women's work-role within the home suggests the need to reevaluate the alleged disorganization of America's immigrant communities. The evidence from a poor working-class area like the Sixth Ward is all the more revealing since its residents, many of whom had fled the Irish famine, would have been particularly vulnerable to these supposed processes of family disintegration. Contrary to the hypothesis, however, the family-centered Irish peasant women adapted to the economic pressures of urban life in such a way as to preserve their traditional role in the family. They did this by combining their economic activity with the functions of childrearing and housekeeping. The large number of the Sixth Ward married women who took in boarders suggests that this was a central means of coping with the multiple demands placed upon immigrant women in America. Even when forced by necessity to work, they did so in ways that would reinforce, rather than disrupt, their traditional familial values.[15]

This point can be further demonstrated by a comparison of the structure of Sixth Ward households headed by Irish, German, and white native-born Americans. We find that the great majority of immigrant households were kin-related while a relatively insignificant proportion were composed of nonrelated adults or adults living alone (see Table 8).[16] Table 8 compares the type of household of Irish, German, and native-born white inhabitants of the Sixth Ward. The native-born significantly had the

[15] These conclusions are not unique to the Irish or to mid-nineteenth-century New York City. For recent studies of women's work experience and its relationship to family structure in other nineteenth- and early twentieth-century communities, see Virginia Yans-McLaughlin, "Patterns of Work and Family Organization: Buffalo's Italians," in Theodore K. Rabb and Robert I. Rotberg, eds., *The Family in History: Interdisciplinary Essays* (New York, 1973) and Daniel J. Walkowitz, "Working-class Women in the Gilded Age: Factory, Community, and Family Life among Cohoes, New York, Cotton Workers," *Journal of Social History* 5 (1972): 464–90.

[16] Most sixth ward immigrant households were composed of nuclear family members only, nuclear family members and relatives (extended household), or nuclear family members, relatives, and boarders (augmented household).

*Table 8.* Type of household

| | Irish | German | Native-born |
|---|---|---|---|
| % of households | | | |
| Kin-related | 94.6 | 90.5 | 86.9 |
| Irregular | 3.6 | 6.1 | 6.9 |
| Single | 1.5 | 3.2 | 6.0 |
| Total | 99.7 | 99.8 | 99.8 |
| No. of households | 2,736 | 943 | 346 |

SOURCE: 1855 N.Y. State Census manuscript schedules.

lowest percentage of kin-related households. If the immigration process had been as disorganizing and disintegrating as is often suggested, it is highly unlikely that the immigrants in this poor, working-class ward, especially those who had fled the Irish famine, would have exhibited this stable structural pattern in the reconstitution and creation of their households in America. Furthermore, native Americans had not been affected by the disorganizing process of immigration across the Atlantic (only one-quarter of the individuals had migrated from outside New York City), and yet the percentage of kin-related households among them was considerably lower than among the German and Irish.

Dividing kin-related households into nuclear, augmented, and extended households demonstrates that the majority of Irish, German, and native-born Sixth Ward residents lived in households composed only of nuclear family members (see Table 9). Slightly higher percentages of Irish and native-born Americans, compared to Germans, took relatives and boarders into their households. The higher proportion of extended households among the native-born perhaps reflected the fact that native-born Americans were more likely than Irish or German immigrants to have had relatives in the city with whom to share their households. Fully 37 percent of the total Irish, German, and native-born American households shared their living quarters with other than nuclear family members. That almost identical proportions in each group found it necessary to do so suggests that Sixth Warders, regardless of ethnic origins, responded in similar ways to poverty, the needs of relatives, and the lack of available housing. While an argument based on household structure obviously tells us nothing about the tensions and conflicts within those immigrant families, it does suggest that the larger outlines of the picture should emphasize cohesion rather than breakdown.[17]

[17] For a further analysis of family and household structure, immigration patterns, and occupational structure in this community, see my "The 'Bloody Old Sixth': A Social Analysis of a New York City Working-class Community in the Mid-Nineteenth Century," Diss. Rochester 1973.

*Table 9.* Composition of Sixth Ward Irish, German, and native-born kin-related households

| | Irish | German | Native-born |
|---|---|---|---|
| % of households | | | |
| Nuclear | 62.9 | 65.3 | 60.8 |
| Augumented | 28.5 | 27.1 | 28.3 |
| Extended | 8.6 | 7.6 | 10.9 |
| Total | 100.0 | 100.0 | 100.0 |
| No. of households | 2,589 | 854 | 301 |

SOURCE: 1855 N.Y. State Census manuscript schedules.

We can further illustrate married immigrant workingwomen's attempts to reduce the strain of their dual roles by analyzing those wives working in occupations other than taking boarders. The evidence suggests that availability of work in the home, and not simply the income level of the husband, determined whether a wife would work. If we divide Irish male heads-of-households' occupations into the two most numerous groups, artisans and laborers, we find that artisans' wives were more likely to work than laborers' wives (see Table 10). At first glance this might seem surprising since laborers, on the whole, tended to receive lower wages than many artisans. Since irregular employment was a problem affecting both artisans and laborers, it cannot account for this apparent anomaly. By analyzing artisans' occupations more closely, however, we find that tailors' wives working in the sewing trades with their husbands, and oftentimes with their children, accounted for most of the difference. The opportunity to work at home and thus combine family and work-roles seemed to be the decisive factor in determining whether or not wives would work.

However difficult it was for a married woman to provide needed income for the family, the problems of the widowed head of household were infinitely greater. According to the New York City Inspector's Reports, large numbers of the foreign-born laboring population, chiefly male heads of households, died in the prime of life, between twenty-five and forty years of age.[18] While the wages of a needlewoman, in combination with a husband's or a father's earnings, might have produced a subsistence wage, those widows who had to support families on these incomes lived on the brink of disaster. Sheer necessity forced widowed heads of households to work in greater variety of occupations than

[18] *Annual Report of the City Inspector of the Number of Deaths and Interments in the City of New York for the Year 1851* (New York, 1852), pp. 448–50.

*Table 10.* Irish working wives by occupations of heads of households and by age

| Head of household's occupation | % of Irish working wives aged 20–29 | 30–39 | 40–49 |
|---|---|---|---|
| Artisan | 32.3 | 40.6 | 25.0 |
| Laborer | 30.4 | 25.9 | 27.5 |

SOURCE: 1855 N.Y. State Census manuscript schedules.

married women. About 25 percent of all employed widows, roughly comparable to the percentage of wives, kept boarders. Most other widows were concentrated in domestic and personal service and in the sewing trades. Younger widows worked as seamstresses, milliners, and cap makers, while those over forty years of age turned to laundering and housekeeping. Very few wives worked in domestic and personal service, but over 20 percent of the widows did. As chief support of the household, these widows, unlike the Sixth Ward wives, were forced to work outside their homes performing the difficult manual labor of a laundress or charwoman.[19]

Comparisons of Irish artisans' and laborers' households with both parents living to households headed by widows also reveal significant differences in pattern of family employment created by the absence of a male breadwinner. For example, in households headed by widows between the ages twenty to twenty-nine, there were fewer persons contributing to the family income simply because these households lacked a second employable adult. Also, a higher percentage of these same households included working relatives. More significant, however, was the tendency, given the extremely low wages paid women workers in the mid-nineteenth century, for widows to send their children to work (see Table 11). Between the ages of thirty and fifty-nine, 13 percent of the artisan-headed households, 14 percent of the laborers' households, and 47 percent of the households headed by widows included working children. At each age interval the children of widows worked in considerable higher percentages than did laborers' or artisans' children.

The death of a husband and father in this period meant both that widows would be more likely to work than women in general and that their children would be forced to work at a younger age and remain in their mothers' households longer than the children of working fathers. We can assume that these children responded to the greater need

[19] Compiled from the manuscript schedules of the 1855 New York State census.

*Table 11.* Workers in Irish artisans', laborers', and widows' households by age of head of household

| Workers | % of household heads aged 20–29 | 30–39 | 40–49 | 50+ |
|---|---|---|---|---|
| Artisans' households | | | | |
| Husband and wife | 32.3 | 39.3 | 20.1 | 19.3 |
| Husband, wife, and child | 0 | 1.3 | 4.9 | 7.0 |
| Husband and child | 0 | 2.2 | 18.5 | 26.3 |
| Husband and relative | 1.5 | 1.2 | 3.4 | 0 |
| Total | 33.8 | 44.0 | 46.9 | 52.6 |
| Husband only | 66.2 | 55.9 | 53.1 | 47.4 |
| Total | 100.0 | 99.9 | 100.0 | 100.0 |
| No. of households | 130 | 229 | 81 | 57 |
| Laborers' households | | | | |
| Husband and wife | 30.4 | 25.9 | 20.2 | 14.9 |
| Husband, wife, and child | 0 | 0 | 7.3 | 7.3 |
| Husband and child | 0 | 1.6 | 8.4 | 20.6 |
| Husband and relative | 1.7 | 5.1 | 2.6 | 1.1 |
| Total | 32.1 | 32.6 | 38.5 | 43.9 |
| Husband only | 67.9 | 67.3 | 61.5 | 56.1 |
| Total | 100.0 | 100.0 | 100.0 | 100.0 |
| No. of households | 240 | 365 | 262 | 262 |
| Widows' households | | | | |
| Widow only | 68.6 | 55.7 | 26.7 | 11.8 |
| Widow and relative | 7.7 | 6.6 | 0.2 | 1.5 |
| Widow and child | 0 | 16.9 | 27.7 | 30.1 |
| Child only | 0 | 1.9 | 20.2 | 36.8 |
| Relative only | 0 | 2.8 | 0 | 0 |
| No workers listed | 23.7 | 16.0 | 25.2 | 19.8 |
| Total | 100.0 | 99.9 | 100.0 | 100.0 |
| No. of households | 38 | 106 | 119 | 136 |

SOURCE: 1855 N.Y. State Census manuscript schedules.

for their earnings created by female-headed households and stayed at home to provide that support. That twenty-five and thirty-year-old sons and daughters remained within their parents' households suggests far more than the family's need for their income. The children's willingness and desire to continue to contribute to the survival of the family unit indicates the tenacity and endurance of strong family ties within this Irish community.

As we have seen, age, family relationships, and availability of work in the home affected both the kinds of work Sixth Ward Irishwomen performed and the likelihood that they would be employed. Did these patterns represent a peculiarly Irish adaptation to a new environment, or did other ethnic groups respond in similar ways? Comparison with the second-largest Sixth Ward immigrant group, the Germans, shows that approximately the same percentage of German and Irish women worked (see Table 12). This confirms what the Irish statistics suggested, namely, that in a poor, working-class community like the Sixth Ward, women's work was necessary for their own and their family's survival. It further suggests that the work patterns we have been discussing do not necessarily reflect responses based on ethnicity, but rather cut across ethnic lines. Working-class women, whether German or Irish, responded in similar ways to the need to secure an adequate family income.

Like their Irish counterparts, many young, unmarried German women in the Sixth Ward worked as domestic servants. This is surprising since an analysis of New York City as a whole indicates that a greater percentage of Irishwomen worked as servants than did Germans or any other immigrant group. This differential is usually attributed to the German family's tendency both to emigrate and to stay together in America. The Irish, on the other hand, allegedly emigrated as individuals.[20] Contrary to this assumption, the majority of Sixth Ward Irish families emigrated as a unit, and a higher percentage (71 percent) of young Irishwomen lived with parents, husbands, children or other relatives than young German women did (65 percent). In fact, the stereotype notwithstanding, a higher percentage (51 percent) of young Sixth Ward German women worked as servants than did their Irish neighbors (43 percent). Because there were numerous large German boardinghouses in the Sixth requiring domestic staff, the language barrier, which existed in the rest of the city and probably contributed to the small overall percentage of German servants, did not prevail. Thus, in the Sixth Ward the general assumptions concerning the low proportion of German servants and the family-oriented explanation for this low percentage did not hold true.

Fully one-third of the German wives between the ages twenty to forty-

[20] See, for example, Ernst, p. 66.

*Table 12*. German and Irish workingwomen by age

| Age | German working-women | | Irish workingwomen | |
|---|---|---|---|---|
| | % | No. | % | No. |
| 15–19 | 50.2 | 89 | 47.9 | 333 |
| 20–29 | 50.4 | 327 | 46.9 | 828 |
| 30–39 | 34.7 | 118 | 39.3 | 435 |
| 40+ | 31.1 | 55 | 37.4 | 402 |

SOURCE: 1855 N.Y. State Census manuscript schedules.

nine worked—a higher percentage in each age category than the Irish. Assuming that both groups had similar economic needs, how can we account for the greater tendency of German wives to work? Although the *percentage* of German working wives is greater, we can see that the facile assumptions concerning family disorganization and breakdown in America's urban centers must be discarded. This is not to suggest the substitution of a roseate picture of immigrant life in America. Grinding poverty, overcrowded unsanitary housing, a high disease and death rate plagued the poor neighborhoods. But despite the physical deprivation which immigrants suffered, strong family and kin ties provided an internal coherence to their daily lives which must be recognized. The relationship between family and work-roles discussed in this paper suggests the dynamics of immigrant adaptation to the pressures of both a new environment and an industrializing society. Even when dealing with the basic problems of survival, these immigrants found ways to minimize the strains of their new world and to reinforce their traditional familial values. Only by recognizing and reexamining this process of adaptation can we begin to understand the mid-nineteenth-century urban immigrant poor.

# III Family and Work Patterns of Immigrant Laborers in a Planned Industrial Town, 1900–1930

*Tamara K. Hareven*

THE ROLE OF the family in adjustment to industrial life has long been one of the central concerns in sociology. However, until very recently sociologists and a relatively few interested historians have proceeded on the basis of a view of the family that stresses its role as a passive agent in the industrial process. This view was reinforced by a commonly accepted theory of social breakdown that emphasizes disorganization as one of the major by-products of modern industrial life. According to this theory, the uprooting of individuals and families from preindustrial environments and their transfer into an industrial and urban setting caused severe social disruption by breaking down traditional family ties and primary reference groups, resulting in dispersal, loneliness, and anomie.[1]

Recent sociological and historical research has begun to question the validity of this stereotype. Studies of migration have begun to show that the adjustment of individuals and families from preindustrial backgrounds to the industrial environments in the United States was not abrupt. It was carried out gradually through an extended chain process by which villagers retained their geographic and cultural ties with their places of origin and joined familiar reference groups in the new setting.

Studies of aculturation and modernization have further contributed to the revision of the old stereotype by emphasizing continuity and gradual transition from village cultures to new industrial and urban settings in

An earlier version of this essay was published in *The Journal of Urban History* 1 (1975): 365–89. It is part of a book in progress, "The Laborers of Manchester, New Hampshire, 1880–1940: The Role of Family and Ethnicity in Adjustment to Urban Industrial Life." The project was supported by the National Endowment for the Humanities and by a research grant from the Merrimack Valley Textile Museum, with matching funds from Amoskeag Industries, the Cogswell Benevolent Trust, and the Norwin and Elizabeth Bean Foundation. The oral history interviews were supported by the New Hampshire Council for the Humanities and the United Textile Workers. I am indebted to Dr. Thomas Leavitt, Director of the Merrimack Valley Textile Museum, whose initial support helped launch this project. Research was carried out at the Manchester Historic Association and the Baker Library, Graduate School of Business Administration, Harvard University.

[1] For the classic formulation of the Chicago School's theory of social breakdown, see Robert E. Park, "The City: Suggestions for the Investigation of Human Behavior in the Urban Environment," *American Journal of Sociology* 20 (1916):577–612; Robert E. Park et al., *The City* (Chicago, 1925).

the United States. Whether individuals migrated from Ireland, Poland, or French Canada or whether they came from the rural United States into the urban environment, they were not suddenly stripped of their traditional culture.[2] Following the route of cultural anthropologists and the work of E. P. Thompson, historians such as Herbert Gutman and David Montgomery have demonstrated that immigrant workers infused their own cultural traditions and work habits into the industrial system and that while they were adapting to it, they also succeeded in modifying that system. The continuous influx of new migrants from the same or similar backgrounds tended to reinforce the impact of preindustrial immigrant traditions on the new system.[3] These new interpretations of the organization of the work process and of the making of a working-class culture have not, however, documented the role of the family in these transitions. The result has been the perpetuation of a grossly oversimplified view of the changes affecting working-class family behavior. E. P. Thompson, for example, writing about the English working-class family, asserts: "Each stage in industrial differentiation and specialization struck also at the family economy, disturbing customary relations between man and wife, parents and children, and differentiating more sharply 'work' and 'life.' . . . Meanwhile, the family was roughly torn apart each morning by the factory bell."[4]

Neil Smelser, on the other hand, when analyzing the transfer of economic functions from the family to the factory in the early Industrial Revolution, has shown that in the textile industry the worker's family carried its own work habits into the factory setting and often continued to function as a unit. Taking a more global view, William Goode has analyzed the role of the family in the process of industrialization, both historically in the West and in contemporary developing societies. He concludes that the family was an independent agent in that process and that it may have acted as a catalyst rather than as a passive recipient. Goode's argument has now been reinforced by a number of historical

[2] For crucial revisions of traditional working-class historiography, see E. P. Thompson, *The Making of the English Working Class* (New York, 1963); Herbert Gutman, "Work, Culture, and Society in Industrializing America, 1819–1918," *American Historical Review* 78 (1973):531–88; David Montgomery, *Beyond Equality: Labor and the Radical Republicans, 1862–1872* (New York, 1967). On recent working-class historiography, see Robert H. Zieger, "Workers and Scholars: Recent Trends in American Labor Historiography," *Labor History* 13 (1972):245–66.

[3] Gutman, "Work, Culture, and Society"; S. M. Miller and Frank Riessman, "The Working-Class Sub-Culture: A New View," *Social Problems* 9 (1961):86–97. For an important revision of modernization theory, see Richard D. Brown, "Modernization and the Modern Personality in Early America, 1600–1865: A Sketch of a Synthesis," *Journal of Interdisciplinary History* 2 (1972):201–28. See also Marc Fried, *The World of the Urban Working Class* (Cambridge, Mass., 1973).

[4] Thompson, p. 416.

studies emphasizing the active role immigrant families played in the migration process and their function as sources of continuity and stability under the pressures of adjustment to new conditions. Rather than positing a breakdown of family life, these revisionists assert that the immigrant family actually controlled its own destiny and charted the careers of its members. This meant that the family made its own decisions in the choices of location, work, and education. As the transmitter of premigration cultural heritage and customs, the family kept ethnic traditions alive and drew on them as sources of resilience and support.[5]

Unfortunately, the studies that have reversed the stereotype of family passivity and breakdown in the industrial process have carried the reversal to the other extreme. The new filiopietism that has been emerging recently attributes seemingly unlimited strength to the immigrant or working-class family and tends to exaggerate its autonomy as an institution. Thus, this neoromantic interpretation of the role of the family could easily result in yet another stereotype, as removed from historical reality as the earlier image of social breakdown.

Now that the ghosts of social breakdown have been driven from historical scholarship, it becomes necessary to consider data more carefully, and to develop an approach to the study of the family's role in the industrial environment that leans to neither extreme. Any such approach must, by necessity, be *contextual* as well as *dynamic*. It must examine the family in its interaction with other institutions, rather than treating it in isolation of the household unit.[6]

The model proposed here attempts to relate "family time" and "industrial time." It emphasizes the interaction between the family and the institutions of industrial capitalism in the context of larger societal processes. In an industrial setting it relates the family to the work process, job mobility, ethnicity, and economic behavior. Within this context, *family* is seen as a sequence of developments over an entire cycle, rather than as a monolithic, uniform, and unchanging structure. As

[5] See Neil Smelser, *Social Change and the Industrial Revolution* (Chicago, 1959); William Goode, *World Revolution and Family Patterns* (New York, 1963); Sidney Greenfield, "Industrialization and the Family in Sociological Theory," *American Journal of Sociology* 68 (1961):312–22.

The best documentation of the revisionist thesis is Michael Anderson, *Family Structure in Nineteenth-Century Lancashire* (Cambridge, Eng., 1971). Specifically on American immigrant families, see Virginia Yans-McLaughlin, "Patterns of Work and Family Organization: Buffalo's Italians," *Journal of Interdisciplinary History* 2 (1971):299–314.

[6] For the emphasis on family and household structure as the major unit of analysis, see Richard Sennett, *Families against the City* (Cambridge, Mass., 1970). Sennett errs in defining "extended family" only within the household, thus ignoring the significant presence of kin outside the household. For a critique of this approach, see Tamara K. Hareven, "The Family as Process: The Historical Study of the Family Cycle," *Journal of Social History* 7 (1974):322–27.

families progress through their development from formation to dissolution, their functions, relationships, and needs differ over the different stages of the family cycle. These changes are critical for the understanding of the family's interaction with the rest of society.[7]

While the term *industrial time* designates the new time schedules and discipline imposed by the industrial system, *family time* describes the internal and external timing of family behavior at different stages of individual and family development. It refers particularly to the synchronization of major demographic events and to the various stages in the development of the family cycle.[8]

This paper will attempt to relate the interaction between the internal timing of family behavior and the external pressures and demands of the world of work. Its basic assumption is that while families adjust their time according to external pressures and conditions, they also often time their own behavior in accordance with their "internal clock." The historian must determine, therefore, under what circumstances the family timed its behavior in reponse to external conditions and under what circumstances its behavior was dictated by internal family customs and traditions.[9]

For the exploration of these patterns, I have chosen to study the immigrant laborers of the Amoskeag Mills in Manchester, N.H., at the peak of this corporation's development during the first four decades of the twentieth century. This particular community was selected for this study for two reasons: the fact that Manchester was a typical New England textile town in many respects, but differed from other communities in that industrial activity was concentrated in one corporation, which continued to exercise sharp controls over the entire town until its shutdown in the 1930s. Under those conditions it is possible to document the family's interaction with the corporation.[10]

[7] For conceptualization and definition of the family cycle, see Paul C. Glick, "The Family Cycle," *American Sociological Review* 13 (1947):164–74; Reuben Hill, *Family Development in Three Generations* (Cambridge, Mass., 1970). On the applicability of sociological stages of the family-cycle approach to historical conditions, see Tamara K. Hareven, "The Family Cycle in Historical Perspective," paper presented at the Thirteenth Seminar of the Committee on Family Research of the International Sociological Association, in press.

[8] On the concept of "industrial time," see Pitrim Sorokin and Robert Merton, "Social Time: A Methodological and Functional Analysis," *American Journal of Sociology* 42 (1937):615–29.

[9] On this point, see my "Family as Process."

[10] On the Amoskeag Mills, see Waldo Brown, *A History of the Amoskeag Company* (Manchester, N.H., 1915). The Amoskeag Mills were the subject of a study by the WPA; see Daniel Creamer and Charles W. Coulter, *Labor and the Shutdown of the Amoskeag Textile Mills*, Works Projects Administration, National Research Project, Report no. L-5 (Philadelphia, 1939).

As a planned industrial town, Manchester did not experience the classic problems of social disorganization that have been generally attributed to urban living. From the late nineteenth century on, Manchester developed cohesive ethnic neighborhoods inside, as well as outside, the corporation tenements. These neighborhoods were tightly organized around kinship and ethnic ties. Thus, the problem that the laborers of Manchester were facing was not urban anomie but rather the pressures of the industrial environment. By proceeding on the basis of this useful concept, we should be able to examine the role of the family in the process of industrialization without being misled by the traditional arguments stressing the disruptive effects of the pressures of city life on the family.

Moreover, the surviving historical record is unusually rich, thus allowing an exploration of conditions and developments from the perspectives of the workers as well as the corporation. The unique collection of cumulative individual employee files kept by the corporation for the period 1910–36 provides detailed data for the reconstruction of the workers' careers. Particularly important are the citations of the laborers' reasons for leaving their jobs and the reasons given by overseers for the dismissals of workers. The linkage of this data with marriage and insurance records permits a reconstruction of the workers' life and work histories.[11]

Once the world's largest textile mill, with an average of twelve to fourteen thousand workers a year, the Amoskeag Corporation employed two-thirds of Manchester's labor force during the first two decades of the twentieth century. Founded in 1831 by the Boston Associates on the model of Lowell, the Amoskeag Manufacturing Company and the city around it were one of a group of planned New England textile communities intended by their developers to prove the moral and educational merits of the new industrial order. For an entire century Manchester was controlled by the paternalistic policies of the corporation that had developed it. Even after the 1850s, when the original ideals of planned New England textile towns were waning in Lowell, Lawrence, and other sister

[11] This project utilizes the following data: A 5 percent random sample of the individual employee files kept by the Corporation from 1912 to 1936. The sample consists of 2,000 individual files. Individual workers' careers were reconstructed from these files over each worker's entire work period. They were subsequently traced through city directories, and wherever relevant and possible, workers' careers were reconstructed for the period before and after their employment by the Corporation, as well as during intermittent periods. The individual records were then linked with marriage records, and were augmented by Corporation records, newspapers, and a collection of oral history interviews of former employees. The records of French Canadian workers were also linked with insurance records. The employee files are located at the Manchester Historic Association. The insurance records are at the Association Canada-Américane, in Manchester.

communities, the Amoskeag Corporation not only retained the tradition of paternalism but actually refined and modernized it.[12]

Like the other textile corporations upon which it was patterned, the Amoskeag Company recruited its early labor force among rural New Englanders. From the 1850s on, however, immigrants from England, Scotland, and Ireland began to replace native workers. In the 1860s, following the textile industry's discovery of French Canadians, widely acclaimed as both "industrious" and "docile," the corporation embarked on a campaign to recruit workers north of the border. By 1900 French Canadians constituted about 40 percent of the labor force in the mill and close to one-quarter of the city's population. While the French migration continued through the first two decades of the twentieth century, the corporation absorbed increasing numbers of Polish and Greek immigrants from 1910 on.[13]

The role of the French Canadians in Manchester is particularly important to an understanding of the developments discussed in this paper. The neighborhood they developed in the city's West End became the most powerful and self-contained ethnic community in the city. Their arrival in the late 1880s coincided with the gradual withdrawal of the Irish from the labor force in the mill and with the corporation's expansion. Since they constituted the group with the highest percentage of workers for one ethnic group, they were able to develop a power base in the mills and to influence the political and cultural life in the city from the beginning of the twentieth century on. By 1918 Manchester, following Woonsocket, R.I., was the second city in the nation to elect a French Canadian mayor.

In response to the transformation of its labor force in the beginning of the twentieth century, and under the influence of the industrial welfare movement, the corporation introduced an efficiency plan intended to modernize and simplify the system of production; it also established a welfare program aimed at socializing the workers into a permanent

[12] On classic planned New England textile towns, see Caroline F. Ware, *The Early New England Cotton Manufacture* (New York, 1931); John Coolidge, *Mill and Mansion* (New York, 1942); John Armstrong, *Factory under the Elms* (Cambridge, Mass., 1968); Vera Shlakman, *Economic History of a Factory Town, Chicopee, Mass.* (New York, 1935).

[13] In 1911 French Canadians constituted 37.6 percent of the labor force, native Americans (many of whom were of Irish and Scotch descent) 18.6 percent, the Irish 14.7 percent, the Poles 10.8 percent, and Greeks 8 percent. By 1923 the French Canadians constituted 46 percent. On the population of Manchester in the context of other textile communities, see U.S., Congress, Senate, *Report on the Condition of Woman and Child Wage-Earners in the United States,* vol. 1, *Cotton Textile Industry*, Document no. 65, 61st Cong., 2d sess. (Washington, D.C., 1910). Manchester, N.H., was one of the communities studied in this report. On the importance of French Canadians in the textile industry and on their migration to New Hampshire, see Ralph Vicero, "The Immigration of French Canadians to New England, 1840–1900," Diss. Wisconsin 1966. Vicero stresses the predominant role of French Canadians in the textile industry.

and cooperative industrial labor force. The efficiency program included the creation of a special employment office intended to counteract informal policies in hiring and firing and, in general, to centralize personnel policies. Directed primarily against labor turnover, the new registration system was designed to demonstrate to the workers that they were being held under close surveillance. At the same time the corporation was hoping to determine, from careful research in the individual records, which immigrant group was most reliable and persistent in its industriousness and discipline and to adjust its hiring practices accordingly.[14]

The welfare measures, introduced simultaneously with the efficiency program, were clearly directed toward families rather than at individuals. These included a home ownership plan that provided land and mortgages for workers staying in the corporation's employ five years or longer, superannuation for a limited number of workers, a playground, baseball field, and vegetable gardens, a dental care program for children, and a visiting nurse and home care instruction for mothers. These programs represented a continuity in the corporation's tradition of nineteenth-century paternalism. Their introduction in 1911 was aimed at preventing potential labor unrest and, in the long run, were intended to develop a permanent, loyal, and stable labor force.

> More than 15,000 persons work in these mills that border on both sides of the river. The wages of these people have permitted them to acquire ease and all seem to be content with their lot. The large company to which they sell their labor treat them as its own children. . . . That is the reason why the Amoskeag Company has never had any trouble with its employees. It treats them not as machines, but as human beings, as brothers who have a right not only to wages but also to the pleasures of life. . . . Its employees work not only to earn a wage but to please their employers, who know how to treat them well and to whom they sell not only the product of their hand but also the best of their technical knowledge.[15]

Thanks to the efforts of the company, farmers in rural Quebec and factory workers in Montreal and Quebec City read this propaganda and similar feature articles accompanied by photographs of the mills. The Amoskeag Corporation and its immigrant workers demonstrated a remarkable fit in their respective ideologies of work, social hierarchy, and authority. In the tradition of industrial paternalism,

[14] On the strike, see Amoskeag Company, *History of the Amoskeag Strike during the Year 1922* (Manchester, N.H., 1924). On paternalism and efficiency in American industry, see Gerd Korman, *Industrialization, Immigration, and Americanization: The View from Milwaukee* (Milwaukee, 1967).

[15] *Le Canado-Américain* (Manchester, N.H.), November 10, 1913.

the corporation viewed itself as a large family, the workers within it as its children, and industrial management as a family affair. The corporation's own management and organization were structured informally along family and kinship lines.

In a paternalistic system such as that of the Amoskeag Mills, the corporation not only perceived itself as a family but was very much aware of the strength of the family in the workers' lives and consciously attempted to utilize the family as an instrument of recruitment and control over the work force.[16] Although the Amoskeag Corporation never pursued a formal policy of family hiring, it encouraged the employment of entire French Canadian families.[17] This was done because family hiring maximized the return in the effort invested in recruitment and transportation. This also held true for housing arrangements, where the corporation preferred to maximize the use of space by giving preference to families with several working members.

On the workers' end, the traditional work ethic and customs of immigrant families were woven around the famiily as a work unit. The workers transferred this tradition into the industrial system and realigned their work relationship in accordance with the realities of industrial employment. Historians who have made much of the alleged discontinuity between agricultural and industrial labor patterns have ignored this point. This is not to argue that the tasks and divisions of labor that the French Canadian farm family had traditionally carried out in rural Quebec were automatically transferred to the American industrial system. The important continuity was in the workers' perception and experience of the family as a work unit even when the location of the job and the nature of the task were different. Daughters and wives, who had earlier contributed to the family's economic efforts on the farm, now transferred these functions to industrial labor. The tasks they were performing differed markedly from those undertaken before immigration, but the basic internal assumptions that guided the respective roles and economic obligations of members to the family economy were not disrupted.[18]

This transition, however, was not without its conflict. Traditional French Canadian views, reinforced by Catholicism, denounced women's work outside the home as a threat to the integrity of the family. Women

[16] This attitude is borne out in the Corporation's welfare program and is continuously reiterated in the Corporation's official publication, *The Amoskeag Bulletin* (1913–21).

[17] On family employment among French Canadian immigrants, see Vicero, "French Canadian Immigration."

[18] These attitudes were articulated in the oral history interviews. Smelser has found a transfer of traditional habits of the family as a work unit into the early industrial systems in England (*Social Change and the Industrial Revolution*). Michael Anderson has argued for the continuation of traditional work habits in nineteenth-century Lancashire (*Family Structure in Nineteenth-Century Lancashire*).

workers in Manchester tried to resolve the conflict with a convenient rationalization, claiming that their industrial work was temporary and looking forward to the day when they would stop working. In spite of this, married women continued to work over extended time periods with only relatively short interruptions for childbirth.[19]

French Canadian workers in Manchester were not preindustrial peasants suddenly exposed to the pressures of industrial life. About 20 percent of all former Quebec workers in Manchester had already worked in the textile industry in Canada before migration. A good number of those workers who had come to the United States from Quebec had worked in the textile industry in Maine before coming to Manchester. Even the rural migrants who had never experienced industrial work on a first-hand basis had been exposed to it through relatives who were going back and forth to mills in Maine and New Hampshire. Under these circumstances, it is likely that traditional customs and work habits had already been modified before their departure to the United States or during their migration through several industrial towns in Maine, for example.

In their daily relations the corporation family and the workers' family could be viewed as two interacting institutions that were exercising checks and balances on each other. Both were flexible institutions whose relationship and patterns of interaction fluctuated over time, in response to internal conditions, as well as under the impact of larger historical processes. The relationship between the workers and the corporation alternated between collaboration and conflict, depending on a variety of factors. On the corporation's side, the relationship was governed by the fluctuation of the textile market, the need for labor, and by competition with other textile towns. In periods of labor shortage before World War I, the corporation was forced to tolerate the independent behavior of the workers. On the other hand, during its decline between 1919 and its final shutdown in 1936, the corporation was gradually curtailing its labor force. As a consequence, it could see to it that the workers had less freedom to maneuver the system.[20]

The worker's response, on the other hand, depended on individual and family values, economic considerations, career expectations, alternative employment opportunities available in the city, and on traditional work habits. Demographic patterns (marriage, fertility, death) also had a crucial impact on the workers' behavior in the factory system. Their work patterns were thus dependent on the stages of the life cycle and on the

[19] This is borne out by the oral history interviews.

[20] On the fluctuation of the textile market and its impact on the Amoskeag Company's hiring policies, see Creamer, *Shutdown*.

particular stage in the family's development. Unmarried individuals in their late twenties, for example, had different attitudes toward their work than did fathers of families of five or widows in their fifties.[21] The degree of their dependence on industrial work, or independence from it, was a function of individual and family needs that changed over different stages of the family's development. Particularly significant in this scheme was the shifting margin of poverty and subsistence at different stages of the family cycle.

The areas in which the family was most effective in making an impact on work patterns and in exercising its own controls over the careers of its members were in directing workers' migration patterns (therefore controlling labor turnover), influencing their job placement, and supporting them in their adaptation to new industrial conditions. The family and the kin group served as the labor recruiter, the organizer of migration routes, and the housing agent. Within the mill itself, the family exercised job controls in the workrooms, directed the work choices of its members within certain limits, and influenced their placement in the mill. Finally, the family also became a major socializer of its members for industrial life. Kinship ties were especially instrumental in affording the workers flexibility in their relationship with the industrial system and in facilitating their experimentation with alternative careers. The kin group acted as a conveyor belt, facilitating the movement of members from one place to another, thus broadening the opportunity base and cushioning the shock of adjustment.

French Canadians were streaming to Manchester in response to the systematic recruitment propaganda issued by the corporation through the ethnic newspapers and through personal communications from relatives already working in the mills. Newly arrived immigrants came to Manchester because their kin were already working in the mill. The relatives met them, placed them on their first job, and located them as temporary boarders in the relative's household until they found a corporation flat or rented in a West Side apartment house.

The case of Mr. R. is typical in this respect. He came to Manchester when he was seventeen years old because a cousin already working in the mills had returned to Quebec for a visit, full of praise for the experience. Upon

[21] On the internal economic conditions of the family and their impact on labor market behavior, see U.S., Senate, *Report on Woman and Child Wage-Earners,* vol. 1, and John Modell, "Family, Economy, and Insecurity," paper delivered at the Annual Meeting of the Organization of American Historians, April 1974. Tamara Hareven and John Modell are embarking on a study of family workers in the early part of the twentieth century. The margin of poverty has been defined by early social investigators of the urban poor. See B. Seebohm, *Rowntree, Poverty: A Study of Town Life* (London, 1922) and Robert Hunter, *Poverty* (New York, 1904).

his arrival in Manchester, he stayed with his aunt, who was a frame tender in one of the weaving rooms. She secured him a job as a helper frame-tender. After two years he sent for his older sisters, and several years later his parents and the younger children came as well. Mr. R. and his sisters boarded with their aunt's family until their own parents came to Manchester.[22]

This pattern of chain migration was not limited to the worker's migration to Manchester. Kinship networks pervaded the entire industrial region of New England. The presence of clusters of kin in a variety of New England industrial towns offered laborers of the Amoskeag Mills the flexibility of moving through a series of mill towns in the hope of improving their conditions. Furthermore, the process of migration was not terminal. Workers migrated back and forth, from relatives in Manchester to family members still left in Quebec, and back again to Manchester. Often leaving the mills for two or three summer months, they went into the Canadian countryside only to return again to the textile mill. Family ties thus formed networks of employment opportunities as well as temporary and permanent stations for migration.[23] The employee records of the Amoskeag Company allow us to reconstruct the worker's migration patterns. Before 1922 about one-fourth of the employees sampled for this study immigrated to various New England mill towns in search of other opportunities, and in most of these instances the presence of relatives in these towns facilitated their sojourns. Migration did not destroy the family and kin group. It transposed a formerly localized family over an entire industrial region in New England.[24]

Flexibility in the corporation's employment patterns before 1922 allowed the family to exercise controls over the recruitment and placement of its members. Workers were able to place their relatives in different workrooms or departments through direct contact with individuals already working there or with the overseers. The character of a department was basically determined by its overseer, and workrooms, frequently containing 100 or more laborers, were still identified by their overseer's name. Even after the introduction of the formal employment office, workers continued to obtain their jobs directly from the overseer. When a vacancy opened up in a workroom, the overseer naturally turned to one of his

[22] Summary of employee file of E. C.

[23] Labor turnover and migration are discussed in detail in Tamara K. Hareven, "The Laborers of Manchester, New Hampshire, 1910–1922: Patterns of Adjustment to Industrial Life," *Labor History* 16 (1975):249–65. See also U.S., Senate, *Report on Woman and Child Wage-Earners,* 1:127.

[24] See also *Lost Time and Labor Turnover in Cotton Mills: A Study of Cause and Extent,* U.S., Department of Labor, Women's Bureau, Publ. no. 52 (Washington, D.C., 1926), pt. 1, pp. 109–13.

workers and asked him to bring in someone he knew. This opened the opportunity for the placement of kin. If one bears in mind that workers were continuously coming and going, it becomes clear how extensive this personal placement network was.[25]

Family groups thus infiltrated the mill and made their direct impact on the composition of the workrooms. Kin and ethnic clusters developed in most workrooms. The pervasiveness of the family group also allowed the workers to try out different jobs in various departments by taking turns going to work and by switching around their employment passes.[26] Members of one family were often threaded through a variety of jobs, always working near one another. Two sisters tended looms next to each other, and childhood friends, cousins, and neighbors often worked side by side for years. "It was like a family when we'd go to work there . . . I was always anxious to go to work."[27]

About one-fourth of all French Canadian workers studied in this group met their spouses in the mill and continued to work there after their marriage. Such arrangements provided support to the workers' attempts to control their work pace. Especially as the corporation was accelerating its pressures for speedups, relatives and friends assisted each other in meeting the work quotas of slow workers even if it meant a loss of pay on their own piece-rate work. The presence of relatives also reinforced the workers' collective strength in resisting corporation pressure, especially when the demand for speedup became overwhelming, in the period following World War I.

In its manipulation of hiring and job placement and in its effort to counteract the faster pace of production, the kin group acted as a surrogate labor union. From the standpoint of the worker, the advantage in such an arrangement obviously lay in the degree of protection and support which the kin group offered its members, particularly to newcomers to the city, and in its socialization of children of newly arrived adults to industrial work. This system of family solidarity also carried its built-in weaknesses. By entrapping individual choices in family decisions, the immediate as well as the extended family exercised considerable control over the careers of its members.

Whether kinship orientation tended to slow down unionization is subject

[25] The overseer was the man in charge of production, management, and discipline in an entire department, which consisted of several workrooms.

[26] The trace of the original 2,000 employee files gathered for the study turned up an additional 500 of their relatives who were also working in the mill. This does not represent all the possible kin combinations. It contains only the immediate ones that could be traced through vital records. If one allowed for second cousins and a variety of relatives that are not mentioned in the interviews, the number of kin could be considerably higher.

[27] Oral history interviews.

to speculation. By comparison to other New England textile towns, Manchester seemed immune to strikes. The Amoskeag Corporation experienced no major strike from 1885, the year of an abortive strike by the Knights of Labor, till 1918, when its first trade union strike—a modest preview of the bitter strike of 1922—took place. The strike of 1922, the company's most serious, was an industry-wide strike protesting a reduction in wages. In the case of Manchester, however, it was intensified by the workers' loss of influence over the circumstances of their employment through informal networks.

The strength and resilience workers derived from their families were reinforced by ethnic ties. Ethnic organizations were strongly enmeshed in the kin networks, thus providing organizational supports for the workers' adjustment to the pressures of the factory and life in the city. The ethnic group offered the commonalty of a cultural heritage and language, residential cohesion, entertainment and rituals, religious ties, and mutual benefit associations. Most of the work and residential pattern were organized around the workers' immigrant culture.

From the late 1920s on, the corporation was becoming nervous about the ethnic and kin alignment in the workrooms: "Refrain from requesting the employment of relatives or persons in charge of units in the same units," read the instructions of management to overseers. An inspector reporting his conversation with a group of overseers to management concluded: "For instance, I did not believe it was really good for any unit of the mill to be wholly comprised of relatives and friends of the operatives also of the same race." In that particular workroom, 90 percent of the labor force was made up of the same ethnic group.[28]

Tight-knit clusters of ethnic neighborhoods appeared in Manchester from the 1880s on. The French Canadians settled on the West Side of Manchester, the Poles in a downtown neighborhood removed from the mills, and the Greeks gradually replaced the Irish on the South Side, each developing their own parishes, clubs, and grocery stores in the neighborhood. Ethnic enclaves developed even in the corporation housing. Although corporation flats had to be secured through individual family applications, workers managed to cluster along kin and ethnic lines in the corporation housing in the same manner in which they succeeded in aligning themselves in the workroom. Officially, applications for residence in corporation housing had to be submitted long in advance, and workers had to wait their turn. In reality, friends and relatives notified prospective tenants of vacancies and managed to secure those flats ahead

[28] Evidence for kin clustering in the workrooms is derived from the reconstruction of kin groups by place of work. See also "memo to Mr. Hagan," Oct. 1934, Amoskeag Files, Baker Library, Harvard University, Cambridge, Mass.

of their turn through the help of acquaintances in the office. Sons of former workers recall the invisible but clearly recognizable boundaries between their gangs, which were organized along nationality lines in the corporation tenements.[29]

Within this context, it is also important to assess the extent to which ethnic background may have been a liability as well as an asset in the workers' interaction with the industrial system. While this study focuses extensively on the French Canadian experience, a cursory comparison of this group with the Poles and the Greeks highlights significant differences. As the first arrivals of a new wave of migration and the largest immigrant group in the city, the French Canadians commanded several advantages. Since they were recruited during a period when the corporation was still at the peak of its production, they were able to penetrate the system with greater effectiveness than the Poles or the Greeks, whose later arrival coincided with the decline of the textile industry. The early entry of French Canadians also enabled them to develop a cohesive neighborhood as well as powerful ethnic organizations. The proximity of New England to Quebec facilitated continuous chain migration to Manchester and encouraged more elaborate kin networks. Proximity to Canada also enabled the French Canadian immigrants in Manchester to maintain vital ties with their places of origin and to visit kin during vacations or periods of unemployment. Particularly during the general layoffs following the strike of 1922, workers frequently migrated back to Canada for temporary work.

The extensive ethnic network in the mill offered opportunities for the socialization of members of the group into the work process—an opportunity that was less available to the more recent arrivals, the Greeks and the Poles. It is not surprising, therefore, that an analysis of the workers' reasons for leaving shows a much higher preponderance of job-adjustment difficulties among Greeks and Poles than among French Canadians. The late arrival of Greeks and Poles and their willingness to work for lower wages placed them at an automatic disadvantage and provoked conflict with the established immigrant groups. Ethnic rivalry thus seriously undermined working-class solidarity.

[29] Based on oral history interviews and on a preliminary survey of the residential clustering in the Corporation's tenements and boardinghouses by Tamara Hareven and Randolph Langenbach. For comparison, see two significant studies of the social space of the urban working class: Pierre Chombard de Lauwe, *La Vie Quotidienne des Familles Ouvrières* (Paris, 1956) and André Michel, "La Famille Urbaine et la Parenté en France," in Reuben Hill and René Konig, *Families in East and West: Socialization Process and Kinship Ties* (Paris, 1970). On ethnicity and residential cohesion, see Herbert Gans, *The Urban Villagers* (New York, 1962). For a comparative experience in a textile community, see Donald B. Cole, *Immigrant City* (Cambridge, Mass., 1957). See also Gerald D. Shuttles, *The Social Order of the Slum: Ethnicity and Territory in the Inner City* (Chicago, 1968).

Whatever the ethnic background, internal family considerations and demographic behavior influenced the stability and persistence of the workers within the mills. The family decided which of its members should go to work, which son or daughter should start first, at what point a wife should stop, when she should return to work, and which of its members should try alternative employment outside the mill. The subtle processes of these decisions were governed by economic needs as well as by traditional values. Aside from involuntary reasons such as illness, accidents, retirement, and death, laborers left for such reasons as these: "husband did not want wife to work"; "wife did not approve of husband's work in the night shift"; "parents want son to go back to school"; "girl takes care of young children at home." As long as the employment system was flexible, family members had control over who should go to the mill and when, who should stay home, at what age a son or daughter should commence work (providing they met the legal age requirement), and to what department or workroom they should be sent.[30]

What factors governed the family's decision as to the timing of its members' entrance into the labor force, into new family obligations, or their migration into new areas? What were the internal and external factors affecting the family's interaction with the world of work?

Family time was governed by demographic considerations as well as by the external pressures of the industrial system. The decisions as to when people left home, gave birth to their first child, and the spacing of subsequent births were timed by the internal clock of family traditions as well as by the external pressures of the system and economic needs.[31] Historians are now only beginning to unravel the specific processes involved in this timing and the ways they varied among different socioeconomic and cultural groups under different circumstances.

For the French Canadian immigrants in Manchester, work meant family employment. Since French Canadians had the highest birth rate of all industrial workers in the United States, it is not surprising that they were recognized as textile workers par excellence. In New England during the first decade of the twentieth century, average family size was 7.2, while the Irish, a group also well known for its high fertility, had an average of 5.0. In the early twentieth century French Canadians also had the highest average number of family members working in the textile industry (3.9). Large families, which had served well the work needs of

[30] The data are derived from tabulations of the "reasons for leaving" in the files of 2,000 employees who left before 1922. Compare with reasons for departure computed by Creamer for the period 1923–35 (Creamer, *Shutdown*, pp. 265–84).

[31] Hareven, "Family as Process," and Anderson, *Lancashire*. For an analysis of women's family cycles, see Pëter Uhlenberg, "A Study of Cohort Life Cycles: Cohorts of Native-Born Massachusetts Women, 1830–1920," *Population Studies* 23:407–20.

farmers, continued to be an asset in industrial work when the immigrants first arrived in Manchester. Changing conditions in the textile industry, however, dictated a modification of demographic behavior after the turn of the century.[32]

The first major impact of the industrial system on behavior patterns was the postponement of marriage, particularly for women. At the beginning of the twentieth century, women who had migrated to Manchester in their teens and young women growing up in Manchester delayed their marriage into their late twenties or early thirties in direct response to the conditions of industrial work. Women's reasons for marrying later were partly that marriage provided no escape from industrial work. Parents also exerted pressure on their daughters to delay marriage, in order to prolong their contribution to the family's income.

Women workers carried a significant share of the burden of their families' support from the moment they were able to work. As unmarried daughters older than sixteen began to work full time, their parents and younger siblings were gradually withdrawing from the labor force. In families of textile workers the daughter's contribution to the family's income was more critical than the son's. A comparative study of several New England textile communities, including Manchester, carried out by the United States Bureau of Labor in 1910, showed that while sons committed only 83 percent of their income to their parents' household, daughters delivered 95 percent of their pay to the family's budget. It was, therefore, in the interest of parents to delay the marriage of their young daughters and thus continue to rely on them as sources of income.[33]

Since marriage failed to provide an escape from industrial work, it actually added the new burden of housekeeping to work outside the home. Caught between the pressures of traditional gender-role definitions in their own culture and the economic need to contribute to the family's income, women found themselves working in the mill as well as tending to their domestic tasks. Women worked after their marriage until giving birth, and returned to the mill as soon as they weaned their infants. Working until the birth of their next child, they left their jobs temporarily, only to return again. The flexibility of the employment system before 1922 facilitated these intermittent work patterns, since women could afford to leave their jobs with the assurance that they would find some work upon their return.[34]

[32] U.S., Senate, *Report on the Conditions of Woman and Child Wage-Earners,* vol. 1.

[33] U.S., Department of Labor, *The Share of Wage-Earning Women in Family Support,* Women's Bureau Bulletin, no. 30 (Washington, D.C., 1923):137–40.

[34] These patterns emerge from the reconstruction of the work careers of 1,000 women from the employee files and from oral history interviews.

One of the important functions of delayed marriage, especially in the second generation of immigrants, was a curtailment in the number of children born to French Canadian mill workers. This decline represented both the changing conditions of the employment market as well as a gradual secularization and relaxation of traditional norms of behavior. With the passing of the New Hampshire Child Labor Law in 1905, the employment of children under sixteen became increasingly risky, and since the production process was no longer dependent on the work of young children, the company willingly cooperated. The decline in the child-labor market not only turned large numbers of children into economic burdens on the family, it also impaired the mother's effectiveness as a breadwinner because it imposed on her patterns of intermittent employment and therefore undermined her chances of occupational advancement.[35]

Children were socialized to the work experience in the mill at an early age. Although the Child Labor Law barred them from employment before the age of sixteen, industrial labor became part of their lives through the work experience of their parents. The proximity in space between their homes and the mills prevented any real separation between the two worlds. The sight of children carrying the lunch pails to the mill at the noon hour was a familiar part of the Manchester scene. School children earned their first money by carrying lunches to unmarried workers from the boarding houses to the mills. Most youths attending high school worked regularly in the mills during the summer. The expectation that children would have to work as soon as the law permitted was strongly conveyed by their parents from an early age. The entire family economy as well as the family's work ethic was build on the assumption that children would contribute to the family's income from the earliest possible age.[36]

By the time they entered the mill, children had become familiar with the entire work experience. Their parents and older brothers and sisters provided a variety of models of occupational behavior. The lack of a true separation between the world of work and the family allowed for children's initiation into the factory experience before they even crossed the gates of the mill yard. They were familiar with names of overseers and second hands, knew the gossip about various transactions in the workrooms, and learned a good number of the shortcuts and tricks. They also knew from an early age that the Amoskeag Corporation was by far the largest employer in the city and that in the shoe industry, Manchester's second largest in-

[35] For a discussion of the decline of the child labor market, see Jeremy Felt, *Child Labor Reform in New York State,* and Tamara K. Hareven, "Child Labor," in Robert H. Bremner et al., eds. *Children and Youth in America* (Cambridge, Mass., 1970), vol. 2.

[36] Oral history interviews.

dustry, employment opportunities were more restricted and the skill requirements more specialized.

Work roles along sex lines were also inculcated at an early age. Girls knew that until their marriage their work would be regulated by their parents and that most of their income would be channeled back into the family's resources. They were also prepared for the fact that if the family could afford to send any of its children to school after age fourteen, the boys would be the ones to go first. Within the limits of the occupational structure, they were prepared for the fact that the highest rank of skill a woman could aspire to would be that of a weaver, while their brothers could become loom fixers, expert dye mixers, master mechanics, and could even eventually reach the most coveted position of all—overseer.

These limits of opportunity cast the daughter into the role of backup person for the son's career. What it meant was that the daughter's work was expected to facilitate the son's occupational mobility. Girls were directed to the mill and were expected to work steadily in order to plug the holes in the family's income so that their brothers could afford the flexibility of experimentation in search of better occupations. As long as the daughters maintained a consistent income, the sons could transfer from one department to another in the mill or could take the risk of experimenting with outside jobs. It is not surprising, therefore, that women who are generally expected to have a higher turnover on the job showed a higher persistence in the Amoskeag Mills than the men.[37]

Commencement of work did not mean independence from parental and family controls. Young men and women working in the mill continued to live in their parents' or relatives' households until their marriage. Those without parents boarded with relatives, usually with married brothers and sisters, under similar arrangements. They were in effect paying for their room and board and using the remainder of their pay for supplies and personal savings. While in large commercial cities young men and women tended to leave their homes and board with strangers, industrial workers in Manchester continued living at home or with relatives until they married. Only those men and women in their twenties and thirties who had no relatives in the city turned to corporation or commercial boardinghouses.[38] Whether they lived with their own kin or boarded with strangers, workers experienced little separation between the world of work and the family. The mill town was a total environment.

[37] Employee files; oral history interviews.

[38] See John Modell and Tamara K. Hareven, "Urbanization and the Malleable Household: An Examination of Boarding and Lodging in American Families," *Journal of Marriage and the Family* 35 (1973):467–79.

Familial organization, or surrogate family organization, thus provided the central organizing scheme in the workers' living and work experience. These arrangements had their own built-in flexibilities, which were governed by both the family's decisions and external pressures. On what basis the family made these decisions is a question still open for exploration.

Immigrant families in factory towns timed their behavior by the internal clocks that were wound by their traditional customs, as well as by the bells of the factory. Under what circumstances did they respond to traditional time, and under what circumstances did they conform to industrial time? This is one of the key issues of social, cultural, and economic history. The data explored in this study suggest that at certain stages of their cycle families were more autonomous than at other stages and that the differences in their behavior over periods of time were governed by demographic considerations as well as by the pressures and requirements of the industrial system.

The family's interaction with the system was based on cooperation and mutual exploitation of needs and opportunities. The family succumbed to the pressures of industrial work during periods of labor surplus but maintained its own controls during periods of labor shortage. While it prepared its members for industrial work, it also cushioned them from potential shock and disruptions they encountered under new industrial conditions, and it offered important resources to fall back on during times of crisis or critical life situations. In its effort to protect its members, the family developed its own defense systems and brought its cultural traditions to bear upon the new environment and the industrial system.

The patterns of family behavior revealed in the Manchester study, particularly their strong association with an ethnic culture, provide yet another dimension to the understanding of the transmission of preindustrial culture into the industrial setting. The evidence on the family presented in this paper reinforces Herbert Gutman's general thesis about the carry-over of preindustrial work habits into the industrial system. At the same time it also raises new questions about continuities and discontinuities in the process of the workers' socialization to the industrial system. The immigrant laborers of Manchester clearly carried over their kinship ties from rural areas into the new setting. However, the patterns of kin organization that emerged in Manchester and the new functions the kin group took on represented new forms of adaptation to industrial life. The organizations and behavior of kin in response to the industrial system were different from those of rural Quebec. Furture research in this field will have to delineate the continuities and transformations in the transmission of traditional patterns of family behavior into the industrial system. The current evidence clearly suggests that the assumption that traditional family patterns were simply transposed into the industrial setting is as simplistic as the earlier assumption that migration destroyed traditional kinship ties.

# IV A Flexible Tradition: South Italian Immigrants Confront a New Work Experience

*Virginia Yans-McLaughlin*

WHAT HAPPENS WHEN peasants immigrate to modernizing societies? What impact does immigration have upon internal family dynamics and upon the family's relationship to the rest of society? How, in particular, do traditional families relate to these new work experiences they find in modernizing societies? These are important, far-reaching questions. The subjects chosen to help answer them are the south Italians who at the turn of the twentieth century immigrated to Buffalo, N.Y., and environs and whose behavioral patterns provide valuable insights into the process of cultural adaptation.

A number of approaches and methodologies are available to historians seeking to examine family change. Conventional sociology, for example, long viewed the family as an end product of socioeconomic forces and as an institution that functions to maintain the existing social order. Thus, by definition, clear dichotomies would exist between folk and modern families. Applied to immigration history, this meant that families who crossed the ocean experienced enormous stress and frequent disorganization as they made their transition from peasant village to industrial nation. At the very least, this transition remolded the traditional family into a mobile, detached, nuclear form whose roles, relationships, and values fit the demands of a more rational industrial economy. In one of the clearest expressions of this position, sociologist Neil Smelser suggests that "almost as a matter of definition we associate the factory system" and other industrial work patterns "with the decline of the family and social anonymity."[1]

Because this approach seemed so inadequate an explanation of evidence I found concerning Italian-American families, I turned to cultural anthro-

This essay also appeared in the *Journal of Social History* 7 (1974):429–45.

[1] Oscar Handlin's *The Uprooted* (New York, 1951) is the most famous example of an immigration historian adopting folk society to modern society dichotomy. The most noted exponent of the more sophisticated functional view is Talcott Parsons. His work on the family is discussed in Morris Zelditch, "Cross-cultural Analyses of Family Structure," in Harold F. Christensen, ed., *Handbook of Marriage and the Family* (Chicago, 1964), pp. 492 ff.; Neil Smelser, *Social Change in the Industrial Revolution* (Chicago, 1959), p. 193.

pologists interested in cultural and historical change. Instead of defining the family as an institution functioning to maintain social equilibrium, some see it as a flexible organization using alternatives within the social order, as well as traditional forms and ways of relating, to suit its needs in a given context. These anthropologists emphasize that tradition—familial or otherwise—plays a significant part in social change and that is satisfies some basic human need, even in modernizing societies. Social change, they argue, does not necessarily imply a systematic fit of institutions, but adaptations of one institution to another. The relationship between modernity and tradition is, then, not dichotomous but dialectical.[2] Using this approach, I was able to understand not only how the family was transformed by modern society, but how the traditional family transformed itself.

We can also learn something from anthropologists about the modernizing societies that play host to these families. These societies do not have the overwhelming and homogenous invincibility they are often assumed to possess as they move toward economic rationality. A range of alternatives exists here too; all kinds of adaptations, reorganizations, and adjustments are possible.[3]

To understand familial change among Buffalo Italians or any other group, we must examine past traditions, historical context, and particular situations. This approach is not a simple linear view which argues that past experiences determine future behavior, that because south Italian families behaved in one way in Italy, we can understand why they behaved in similar ways in America. Nor is it a static functional explanation that sees culture and social structure as mere "reflexes" or "mirror images" of one another.[4] We are examining a dynamic process, a give and take, between new conditions and old social forms.

This theoretical perspective facilitates historical understanding of immigrant family behavior, especially the work experiences of these families. Persisting traditional modes and their relatively smooth transition from folk to modern society cannot be well understood without it. This became evident when I examined evidence for Buffalo Italians, who endured all the economic and social deprivations usually associated with lower-class family instability. Most of the men, for example, were low-

[2] I am indebted to Lloyd I. Rudolph and Susanne Hoeber Rudolph, *The Modernity of Tradition* (Chicago, 1967) for this approach. See especially their introduction. Although these authors are concerned with Indian politics, they adopt the flexible approach used by many anthropologists.

[3] Clifford Geertz, *Peddlers and Princes: Social and Economic Modernization in Two Indonesian Towns* (Chicago, 1963), p. 145, takes this position.

[4] Clifford Geertz, "Ritual and Social Change," *American Anthropologist* 59 (1957): 32–54 is a critique of such a position.

paid, unskilled seasonal workers, unemployed six or seven months out of twelve. They experienced little vertical or horizontal occupational mobility. These Italians found themselves residentially and socially segregated. They were denied political power. The last large immigrant group to enter the city, they became the unfortunate target of nativist stereotypes and discriminatory practices. Black Americans, who did not begin significant Buffalo settlement until relatively late, did not assume this burden from them until the 1920s and thirties.

Despite these pressures, all the usual indices indicate remarkable family cohesion. Italians had low desertion rates, low illegitimacy rates, few broken families, and they requested welfare aid infrequently. Other evidence points to the persistence of traditional values, especially among the first generation.

Struggling to fill their economic needs, these families entered a new work world.[5] Buffalo's peculiar occupational structure and job discrimination limited their options, but they nevertheless perceived alternatives for themselves. They chose work styles and occupational modes that permitted minimal strain upon accustomed family arrangements. By constructing and interpreting their own social reality in terms of past experiences, they managed to adapt themselves to a new social context with relative ease.

If past experiences help explain Italian family behavior, in order to understand this behavior, we must journey backwards in time to nineteenth-century southern Italy. Our goal is to examine family work experiences there to achieve more empathetic understanding of how these immigrants perceived their new situation.

In southern Italy clear connections existed between an individual's economic role and his or her family role. But strong cultural traditions frequently intervened, so that any statement positing equivalence between the two would be hazardous. Consider the father first. He presided over his family, whose economic well-being depended on his labors. Because he rarely owned or rented land enough to support his family, he generally hired himself out as a day laborer. Seasonal unemployment or underemployment—the usual facts of peasant life—and the daily and sometimes weekly absences from home required by his work search did not seriously undermine his authority. Cultural traditions supported it strongly.[6]

[5] Virginia Yans-McLaughlin, "Like the Fingers of the Hand: The Family and Community Life of First-generation Italian-Americans in Buffalo, New York, 1890–1930," Diss. Buffalo 1970, contains evidence supporting these statements.

[6] Leonard W. Moss and Walter H. Thomson, "The South Italian Family: Literature and Observation," *Human Organization* 18 (1959): 40, 38, argue that the male's high status could not have derived entirely from his economic role because he retained it even if unemployed. They argue, therefore, that the dominant cultural tradition

But he had a competitor. The Italian family has been described as "father-dominated, but mother-centered." Some argue that matriarchal traditions without any immediate economic basis help explain the mother's relatively powerful position, but her economic importance to the family played some part.[7] Wifely functions were extremely important in this peasant economy; it would be unwise to undervalue them by projecting backwards in time present-day market values that define work in terms of wages received for services performed outside the home. The fact of the matter is, however, that Italian peasants themselves attributed greater prestige and importance to male contributions to the family economy. A wife's clearly defined family and household responsibilities included obedience to her husband, family loyalty, thrift, and most important, childbearing. She oversaw family resources, prepared and purchased food, mended and made clothing, and ordered children in household tasks.

Peasants looked disdainfully at wives who sought work outside the context of the family, and few did so unless poverty required it. Sicilians held very strictly to this rule. On the other hand, an expected part of a wife's year-round labors could include joining the family in crop harvesting. Seasonal migrations also drew entire peasant families away from

---

tended to support the male. See also Constance Cronin, *The Sting of Change: Sicilians in Sicily and Australia* (Chicago, 1970), p. 104.

[7] Moss and Thomson, p. 38, and Leonard Covello, "The Social Background of the Italo-American School Child: A Study in Southern Italian Family Mores and Their Effect on the School Situation in Italy and America," Diss. New York University 1944, p. 377. I am indebted to Louise A. Tilly for her comments on an earlier version of this paper presented at the Anglo-American Conference on Comparative Labor History, April 1973 for the distinction made here between "market" and "peasant" economic values.

[8] As Tilly wisely points out, because conditions varied considerably throughout Italy, generalizations concerning women's work roles are hazardous. But figures from the 1901 census do support my generalization that southern women rarely labored outside the home in nonagricultural occupations. The figures for females nine years of age and over engaged in work outside the home (including domestic servants) are: Abruzzi and Molise, 11 percent; Basilicata, 11 percent; Calabria, 30 percent; Campania, 19 percent; Sicily, 15 percent. Figures are computed from Italy, *Annuario Statistico, 1905–1907* (Rome, 1907), pp. 111 ff. And as Tilly correctly pointed out, these are gross figures making no allowance for urban and rural distinctions. I suspect that the figures for women working outside the home would be lower if peasants alone were considered. I would also like to suggest that even if this small percentage of women did work outside the home, we cannot assume that their behavior was socially acceptable.

Seasonal migrations are discussed in Robert E. Dickinson, *The Population Problem of Southern Italy* (Syracuse, N.Y., 1955), pp. 67–74; Italy, *Atti della giunta per la Inchiesta Agraria e sulli Condizione della Classe Agricola,* vol. 13, Tome 2, Fas. 4 (Rome, 1885), pp. 20 ff.; Robert Foerster, *The Italian Immigration of Our Times* (Cambridge, Mass., 1919), pp. 532–33 discusses family migrations; see also Sydney Sonnino, *La Sicilia nel 1876,* Libro Secondo, *I Contadini* (Florence, 1877), pp. 84, 98, 117. Louise Odencrants, *Italian Women in Industry: A Study of Conditions in New York City (*New York, 1919), pp. 27 ff. and U.S., Congress, Senate, *Reports of the Immigration Commission,* 61st Cong., 3d. sess., vol. 4, *Emigration Conditions in Europe* (Washington, D.C., 1910), p. 160 comments on the lack of industry in the Italian south.

their villages, but girls and women rarely worked in nonagricultural occupations because factory towns existed in the *Mezzogiorno.*[8] Women who left home to labor generally worked as members of a family unit earning a portion of the family wage. They did not regard themselves, nor were they regarded, as independent wage earners. Women did not derive their status within the family from their position as wage earners, nor did the wages they earned challenge the husband's position. His frequent absences from home suggest that even her household powers—always subject to his will—accrued to her by default. A Sicilian study reports, for example, that the father's "authority in his house is final, and there is no official redress to his commands."[9]

Although the peasants loved their children and treated them well, they too had responsibilities. As Covello observes, "The economic basis of married life was reflected in the evaluation of children primarily as an economic asset."[10] Their economic value as workers shortened the period of childhood. Despite government efforts to curb child labor, in 1911 almost one-half of all children ages ten to fifteen were gainfully employed. Peasants completely ignored child labor legislation applying to agricultural work.[11]

Returning to the American scene, we can see how these family relationships fared in a new context. Buffalo Italians, most of them Sicilians, who journeyed to northwestern New York's food-processing factories and the fields surrounding them, are the basis for our discussion. Although some assume that the factory's impersonality, industrial discipline, and work routines prevented possibilities for continuity, these Italians had a very different experience.

Early in this century rapidly growing fruit- and vegetable-processing companies throughout the nation recruited employees from rural areas and immigrant quarters in nearby cities. Processing these perishable products required many hands working long hours during the busy June to October season. Although precise figures are not available, contemporary reports establish that Buffalo Italians commonly journeyed all over the state to join other *paesani* engaged in this labor.[12]

Substantial Italian colonies existed in all large cities near the canneries, but upstate manufacturers still reached far west to Buffalo for their labor

[9] Moss and Thomson, p. 38; Cronin, p. 104.

[10] Covello, "The Italo-American School Child," pp. 357, 359.

[11] Ibid., p. 365.

[12] Amy Bernardy, "L'emigrazione delle donne," *Bollettino dell'Emigrazione,* 1909, no. 1, pp. 69, 85–87; U.S., Congress, Senate, *Reports of the Immigration Commission,* 61st Cong., 2d sess., vol. 22, *Immigrants in Industry,* pt. 24, *Recent Immigrants in Agriculture,* vol. 2, p. 500; New York, *Second Report of the Factory Investigating Commission* (hereafter cited as *FIC*), 2 (Albany, 1913):792.

forces. Buffalo's peculiar economic structure partly explains this phenomenon. Other nearby cities, such as Rochester, Syracuse, Utica, and Troy, had enough homework and light industries to absorb female and child workers, but Buffalo had different labor demands. Heavy industry and transportation, its most rapidly expanding sectors, presented greatest demands for male labor. Although opportunities existed in these industries for unskilled women and children, and other ethnic groups took them, Italians generally did not. Husbands and fathers feared the liberalizing influence contact with American workers might have.[13] Instead, Italians opted for employment in the fields and canneries of the region.

While south Italians seemed to have a special preference for this type of work, manufacturers found it difficult to employ American-born workers, who preferred regular employment of fathers to seasonal employment of the whole family. Italian males, who found themselves restricted to seasonal dock and construction work, did not have this option. Each year more and more Polish women, who had once labored in the canneries, expressed their preference for year-round domestic work in Buffalo's private homes. Because Italian family mores concerning women working in another man's home discouraged it, this option presented no realistic alternative for unskilled women. Cannery work, on the other hand, presented the possibility of extending community controls upon the family into the factory, and this explains why it seemed more respectable to Italians than other occupations did. The canneries provided a unique work opportunity where laboring and living spaces existed in close proximity. In the living quarters, ever-present parents and kin kept a watchful eye on all community members. That children remained directly under parental control was only one asset. Adults could work assured that their young ones were safer than they would have been left home alone or playing in the streets.[14]

Come summer, south Italian women and children became migrant laborers and left their Buffalo homes—sometimes without fathers and husbands, who were forced to seek summer construction jobs in the city because so many could not obtain year-round employment. At first glance such an arrangement seems surprising. South Italian mores required a husband to guard his wife and daughters jealously.

[13] For a discussion of these points, see Virginia Yans-McLaughlin, "Patterns of Work and Family Organization: Buffalo's Italians," *Journal of Interdisciplinary History* 2 (1971): 299–314.

[14] U.S. Senate, *Recent Immigrants in Agriculture,* indicates the decreasing popularity of canning work among Poles and American-born workers (2:491). Even Italian men looking for work considered canning work more respectable for themselves than railroad work (ibid., p. 491). The importance immigrants assigned to control of their young is indicated in Consumer's League of New York, *Behind the Scenes at the Canneries* (New York, 1930), p. 48; and in 2d Report, *FIC*, vol. 2, 1913, p. 1297.

But was going to the cannery really such a break with tradition? Seasonal migrations had not been an unusual recourse for peasant families who followed harvests throughout the *Mezzogiorno*. And temporary family dissolution was no strange experience either. Immediate need had justified its risks before, when many job-seeking fathers journeyed throughout the Italian south or across the sea, not to escape family responsibilities, but to fulfill them. Once in America, the same kind of thinking motivated risks and adjustments. And though many fathers remained in Buffalo, some could find employment with their families, as factory mechanics or harvesters.[15]

Removal of the family to the country had another aspect reminiscent of the Italian situation: the profitable use of children could continue without fear of reprisal for violation of factory codes or child-labor laws. Legislation limiting the number of hours women could work was also difficult to enforce. The canners, for their part, tended to ignore statutes limiting weekly work hours for women and for children under sixteen on the grounds that their trade's special conditions exempted them. And although processing-shed labor was industrial in character, not until 1913 did factory legislation codes attempt to control these establishments, and even then enforcement was lax. In the meantime canners worked their employees for thirteen and one-half hours per day or more. Because the season lasted from mid-June to mid-October, parents also violated and avoided compulsory school attendance laws. In the country, school authorities could be easily circumvented.[16] The work situation, then, made it possible for the immigrant family to maximize its income over a very short period.

Employers paid by the piece for both shed and field work, and hence cannery wages varied according to speed and skill. In a typical cannery, no one earned less than $1.00 a day; most foreign-born men and women earned from $1.25 to $1.75. Family income sometimes exceeded what a male head alone could earn in the city in summer railroad or industrial work.[17] Further enhancing the appeal of cannery work were wage supple-

[15] Maria Maddalena De'Rossi, Segretariato femmenile per la tutela delle donne e dei fanciulli emigranti, Relazione, "Le donne ed i fanciulli italiani a Buffalo e ad Albion" (Rome, 1913), p. 18.

[16] The labor law was amended a number of times regarding the number of hours women and children could legally work in factories. The New York State Factory Investigating Commission was particularly interested in including the canneries under the factory acts and eventually succeeded in doing so. See Jeremy Felt, *Hostages of Fortune: Child Labor Reform in New York State* (Syracuse, N.Y., 1965), pp. 25, 170; Bernardy, "L'emigrazione delle donne," p. 66; 2d Report, *FIC*, vol. 1, 1913, p. 125; editorial by Virtus, "La schiavitu delle donne e dei fanciulli," *La Fiaccola*, (Buffalo), July 28, 1910, p. 1.

[17] U.S. Senate, *Recent Immigrants in Agriculture,* 2:508, 494.

ments, which lowered family living costs for the season. In many cases canners provided housing, fruits, and vegetables gratis, or at a nominal fee.

Italians laboring in New York canneries could get along on as little as $0.50 to $1.00 a week per person. "Very thrifty" families, the Immigration Commission reported, saved "considerable sums" every summer, enough to get through a winter of probable unemployment of fathers. For some who could not find work, it presented the only opportunity to earn a living.[18] Foremost among the economic assets of working in the canneries, however, was the fact that Italians could earn a family wage. An Italian social worker described the immigrants' practical conception of family economics in a manner recalling the south Italian situation: "dal numero delle braccia di una famiglia dipende la prosperita della medisma" (a family's wealth depends upon the number of hands it has).[19] Because these immigrant families chose to earn their livelihoods in this fashion, they discovered a way to minimize the tensions which their low urban living standard could have produced.

A work situation that minimized family strains because it permitted mother and child to labor together constituted reason enough for Italians to become migrant laborers. Even in cases where mother and children went alone to the canneries, they stayed away from home for only short periods, and apparently immigrants did not perceive their absence as a serious challenge to the family's well-being. One gets the impression that they may have viewed it as a chance for wife and children to return to a familiar agricultural environment. Recall also that in Italy the mother supervised household tasks and production independently of her husband. Several observers noted that south Italians especially tended to organize cannery work along family lines. The labor—weeding, harvesting, and preparation for preserving—was light enough for women and children to engage in and, a government investigation reported, "since the women and children can work efficiently, the laborers, particularly the south Italians, make the family the working unit. This means that the whole family engages in farm labor or berry picking and the earnings all go into the family fund.[20]

The canners' mode of recruiting south Italians reflected their recognition that priority must be given to their family needs. The companies usually brought migrant workers from the city in family groups. An Albion company, which employed about three hundred Buffalo Italians, instructed its *padrone* to "secure families whenever possible." "It is found," the

[18] Ibid., pp. 494, 496, 150; see also Virtus, "La schiavitu," *La Fiaccola,* July 28, 1910, p. 1, and Buffalo, *Il Corriere Italiano,* Dec. 2, 1905, p. 1.

[19] De'Rossi, "Le donne ed i fanciulli," p. 18.

[20] Bernardy, "L'emigrazione delle donne," p. 88; U.S., Senate, *Recent Immigrants in Agriculture,* 2:491.

Immigration Commission stated, "that when the family is employed as a whole on the farm all are more contented and more apt to remain for the season than when part remain in the city and part go to the country."[21]

Those who defended recruitment of families for migrant labor and use of child employees claimed that the foreign parents would not come to the rural areas without their children. Some canners stated that they actually did not wish the children to work there, but the parents insisted. Eager adults worked their children in the fields, even when employing farmers, who feared the young ones might damage crops, opposed it.[22]

The general division of work among family members at the canneries shows further adaptations of south Italian practices. Close integration of economic and family roles as well as sex-role differentiation continued. Fathers either remained in the city or worked apart from women and children, so disciplinary activity and work direction stayed in the mother's hands. If a woman had evening work, the father sometimes cared for the family's young, but an elder daughter or some older woman more typically assumed these responsibilities. The entire family together might work the bean, pea, and corn fields in weeding and harvesting processes, just as it had in Italy. In grape-growing areas all tended vines and picked the fruit.[23] Until child-labor legislation was enforced in the canneries, children who once assisted in domestic chores in Italy now helped their mothers prepare crops for canning or snipped and husked vegetables while the women packaged and labeled them.[24]

Comparison of Italian and native-born working-class conceptions of the child's role and the use each made of their children points to some useful distinctions. While 90 percent of American-born children, many of them local residents, came to the canneries as independent workers, all foreign youngsters worked and traveled with their parents. This suggests the foreign parents' unwillingness to relinquish economic and familial control over their offspring.[25] A "working investigator" disguised as a laborer noted

[21] Ibid., pp. 507, 492. The agent who went into the Italian quarter claimed he always received more applications than he needed. Important abuses normally associated with the padrone system, however, especially that recruits pay the padrone for securing employment, do not seem to have been serious. By 1911, for example, many farmers did their own contracting, wages had become better established, and workers could find positions on their own without using agents as go-betweens (ibid., p. 493).

[22] 2d Report, *FIC*, vol. 1, 1913, p. 141; see also testimony of the plant supervisor where Buffalo Italians were employed (ibid., vol. 3, 1913, p. 423); Luciano J. Iorizzo, "Italian Immigrants and the Impact of the Padrone System," Diss. Syracuse 1966, p. 190.

[23] "Looking Over the Canneries," *Express,* (Buffalo), Aug. 16, 1912, p. 7; Consumer's League of New York, p. 47; 2d Report, *FIC*, vol. 2, 1913, p 954; U.S., Senate, *Recent Immigrants in Agriculture,* 2:509.

[24] George Mangold, *Migratory Child Workers* (New York, 1929), p. 4; U.S., Senate, *Recent Immigrants in Agriculture,* 2:509; 2d Report, *FIC*, vol. 2, 1913, p. 775.

[25] 2d Report, *FIC*, vol. 2, 1913, p. 802.

that where "American" help was used in snipping or husking, work rarely commenced before seven in the morning. Where foreigners—that is, Italians—labored, work began as early as 4:00 A.M. in rush season. Where Americans were employed, children seldom did other work during the day, but Italian parents often roused their children at dawn to snip beans until daylight, when they went to the fields to pick beans. At night they went to the sheds and worked again. The investigator claimed that "cases in which American mothers force their children to work are, however, the exception and not the rule." Even when American children did work, she claimed, they eagerly awaited going to the "sheds where there are many other children and where they can earn a little spending money."[26]

Parental motivations in forcing the children to work are clear. A social worker at Albion's Olney Canning Company observed that strong economic motives drove the Buffalo Italians working there. The Italian people, she said, considered their "children as so much money value." The social workers had great difficulties manipulating intractable parents who failed to accept that the children belonged in cannery schools, not in factory sheds. Throughout the entire summer, the social worker claimed, she and her colleagues frequently failed to keep children under ten—the legal working age for labor of this kind—out of the sheds and off the harvest fields. "You understand," she reported, "the disposition of the mothers . . . was to make money out of the children." An Italian government agent who visited the canneries at about the same time concurred. "The canners," she said, "like the cheap labor of the Italians and their children, and the parents for their part go with pleasure because it gives them a way to earn off their children." Italian adults, she noted, were the hardest drivers. Lamenting the "precocious old age" of Italian youth, she observed that little ones, "old enough to hold a bean are made to work by their parents." While softer American parents permitted their young ones to leave work, the *Mezzogiorno's* children struggled on.[27]

The organization of labor in the sheds, to the extent that parents determined it, indicated juvenile subservience to adults among all groups. Whether they wanted to or not—and these children, like most, had a special proclivity for not wanting to—young ones followed parental orders. Adults, especially the Italians, definitely maintained the upper hand in delegating work tasks. An Italian-born social worker who visited canneries where Buffalo Italians labored elaborated further. The mothers were "hard on the children," she commented: "Although they love their children, they do not love them in the right way sometimes. They think they must

[26] Ibid., vol. 1, pp. 135–38.

[27] Testimony of Jennie Bowen, Dec. 10, 1912, 2d Report, *FIC*, vol. 4, 1913, p. 1933; Bernardy, "L'emigrazione delle donne," pp. 67, 62–64.

bring in something and that is the Italian idea. They like to have children because they help to lift the burden. Q. 'The more children the more work?' A. 'Yes.' " Noting that children in Italy were expected to work, she continued that she saw nothing wrong in this because it prevented them from becoming lazy.[28] Like the migrant laborers she commented upon, this woman also interpreted the situation in terms of her own cultural attitudes.

The style of parental discipline of Italians and Americans varied, the former being particularly relentless, the latter more indulgent. The Italian investigator who asked children in a corn husking shed why they continued to work so long received the reply, "We'd get licked." Testimony given the Factory Investigating Commission relating to the situation at a cannery where many Buffalo Italians worked speaks for itself:

> The parents were constantly urging the children to work. One little boy, aged 11, was throwing some bean snippings at another little fellow and had stopped work a second. His father hit him brutally across the face and set him again to work. Everywhere parents were forcing children to work. . . . If they did not work they would shake them and sometimes hit them depending on the parent. This is not true of all parents, but the majority of Italian parents were forcing their children to work. Most of the American parents were not forcing them to work. Take for instance, the woman, Mrs. McGaffie, the woman I have mentioned here. She had a little girl aged 10 in the factory. She did not use such stringent methods of forcing the children to work as the Italians did, but she kept the child constantly at work for 6 or 7 hours a day. But she was not so brutal about it as the Italians were, and she let the child go home to meals, and stopped when she pleaded and pleaded with her mother that she was tired.[29]

A Factory Commission inspector's report concerning a cannery where many Buffalo Italians worked tells of a twelve-year-old Italian child, little Jack, whose family woke him at three in the morning. He snipped beans from 4:30 A.M. to 10:00 P.M. with only a few minutes off for supper. After this long day's work, his only comment to the investigator was, "My fingers is broke." That day he went to sleep at midnight and woke up at 3:00 A.M. He was, he said, "awful tired," but his mother made him work. Finding his hands swollen, he tried to leave work several times. His mother also constantly scolded his ten-year-old sister, who could "hardly keep her

[28] Testimony of Mary Chamberlain, social worker disguised as laborer, 2d Report, *FIC*, vol. 3, p. 1013; testimony of Madeline De'Rossi, social worker, North American Civic League for Immigrants, Dec. 10, 1912, 2d Report, *FIC*, vol. 4, 1913, p. 1945.

[29] Bernardy, "L'emigrazione delle donne," p. 67; testimony of Mary Chamberlain, taken from the diary she kept when working as a disguised laborer at the cannery, 2d Report, *FIC*, vol. 2, 1913, p. 1007.

eyes open," to continue her work. Jack earned $1.40 that day. He could keep none of his wages. But, he said, labor like this was nothing compared to the pea season, when his mother and sister returned home at 1:00 and 2:00 A.M., and "they was so sick they fell down and vomited."[30]

The Factory Investigating Commission neatly summarized differences between Italian and American attitudes toward work and childrearing. For foreigners the shed was "distinctly a place for work." But for the American child the shed was more like a "playground where they play at work till they get tired and then quit." The disposition of the funds earned by Italians and Americans also tells us something about their differing cultural attitudes toward the child's family role. American children, the Commission's report noted, worked to earn spending money, to buy a bike, a toy, or shoes. But Italian and Polish parents required their children to submit their wages to the family budget. Indeed, since parents, not children, received the wage, it is highly unlikely that the latter ever saw their earnings. An Italian government reporter's comments put it well: "In general the child is considered as a tool and appendix of the mother, and it is she who is paid, not them."[31] As in Italy, the child did not achieve even this symbolic recognition as a wage earner.

Because of this transference of family discipline into the factory, canners had few problems obtaining the highest possible output from children. As one factory investigator put it, the "severe manner of the mothers rules the house and family in largely the same manner as she controls the family in the shed or field." Goaded by sheer economic necessity and in some cases the need to earn enough for the whole year during the summer, such parents were far more effective taskmasters than the factory owners could have been. Indeed, the chief factory inspector testified that so far as the canners were concerned, children remained free to come and go: the parents, he claimed, especially the foreigners, forced the children to work. Similarly, Italian parents, not the manufacturers, sent their children running away when the canning inspector, representative of the public interest in their young ones, arrived.[32] The canners felt no compulsion to keep records of the children's working hours for, as one student of child labor put it, "They knew that the parents would keep their offspring at work, just as tenement parents did, in order to increase the family 'piece work pay.'" Or, as aptly put by the Commission, "The canners supply the materials to work on, the parents do the driving."[33]

At least one canner permitted a school on his premises for children under working age, but Italian mothers resisted allowing their children to attend.

[30] 2d Report, *FIC*, vol. 2, 1913, p. 785.

[31] Ibid., pp. 781, 786, 789; Bernady, "L'emigrazione delle donne," p. 67.

[32] 2d Report, *FIC*, vol. 2, 1913, p. 1296; ibid., pp. 949, 775.

[33] Felt, p. 174; 2d Report, *FIC*, vol. 1, 1913, p. 166.

In fact, the women began what was described as "practically a riot . . . [though] not as bad as that," when a plant superintendent, attempting to comply with labor codes by keeping children under ten out of the sheds, was besieged by angry Italian women, one of whom bit his finger "right through."[34] The Commission did not fully clarify the circumstances of this disturbance, but all witnesses agreed that many mothers, wishing their children to work rather than attend school, participated—not just the single female assailant. And clearly this "riot" resulted from the factory supervisor's interference into what the parents considered their exclusive domain.

Most observers did not attribute the harshness of this situation to parental hardheartedness, but to low family wages. The Factory Investigating Commission noted, for example: "Nor are the parents alone to blame. Their parental love is often dulled by the hard grind of necessity. Manifestly a canner who pays low wages to parents cannot argue convincingly that the children should not be permitted to snip beans to increase the meager earnings of the family. If children should not be permitted to work, the cannery owner would still be under the necessity of obtaining the labor of their parents and unquestionably would soon have to pay the parents approximately what is now the total family income." Apparently American working-class parents could better afford to be "much more careful in caring for their children" than less fortunate foreigners who had little choice but to conceive of their children as economic assets and use them accordingly.[35]

Italian parents avoided, ignored, or protested against state intervention in family affairs, just as they had in the Old World. Although the goals of parents and canning manufacturers differed, the effective results were the same. Usually the two formed a cooperative partnership to avoid child-labor and truancy regulations. It is easy to understand the employers' motivations. Manufacturers generally perceived that so long as they made no attempt to undermine Italian family organization—take, for example, their recruitment policies—they could expect to receive optimum output from every family member. Moreover, the use of child labor usually worked to their advantage, so why—except for an occasional public demonstration of good will, such as allowing the North American Civic League to establish immigrant schools on their premises—attempt to challenge it?

The economic needs of immigrant parents led them to reject the

[34] De'Rossi, "Le donne ed i fanciulli," pp. 19–21; testimony of Jennie Bowen, Dec. 10, 1912, 2d Report, *FIC*, vol. 4, 1913, pp. 1916–23; testimony of Robert Mulree, Superintendent of Olney Canning Co., Aug. 15, 1912, 2d Report, *FIC*, vol. 2, 1913, pp. 423–24; see also testimony of Miss De'Rossi, Dec. 10, 1912, ibid., vol. 4, p. 1943.

[35] 2d Report, *FIC*, vol. 1, 1913, p. 166; ibid., vol. 2, p. 781.

American legal endorsement of community interest in the disposition and care of their children. Legal definitions of the child as a separate personality with rights more important than his family obligations made no sense to them, simply because such individualistic notions conflicted with more familial south Italian ones. The former peasants saw the child as a member of the family group in which no outside influence had a right to interfere. What one student of child labor wrote of nineteenth-century American parents, who also brought a traditional culture with them to the factory, applies equally to Italians of this later period. "The average New Yorker," he wrote, "was as opposed to interference in the family as he was to state meddling in the market place."[36]

Because Polish, Italian, and an earlier generation of American-born parents exhibited similar attitudes to child labor, one could argue that similarities in class and economic position, not cultural tradition, explain their behavior. And indeed our evidence suggests the beginnings of a lower-class subculture cutting across ethnic lines. But I do not see the cultural and class explanations as mutually exclusive. The choice of explanations, it seems to me, depends upon what one wishes to explain. In this instance I am less concerned with proving that most peasant cultures adapted uniformly to industrial society than I am with adaptation of one traditional culture to that society. Others will have to assume the larger task. In the meantime I would hazard the guess that original distinctions among traditional cultures moving into American society played some role in differentiating each group's response.

Additional evidence points to the persistence of traditional Italian cultural attitudes despite the new work situation. Extremely poor housing conditions, which certainly encouraged the deterioration of sexual controls and "moral degeneration," failed to undermine Italian morale. Housing arrangements generally allowed little or no separation of the sexes. Facilities varied according to the cannery. Tenements, barracks, and separate houses were each used in different places. Not uncommonly, entire families, regardless of their size, resided in one room. Worse, several families might be housed together, separated only by a canvas. Adults of both sexes slept, dressed, and washed in the same area. Often, young adolescent children, male and female, used the same sleeping quarters. Boarders frequently intruded into a family's already limited privacy. In one colony, unmarried men and women of an undetermined nationality lived in the same barracks with only a broken partition separating them.[37] In spite of these circumstances, community pressures prevailed

[36] Felt, p. 9.

[37] Bernardy, "L'emigrazione delle donne," p. 88; 2d Report, *FIC,* vol. 2, 1913, pp. 884–87; Virtus, "La schiavitu," p. 1.

in the Italian quarters, where the people kept "good humor." Other ethnic groups living under similar conditions apparently did not exercise the same degree of control. Fòr example, Buffalo's health commissioner, himself of Polish origin, traced a number of illegitimate births in the Polish community to these circumstances. Despite his knowledge of Italian living conditions both in Little Italy and at the canneries, he made no mention of Italian illegitimacy.[38]

The work situation itself also challenged traditional moral concepts. The manager of a Geneva, N.Y., cannery which employed Buffalo and Syracuse south Italians noted that despite the close association of the sexes both in the dormitories and at work, moral conditions remained "excellent." But there is no doubt that factory organization tested Italian female morality. A social worker, disguised as a laborer, wrote in her diary of "fresh" bosses and timekeepers at the canneries, each of whom had power over the women. "The situation," she said, "is much like that of a department store where the floor walker has a lot of girls under him, receiving low wages and all more or less at his mercy." Male cannery superintendents apparently did not consider it beneath their dignity to offer the young women an opportunity to earn extra money, and the fact that much cannery work took place at night made the situation more threatening for the women. Another social worker had actually been drawn by the women into their protective community. They warned that the timekeeper was "fresh" and that she had best avoid him. Protection extended outside the immediate Italian community and the basic family group when an Italian girl warned her that "one must be careful not to get fresh with the Italian boys, because they are dangerous."[39] Sexual identification apparently triumphed over ethnic loyalty.

An additional circumstance reinforcing community feeling among the Italians, despite the shifting nature of the migrant population, was that the work force contained other, sometimes hostile and competitive, groups—country people living near the canneries, Poles, and Syrians. As one commentator has put it, "Confined in a single rural factory [they] were unlikely to form much of a bond with another." This same person observed that considerable conflict existed between the Syrians and Poles, who gladly accepted low salaries, and the Italian women, who wished to strike for higher pay. As for the Americans, they would side with the American employer rather than join the "Eyetalians" in a strike. Those strikes that occurred were attributed to the Italians; they provide testimony to their sense of solidarity, especially where bread-and-butter issues were

[38] Bernardy, "L'emigrazione delle donne," p. 88; 2d Report, *FIC*, vol. 2, 1913, p. 887.

[39] U.S., Senate, *Recent Immigrants in Agriculture,* 2:502; testimony of Mary Chamberlain, Nov. 26, 1912, 2d Report, *FIC*, vol. 3, 1913, p. 1014; ibid., p. 1016.

concerned.[40] The closely knit Italian women frequently joined together, hoarding work under their skirts and chairs in an effort to save piecework for themselves. In this manner they earned the resentment of less united, but equally discontented, women. The same sense of solidarity prevailed between an Italian foreman and female workers when the foreman gave the "Buffalo tables" more than their share of the work.[41]

Italian immigrants sought other occupational arrangements in American cities which permitted easy adaptation of traditional practices. For example, they found homework, another semitraditional occupation, attractive. Like the canneries, it provided a transitional step for recently arrived peasant groups attempting to cushion the full leap into industrial society. A New York State factory investigating commission report on 300 New York City families emphasized the peculiar preference Italians seemed to have for this work style:

> The large proportion of Italians engaged in homework is significant of the fact that their home traditions lend themselves with peculiar readiness to the homework system. The Germans accept homework as a trade and adapt themselves to specific phases of it at which they may become expert. They do not do finishing, but do fine custom tailoring, making vests complete or fine handmade button holes. . . . The Irish and Americans adopt homework only as a last resort. They do it only when they are poverty stricken and driven to it by necessity. The Italians come usually from rural districts and know little about factory work and organized industry. The men become laborers and fall into seasonal trades where the wages are small and irregular and must be supplemented. As a rule they have strong home associations, they expect their girls to marry young, and they do not like them to go out into factories. Accustomed in Italy to depend upon the labor of their children in the fields, they expect them in this country to yield a financial return at the earliest possible moment and are, therefore, ready to have them adopt homework, a system that lends itself to the exploitation of women and children.[42]

In both homework and cannery industries, the family continued as the basic productive unit, and the organization of work, if not its substance, closely resembled Italian practices. The mother's role as arbiter of household tasks and disciplinarian of children was reinforced by her economic position as work manager, be it making artificial flowers, sewing, or canning. However, she retained her inferior position to her husband be-

[40] Felt, p. 170; Consumer's League of New York, p. 44; 2d Report, *FIC*, vol. 1, 1913, p. 167; ibid., vol. 2, 1913, p. 872.

[41] Testimony of Mary Chamberlain, 2d Report, *FIC,* vol. 2, 1913, p. 1016; Consumer's League of New York, p. 45.

[42] 2d Report, *FIC,* vol. 2, 1913, Appendix 4, "Manufacturing in the Tenements," pp. 684–85.

cause she had not become the chief breadwinner. As in Italy, these families viewed income earned by wives and children who ventured to migrant labor camps or worked at home as a supplement to the father's wages, not a replacement. In neither case did the Italian male relinquish his support obligation, nor did he forfeit his control and authority. A close association of economic and family functions similar to what existed in Italy prevailed in both situations. Italians found such arrangements agreeable because they brought income in but minimized sex-role conflict.

Other studies suggest that these kinds of adaptations were not peculiar. They also show that employers seeking high output at cheap prices had a flexibility of their own. New Jersey silk weaving firms, for example, often hired whole Italian families, probably because these employers, like cannery owners, recognized the family's potential as a well-disciplined work unit. Smelser's study of the English industrial revolution observes similar phenomena in the recently mechanized weaving industry, and studies of modern Japan emphasize how its economic institutions operate under traditional political and personal concepts. Finally, a study of south Italian factory laborers in Pittsburgh shows the same transference of kin control occurring in an urban situation. In this instance Italians did permit women and children to enter industrial occupations outside the home because proximity to the ethnic neighborhood and the presence of other Italians in the work force provided props for expected behavior.[43]

One could argue that both the canneries and homework industries were semitraditional occupations and that immigrant adjustment to them does not challenge customary notions concerning the relationship between the family and industrialization. But such an argument does not explain the immigrants' behavior in more typical urban settings, and it obscures some important distinctions about them and the industrial society they helped to create. We tend to simplify what the creation of such a society means. Geertz reminds us that "economic development can take place within a context of general social and economic conservatism in which essentially traditional values and social structures are so adapted as to be capable of integration with more efficient economic practices."[44]

Sometimes with their employers' cooperation and sometimes without it, Italian immigrants transformed canning factories into communities where Old World social attitudes and behavior could continue and where kinship

[43] Foerster, p. 346, discusses the New Jersey situation; Smelser, pp. 182, ff.; Geertz, p. 144, mentions a Japanese study by James G. Abbegglen, *The Japanese Factory: Aspects of Its Social Organization* (Glencoe, Ill., 1958); George H. Huganir, "The Hosiery Looper in the Twentieth Century: A Study in Family Occupational Processes and Adaptation to Factory and Community Change, 1900–1950," Diss. Pennsylvania 1958 discusses Pittsburgh Italians.

[44] Geertz, p. 144.

ties operated to maintain them. The way in which these families fit themselves into their new context confirms that, despite requirements for efficiency and rationality, modern economic institutions were quite capable of incorporating such traditional needs.

There was a lot of room in industrial America for immigrants wishing to avoid a head-on collision with a new way of life. But immigrant preference for fringe occupations shows how tradition influenced both their perception and their use of work options. Without taking their perceptions into account, we cannot understand them *or* their history.

# V Political Leadership in the Industrial City: Irish Development and Nativist Response in Jersey City

*Douglas V. Shaw*

AMERICAN CITIES IN the nineteenth century developed simultaneously as centers of industry and as areas with high concentrations of immigrants. Immigrants worked disproportionately in the unskilled and semiskilled jobs available in the city, and it is here that they developed communites that attempted to reenforce and sustain the cultures with which they arrived. By the Civil War many American cities had populations with an adult majority of non-native-born citizens, and these majorities came to play a prominent, if not a controlling, role in the political fabric of numerous communities.[1]

The growth of an immigrant political presence both reflected and heightened the cultural tensions existing in urban America, and the possibility of American cities controlled by non-Americans haunted members of the native-born elite. Styling themselves as reformers, they attempted to beat back and constrict the role played by immigrants, blurring the distinction between the expression in politics of different cultures and the arrival of incompetence and corruption. The reformers' image of the immigrant in politics stuck, and historians have tended to view nineteenth-century municipal history from this perspective.[2]

In Jersey City the Irish developed a political leadership class by 1865 and dominated the city's municipal institutions by 1870. A close examination of the issues, personalities, and rhetoric involved in this transference of power reveals much about the nature of the Irish and native-born communities and about the conflicts that existed between them: conflicts involving ethnicity, social class, and religion.

The 1860 census data for Jersey City establish the relationship between

[1] Herbert G. Gutman, "Work, Culture, and Society in Industrializing America," *American Historical Review* 78 (1973):560–62.

[2] In treating municipal government, historians have been most concerned with governmental structure and with corruption versus reform. By not fully exploring and developing the impact of urban ethnocultural conflicts, they have underestimated the role these conflicts played in forming both the structure of nineteenth-century municipal governments and the motivation of many reform groups. See, for example, Charles N. Glaab and A. Theodore Brown, *A History of Urban America* (New York, 1967), chaps. 7 and 8; Alexander B. Callow, *The Tweed Ring* (New York, 1965); Melvin G. Holli, *Reform in Detroit: Hazen S. Pingree and Urban Politics* (New York, 1969).

class and ethnicity (see Table 13).[3] Each nationality had a distinct occupational grouping, with the most striking differences being those between the two groups that each constituted almost 40 percent of the population, the native-born and the Irish. Almost half of the native-born did not work with their hands; virtually all of the Irish did. Thus the lines of class cleavage and the lines of ethnic cleavage overlapped: the native-born constituted the city's economic and social elite; the Irish comprised a disproportionate number of the poor. A third line of cleavage, and perhaps the most important in terms of the conflicts that followed, cut through the community in much the same way. The native-born tended to be Protestant, while the Irish were almost all Catholic. Thus, ethnic, religious, and class cleavages were cumulative rather than cross-cutting, intensifying the cultural and political conflicts between the different groups.[4]

Located across the Hudson River from lower Manhattan, Jersey City had first developed as a residential suburb of New York City, populated largely by middle-class merchants and clerks. Only after 1850 did the selection of the city as an eastern terminus by the trunk-line railroads bring industrialization and large numbers of lower-class Irish immigrants.[5] The traditional native-born elite responded to this ethnic heterogeneity by creating and manipulating institutions that had as their goal Americanizing and Protestantizing the Irish.

Officially and unofficially the city was unabashedly Protestant. In 1853, at the suggestion of the aldermanic committee on alms, the Protestant churches created the City Mission and Tract Society to act as the quasi-official voice of Protestantism in city affairs. The paid City Missionary preached compulsory Sunday services to the largely Irish inmates of the almshouse and the jail, and, with the Tract Visitors, attempted to deliver a piece of Protestant literature to every family each month.[6] The Mission and Tract Society, with its allied Bible Society, also exercised a heavy influence on the public schools. Throughout the 1860s, from one-third to

[3] For a more complete discussion of these data, see Douglas V. Shaw, "The Making of an Immigrant City: Ethnic and Cultural Conflict in Jersey City, New Jersey, 1850–1877," Diss. Rochester 1972, pp. 14–47.

[4] For a discussion of the effects of cultural cleaverage on political institutions, see Robert A. Dahl, *Democracy in the United States: Promise and Performance,* 2d. ed. (Chicago, 1972), pp. 293–312; *Polyarchy: Participation and Opposition* (New Haven, 1971), pp. 105–23. See also Michael Hechter, "The Political Economy of Ethnic Change," *American Journal of Sociology* 79 (1974):1151–78.

[5] Alexander McLean, *History of Jersey City, N.J.* (Jersey City, 1894), pp. 56–59; *New York Times,* Aug. 21, 1870.

[6] *Daily Sentinel and Advertiser* (Jersey City), Nov. 5, 1853, May 6, 1854; *American Standard* (Jersey City), Dec. 15, 1873. All newspapers cited are from Jersey City unless noted otherwise.

*Table 13.* Nativity by selected occupations, white males twenty and older, Jersey City, 1860

| | White males | | | | | | | |
|---|---|---|---|---|---|---|---|---|
| | Native | | Irish | | British | | German | |
| Occupations* | No. | % | No. | % | No. | % | No. | % |
| Nonmanual | 1,180 | 42.1 | 168 | 6.6 | 236 | 25.7 | 110 | 13.6 |
| Skilled | 969 | 34.4 | 743 | 28.2 | 498 | 54.3 | 482 | 59.6 |
| Unskilled | 254 | 9.0 | 1,472 | 55.9 | 106 | 11.5 | 109 | 13.4 |
| Other | 415 | 14.5 | 253 | 9.3 | 78 | 8.5 | 109 | 13.4 |
| Total | 2,818 | 100.0 | 2,636 | 100.0 | 918 | 100.0 | 810 | 100.0 |

SOURCE: Census data are derived from the federal manuscript census schedules for Jersey City, N.J.; National Archives Publication, roll 653–93.

**Nonmanual* includes merchants, manufacturers, professionals, clerks, and other white-collar workers; *skilled* are predominantly artisans and men in the building trades; *unskilled* are largely laborers; *other* includes shopkeepers, policemen, and those listed without occupation.

one-half of the school board interlocked with the directorates of the Protestant missionary organizations.[7]

The processes of justice also tended to work against the Irish, if not because of their ethnicity, then because of their social class. The Irish regularly made up about 70 percent of those arrested in each monthly report by the city marshal, and offenses involving liquor constituted over half the arrests.[8] As with the schools, nativism played an important role in police work. In 1857 a nativist weekly newspaper, reviewing the party affiliation of city officialdom, claimed that eight of the twenty policemen were Know-Nothings.[9]

The Know-Nothing movement was strong in Jersey City, a reflection of the strength of nativism and anti-Catholicism among the native-born. From 1853 to 1857 the city supported two Order of United Americans lodges, and in 1856 the American party presidential candidate, Millard Fillmore, attracted approximately a third of the native-born vote. While the Know-Nothing movement as a coherent organizational force collapsed in the late 1850s, members of the movement continued to oppose Irish penetration of the city's political institutions. In the cultural

[7] McLean, pp. 145–47. The twelve-man school board that took office in 1857 was typical. It contained five men associated with the missionary and Bible societies, three Know-Nothings, and the superintendent of the temperance Sabbath School (Shaw, p. 68).

[8] See, as examples, the marshal's report for November 1860 (*American Standard,* Dec., 1860), or the 1856–67 prison statistics (*Jersey City Courier,* July 9, 1857).

[9] *Jersey City Courier,* June 18, 1857.

and political conflicts of the next decade, former Know-Nothings played a disproportionate role.[10]

Thus the native-born attempted to use the city's institutions to coerce the Irish into new cultural and behavioral norms. This was the context in which independent Irish political activity began. More specifically, Irish protests were directed against the nativism and anti-Catholicism of the native-born and the institutions they controlled. During the 1850s the Irish had unsuccessfully protested proselytism in the almshouse and schools, but after 1860 they were able to blunt, by means of successful political activity, the nativistic thrust of city institutions.

The first successful revolt against native-born hegemony came in 1861 with the campaign for city recorder, a local judicial post that dealt with minor cases such as drunkenness and disorderly conduct, in which the law and the poor collided. Eight Irish delegates walked out of the Democratic city nominating convention after that party renominated the incumbent recorder, Thomas E. Tilden, a former Know-Nothing who had compiled a harsh record. Forming an independent political organization that drew strong support from the German community, the dissident Irish nominated Cornelius Martindale, a nonevangelical English-born accountant of lower-class origins. Opposing two candidates allied with nativism and temperance, Martindale won with 55 percent of the vote, capturing 84 percent in the most heavily Irish ward. A first success led to a second: in the following year, 1862, Irish Democrats forced an Irish nomination for police chief, carrying the convention by only one vote, but then securing a 51 percent victory for their candidate.[11]

Throughout the 1860s the Democratic party was the dominant political force in Jersey Cty, but it was by no means a harmonious political unit. Led by its native-born wing, many of whose members had strong ties to temperance, evangelicalism, and nativism, it depended upon the Irish for electoral success. But as the decade advanced the Irish became increasingly less willing to support native-born candidates, and the old elite fought hard to retain their pre-eminence.[12] Clearly, the most important political tension in Jersey City was within the Democratic party. The

[10] On September 4, 1856, the *Hudson County Courier* printed a list of almost 600 ratifiers of the Fillmore presidential nomination, almost three-fourths of the Jersey City Fillmore vote of 840 that November. The list thus provides a good indication of nativist strength in the 1850s; it also contains a large percentage of the men who became prominent in politics after 1860. Occasional independent candidates used the American party label until 1868 (*Evening Journal*, Nov. 28, 1868).

[11] *American Standard,* Mar. 14, 16, Apr. 4, 17, 1861; *New York World,* Apr. 9, 1861; *American Standard,* Mar. 27 and Apr. 1, 1862. The office of police chief was made non-elective in 1866; that of recorder in 1871.

[12] See, for example, the "Junius" letters, *Jersey City Chronicle,* Apr. 1–4, 1863; see also *Evening Journal,* May 25, 1867, and Dec. 2, 1868.

native-born leadership of necessity began to run more and more Irish candidates for important elective offices. But it tried to choose these candidates carefully, and the first generation of elected Irish officials tended to be subordinate to the native-born and subject to manipulation. A Republican newspaper observed that "great care" had been taken "to exclude Irishmen of character and intelligence" from office.[13]

How the native-born Democrats maintained ties to the Irish community remains obscure, but money undoubtedly played an important role. An Irish candidate who opposed a native-born incumbent in 1870 claimed that the native-born leadership relied upon "the lowest class of Irishmen" and that they "debauch young men, and give them money and make them the tools of politicians." Patronage was also important. Throughout the 1860s the police force and less important city offices became increasingly filled with Irish.[14]

This alliance between native-born Democrats and a number of pliant Irish officeholders outraged both the Republicans and some elements of the Irish community. But in a sense it served both groups well. Irish aldermen regularly voted for native-born former Know-Nothings for such important offices as overseer of the poor, treasurer, city clerk, and city marshall. The city in return employed Irish laborers on city projects and also employed numerous Irish policemen. This employment was important and was valued in the Irish community. When an Irish revolt split the Democratic party at the county level in 1870, local Fenian leaders urged support for the regular Democratic ticket on the grounds that a party split would result in a Republican victory, and that, in turn, would result in massive removals of Irish police and laborers.[15] Further, the Irish in the Democratic party forced the native-born to hedge their positions on temperance and Sabbatarianism. When Cornelius Martindale ran for a second term as recorder in 1866, for example, he received support from native-born as well as Irish Democrats.[16]

Although the first generation of Irish officeholders was generally subservient to native-born dictates, the second was not. The Irish achieved political dominance of Jersey City between 1867 and 1870. It did not come from a determined drive for control, but from force of numbers and the importance of ethnicity in local politics. One newspaper accurately noted in 1868 that the "old Know Nothing Democrats" had, until recently, "been smart enough to honeyfugle the Irish into doing all the heavy voting

[13] *Jersey City Times,* Apr. 11, 1871.

[14] *Evening Journal,* Nov. 1, 1870. In 1860, according to the manuscript census, the Irish constituted 38 percent of the police force. In 1870 they constituted 66 percent (*Jersey City Times,* May 9, 1870).

[15] *American Standard,* Nov. 2, 1870.

[16] *Jersey City Times,* Apr. 11, 1866; *Jersey City Herald,* July 9, 1870.

and yelling while they took all the fat offices themselves." But now "Pat has worked up to a conscious sense of his power, and demands the offices himself."[17] By 1870 the native-born elite had lost control of Jersey City.

A look at the changing ethnic composition of the board of aldermen demonstrates both the rapidity and the completeness of that change (see Table 14). Although the total number of aldermen changed over time, the native-born retained indisputable control from the 1850s through 1867. By 1869 the native-born had lost 60 percent of their representation, and the board was almost half Irish. One newspaper reported aldermanic dialogue in brogue. In 1870, when the city consolidated with two of its suburbs, doubling the number of wards, the number of aldermen increased correspondingly, but the proportion from each group remained much the same.[18] This change in ethnicity was compounded by a sharp increase in the independence of immigrant aldermen.

Extensive biographical information exists for the aldermen elected in the spring of 1870.[19] An analysis of these men—and how they acted as aldermen—can tell us much about the sources of Irish leadership and the adaptation of the Irish community to industrial America. But it is a mistake to think only in terms of the immigrant communities as making that adaptation. Of the eleven native-born aldermen, only two had been born locally. Of the other nine, seven had farming or small town backgrounds and had entered an urban environment as adults. Yet as members of the dominant group in American society they had achieved a fair measure of economic success. Eight were clearly of the economic elite, and the other three were young, prospering businessmen.

Just as the native-born aldermen came from the elite of the native-born community, the fifteen Irish aldermen came from the elite of the Irish community. Since the Irish community was largely working class, the Irish aldermen represented the working-class elite and small proprietors. Significantly, not only were none of the Irish aldermen unskilled, but of the nine whose fathers' occupations are known, only two were laborers. Irish political leadership did not come from those with their roots deepest in Ireland's peasant culture; it came from those least foreign to the industrial aspects of American society.

In 1870 Jersey City's nine Irish-born Catholic aldermen included a butcher, a produce marketer, a carriage maker, the owner of a small quarry, a cattle dealer, and a saloon keeper. None did business on a large scale and none were financially independent. The occupations of the six

[17] *Evening Journal,* Nov. 20, 1868.

[18] *Evening Journal,* Oct. 21, 1868; McLean, pp. 79–83.

[19] The *Jersey City Herald* printed one biography in each weekly edition between July 30, 1870, and Feb. 25, 1871. Briefer accounts appeared in the *Jersey City Times,* May 10, 1870.

*Table 14*. Jersey City aldermen by ethnicity

| Aldermen | 1857 | 1867 | 1869 | 1870 |
|---|---|---|---|---|
| Native-born | 13 | 10 | 4 | 11 |
| Irish | 3 | 4 | 6 | 15 |
| German | 0 | 0 | 2 | 3 |
| British | 0 | 0 | 2 | 3 |
| Total | 16 | 14 | 14 | 32 |

SOURCES: *Jersey City Courier*, May 7–June 25, 1857; *Jersey City Times*, May 10, 1870; Mclean, pp. 97–100.

second-generation members were similar, including a machinist, a milk agent, two factory supervisors, and a saloon keeper. An Irish editor referred to these aldermen as "active, intelligent hard-working artisans who are among the bone and sinew of our city."[20]

These men related to their wards and neighborhoods in ways not understood by the native-born elite. The career of John Maloney, owner of the Prospect Shades saloon near the Erie Railroad repair shops, is illustrative. Employed as a machinist in repair shops for a number of years, Maloney had taken an active role in two strikes over late pay. Blacklisted after the failure of the second strike in early 1870, he opened a saloon shortly thereafter and was elected an alderman later that spring. As a labor leader and then as a saloon keeper, Maloney played a vital role in his local community. Saloons offered their patrons more than recreation and escape. They provided meeting places for fraternal and benevolent organizations as well as labor unions, made newspapers available, and, of course, were places of political discussion and organization.[21]

Although all of the Irish aldermen seem to have been sympathetic to the cause of Irish freedom, none were conspicuous in post-Civil War Irish nationalist activity. Many, however, participated actively in local parish affairs. For example, Patrick McNulty, president of the board, was a trustee of Saint Joseph's Church and a participant in the Catholic temperance movement, and John Hogan, who had lived in New York City, had been instrumental there in securing the use of the Douay Bible in his ward school.[22]

The Irish communities were complex social organisms with their own in-

[20] *Jersey City Herald*, July 2, 1870.

[21] Andrew Sinclair, *Era of Excess: A Social History of the Prohibition Movement*, Harper ed. (New York, 1964), pp. 73–76; Brian Harrison, *Drink and the Victorians* (Pittsburgh, 1971), pp. 45–55.

[22] *Jersey City Herald*, Sept. 24 and Nov. 10, 1870.

ternal organization and values, and this was reflected in their choice of political leaders. Irish regional factionalism played an obscure, but probably important, role. In 1857, for example, Connaughtmen and Munstermen rioted for three days over whose shanties would be built where at a construction site. In 1868 in a ward primary where, as one editor noted, three-fourths of the Democratic voters were "of Irish persuasion," a Corkonian squared off against a Tipperary man on the issue of where in Ireland an Irish alderman should come from. Although railroad domination of the city was an important issue elsewhere in the community, in the fifth ward the candidate from Cork, an Erie freight supervisor, won the election.[23] The continuity of Irish regional attachments was important, and it affected, in ways that remain obscure, attitudes toward Irish nationalism and participation in American politics.

Given the limited nature of nineteenth-century municipal government, these men worked no revolution in Jersey City, and their acts indicate few traces of social radicalism. But they did respond, in ways both symbolic and real, to the needs and aspirations of Jersey City's Irish laboring community. Sympathy with Irish nationalism led to use of the city armory by Irish drill companies, and when Jeremiah O'Donovan Rossa and other Irish revolutionaries visited the United States in early 1871, the aldermen appropriated $500 for a public reception. Catholics, rigidly excluded from the school board until after the Civil War, approximated their proportion of the population by 1870. Nativists no longer controlled the almshouse or prison, and the police reflected Irish, not native-born, attitudes towards the enforcement of sumptuary legislation.[24]

Nothing better symbolized the change in aldermanic cultural background than the response to a strike of Erie machinists in early 1870. After the police force broke the strike by protecting strikebreakers brought over from New York City, the aldermen, led by Patrick Sheeran, an Irish carriage maker, censured the police force. Sheeran justified the censure in words that illustrated the new constituency to which the city government was responsive. "These strikers should be respected," Sheeran proclaimed, "and I want to know what business this man Chief Fowler had to take the police force . . . to protect the property of the Erie and prevent a riot. How dare he prevent a row and keep the New Yorkers from getting licked?"[25]

Although the Irish community accepted leadership from the working-class elite, it rejected leadership from men outside that class. In the fall of

[23] *Hudson County Courier,* Feb. 19, 1857; *Evening Journal,* Nov. 20, 23, 28, 1868.

[24] *American Standard,* Mar. 10, 1871; *New York Times,* Feb. 22, 1871; *Manual of the Board of Aldermen of Jersey City, 1870–1871* (Jersey City, 1871), p. 258.

[25] *Evening Journal,* Jan. 28 and Feb. 2, 1870. Sheeran represented "the shanties of Sheeranville" (*New York Sun,* Nov. 17, 1870).

1870 Irish Democrats from the relatively small Irish middle class attempted to end native-born domination of the party at the county and congressional-district levels. Calling themselves the Young Democrats, they nominated Aeneas Fitzpatrick, a wholesale merchant, for Congress, and a slate of candidates selected from the Irish elite for the state assembly.[26] They appealed to the Irish electorate to reject the regular Democrats in favor of an independent Irish slate and campaigned explicitly against the Know-Nothing past of the incumbent Democratic congressman, Orestes Cleveland. But their revolt failed. Fitzpatrick received only 3 percent of the vote in Jersey City and less elsewhere. None of the assembly candidates carried their districts. Here, dissimilarity of class and experience seems to have overridden ethnic ties; middle-class Young Democrats were not accepted as political leaders by the Irish poor.[27]

Thus by 1870 Jersey City was governed by a majority of men who were immigrants and chiefly Irish, but they were largely of the working-class elite or small proprietors with working-class roots. In office they had attempted to diffuse the force of nativism and anti-Catholicism and had responded—but in ways that were in no sense economically or socially radical—to the needs of their communities. They had entered American democratic politics as they had found it and had mastered it.

The native-born elite did not see this Irish leadership as "active, intelligent hard-working artisans . . . among the bone and sinew of [the] city." They saw them as unintelligent, unreliable, and corrupt. They were ridiculed and reviled in the press, and corruption became the code word for their perceived collective sins. Elite response to Irish control of Jersey City was swift and decisive. It illustrated the continuity of elite nativism and the ideological, if not the organizational, coherence of the nativist movements of the 1850s through and after the Civil War.

Less than a year after the aldermen elected in 1870 took office, the process of their removal began. In the winter of 1871 local Republicans, with support from some native-born Democrats, wrote and passed through the New Jersey legislature a new city charter that had the effect of virtually abolishing local government in Jersey City. While the mayor and aldermen retained their offices, most municipal functions were transferred to

[26] The Young Democrats received extensive coverage in the *Evening Journal, New York Herald,* and *Newark Advertiser* during October and November 1870. For an interview with Fitzpatrick (who was described as living in "a plain comfortable mansion"), see *New York Sun,* Oct. 29, 1870. The regular Democratic assembly ticket included four Irish allied with the native-born elite, one German, and one native-born (*American Standard,* Nov. 9, 1870).

[27] Fitzpatrick received only 1.1 percent of the vote in the district as a whole, which included much of northeastern New Jersey. Although soundly trounced, the Young Democrats drew enough votes away from the regular Democratic ticket to aid a general Republican victory (*Jersey City Times,* Nov. 9, 1870).

three commissions—public works, fire, and police—whose members were appointed directly by the state legislature. Additionally, the charter replaced the sixteen wards with six aldermanic districts, drawn in such a way as to minimize Irish influence. As many of the Irish as possible were concentrated in one large horseshoe-shaped district.[28]

The motivation behind the revised city charter was to remove the Irish from power by sharply reducing the role of local elected officials and vesting the appointive authority in the largely native-born Protestant state legislature. The Republican *Evening Journal*, published by men who had been Know-Nothings in the 1850s, claimed that the 1871 charter would "give somebody besides Irishmen a chance to hold office and find employment under the city government." The role played by nativism and anti-Catholicism in this municipal reconstitution became apparent five years later, in 1876, when a local Irish-edited newspaper printed the membership lists of the Order of American Union, a secret organization devoted to protecting the Protestant orientation of the public schools and to preventing any diversion of public money to Catholic schools. Among the 400 names printed were many of those who had supported charter reform in 1871, as well as seven of the seventeen original state-appointed commissioners.[29]

Not only was the charter supported by the native-born elite of both parties, but native-born Democrats then "redeemed" their own party by excluding the Irish from any role in the municipal elections held directly after the charter took effect. Abandoning the large Irish district to itself, native-born Democrats nominated for the now relatively unimportant body of aldermen a slate that was a study in nativism: of the six candidates resident in the city in the 1850s, five had been Know-Nothings. "It is serving notice on the Irish voters to take a back seat," claimed one newspaper, "telling them they are good enough, as of old, to do the voting, but not the sort to put on the lead or be put into office. We knew they would get this back-handed slap someday; but they must settle the hash themselves."[30]

Thus the government of Jersey City returned to native hands. Native members of both parties refused to countenance a city government dominated by working-class Catholic Irishmen, men whom they neither trusted

[28] *Charter of Jersey City and Supplements* (Jersey City, 1873); Shaw, pp. 208–9.

[29] *Evening Journal*, Feb. 3, 1871; *Argus*, Apr. 5–12, 1876. When the police commissioners organized in 1871, they refused to reappoint many Irish Catholics to the force (*New York Sun*, Apr. 3, 1871; *Irish World* [New York], May 6, 1871).

[30] *Evening Journal*, Apr. 10, 1871; *American Standard*, Apr. 10, 1871; *Jersey City Times*, Apr. 10, 1871.

nor knew. The Irish did not play a prominent role in Jersey City politics again for another fifteen years.[31]

These findings demonstrate clearly how difficult it is to understand the role of immigrants in industrializing America without exploring the cultural conflicts between immigrants and the society into which they moved. Often these conflicts were expressed in ways open to historical study through a close examination of local politics. Historians have tended to overlook both the persistence of nativism in the nineteenth-century and the manner in which nativism defined the terms of cultural adaptation for immigrant groups.[32] For the Irish of Jersey City that backdrop of nativism provided both the initial issues for political involvement in the early 1860s and the pretext for their removal ten years later. During that interval the Irish community elected men who had achieved success within the working-class community and who possessed the articulateness to speak for the worth and dignity of Irish identity. This was the important issue in the Irish community, although the native-born perceived only corruption and deceit instead of dignity and hard work. This cultural clash of immigrant and native-born will be illuminated as we develop comparative studies of both cultures. The nineteenth-century city was largely a place of rural immigrants and rural migrants. Jersey City's nativists were about as rural in their origins as Jersey City's Irish. Only when both are studied from similar perspectives, as adapting in different ways to industrialization and urbanization, will the cultural and political conflicts of the era come clearly into focus.

[31] Richard J. Connors, "The Local Political Career of Mayor Frank Hague," Diss. Columbia 1966, pp. 15–16.
[32] Gutman, pp. 580–85.

# VI Immigrant Workers and Managerial Reform

*David Montgomery*

"Our immigrant labor supply has been used by American industry in much the same way that American farmers have used our land supply," wrote William M. Leiserson in 1924. "But just as the disappearance of free land has led farmers to conserve their soil and to put a considerable investment into maintaining and improving it, so the restrictions on immigration brought about by the war and legislation have led employers to conserve the skill and strength of their labor and to put a considerable investment into training and improving it."[1] Leiserson's description of the use of immigrant workers early in the twentieth century was accurate, even if his depiction of more recent practice was overly optimistic. A closer look at the interaction between immigrant behavior and the reform of managerial practice, however, suggests that important changes in that practice began even before America's entry into the war and that the immigrants themselves were active agents in bringing the changes about.

There were, in fact, three types of reform in managerial behavior during the first two decades of this century that need to be distinguished. The first, which may be called corporate welfare, involved paternalistic measures initiated by employers with the primary intention of changing their employees' social attitudes, work habits, and life-styles. The endeavors of corporate "sociological departments," like those of later "Americanization" plans, can best be understood by reference to Herbert Gutman's discussion of the "recurrent tension over work habits" generated by the encounter of newcomers steeped in preindustrial cultures with the demands of modern industry for orderly, regular habits. The basic thrust of welfare reform, seen in this context, was to hasten the cultural transformation of the immigrants by promoting the attitudes of "thrift, sobriety, adaptability, [and] initiative" that would allow employers to assign them easily to industrial tasks.[2]

The research for this study was assisted by a fellowship from the John Simon Guggenheim Memorial Foundation.

[1] William M. Leiserson, *Adjusting Immigrant and Industry* (New York, 1924), p. 105.

[2] Herbert G. Gutman, "Work, Culture, and Society in Industrializing America, 1815–1919," *American Historical Review* 78 (1973):531–88; Don D. Lescohier, *The Labor*

The second type was the professionalization of personnel management. Born of a sense that labor turnover had reached crisis proportions in the years after 1910 and propelled forward by the rapidly mounting tendency of immigrants and native workers alike to strike and to restrict output in organized fashions, the personnel management movement developed trained executives whose mission it was to cope with grievances arising at work and thus to stabilize and pacify the daily operations of the concern. Proponents of the new profession claimed credit for "a reduction in working time lost, a reduction in labor turnover, the elimination of serious labor disputes, the development of esprit de corps, greater production, betterment of physical and social conditions of employees, a reduction of sickness and accidents, and the Americanization of aliens."[3] It was through their efforts that the three species of reform were ultimately blended into the American Plan of the 1920s.

The third type was scientific management, or Taylorism, in the strict sense of the term. It was concerned with the systematic organization of production and with instructing and enticing the employee to perform his specific work assignment in "the one best way." Frederick Winslow Taylor himself considered welfare reforms "of secondary importance" and insisted that they "should never be allowed to engross the attention of the superintendent to the detriment of the more important and fundamental elements of management." The goal of scientific management, in Frank Gilbreth's words, was "the establishment of standards everywhere, including standard instruction cards for standard methods, motion studies, time study, time cards, [and] records of individual output."[4] Although personnel management was to develop in part as an effort to resolve some of the failures and internal contradictions of scientific management, Taylor and his colleagues clearly believed that careful selection and training for job assignments, a well-organized flow of work and incentive for job assignments, and incentive pay would suffice to keep labor contented and loyal.

Scientific management could "barely be said to have made any impression outside of machine shops," observed President John Calder of the Remington Typewriter Company in 1913.[5] Even if Calder had overstated the point, the direct impact of scientific management had been felt primarily by skilled workers, whose control over the way they performed

---

*Market* (New York, 1919), pp. 251–75. The phrase quoted is from W. H. Beveridge, in Lescohier, p. 268.

[3] E. C. Gould, "A Modern Industrial Relations Department," *Iron Age* 102 (1918): 832–33.

[4] Frederick Winslow Taylor, "Shop Management," *Transactions of the American Society of Mechanical Engineers* 24 (1903): 1454; Frank B. Gilbreth, *Primer of Scientific Management,* 2d. ed. (New York, 1914), p. 36.

[5] John Calder, "Overvaluation of Management Science," *Iron Age* 91 (1913):605.

their tasks it challenged. Before the economic crisis of 1907–9, therefore, corporate welfare was the only one of these three types of management reform that had affected immigrant workers, and even its influence was not particularly widespread.

In the first decade of this century employers apparently felt little need to conserve, train, or improve their immigrant workers. Those immigrants who came with artisan or industrial skills tended to abandon their old trades in America, largely because they found little demand here for the ancient crafts they had learned abroad. Although almost 100,000 shoemakers came to America between 1900 and 1910, the number of immigrants engaged in that occupation actually declined during those years from 75,000 to 55,000 (about a fourth of the industry's total force). Similarly, the number of curriers, blacksmiths, bookbinders, and cabinet makers who deserted their former occupations exceeded the number of new arrivals in that decade. Some immigrant artisans, like Italian marble cutters, did practically monopolize a shrinking trade here. Others, like the 214,000 foreign-born carpenters, were sufficiently numerous (26 percent of all carpenters) to discourage metropolitan employers from training apprentices. Nevertheless, almost half of the newly arrived carpenters left the trade.[6]

Most immigrants at that time, however, had no artisan skills to abandon. By the estimates of the Immigration Commission, 54 percent of the men and 44 percent of the women among the immigrants it studied had worked in agriculture in Europe, and not more than 10 percent of them entered farm work in the United States. To turn the point around, in only two of the major industries it examined had two-thirds or more of the immigrants worked at the same occupation abroad, clothing and silk manufacture.[7] Athough silk manufacturing in the United States differed little from that in Western Europe, the factories that employed about half of the clothing workers by 1910 demanded very different work habits from those of the *shtetl* tailor.

For the great mass of twentieth-century immigrants, therefore, the skill and knowledge required by manufacturing occupations in which they were engaged were embodied not in their training but in the technical organization of the factory itself. The mental component of their labor was not their property, but their employers'. They were, to use Karl

[6] "Occupations of Immigrants before and after Coming to the United States" (typescript), David J. Saposs Papers, box 21, State Historical Society of Wisconsin, Madison, hereinafter cited as "Occupations of Immigrants"; U.S., Bureau of Census, *Sixteenth Census of the United States: 1940, Populations, Comparative Occupational Statistics for the United States, 1870–1940* (Washington, D.C., 1943), pp. 104–12.

[7] "Occupations of Immigrants." It is noteworthy that these two industries are among the very few in America where socialism and communism ever enjoyed large numbers of followers.

Marx's vivid phrase, "brought face to face with the intellectul potencies of the material process of production, as the property of another, and as a ruling power." Science, "a productive force distinct from labour," had been pressed "into the service of capital."[8]

Where laboratory science and production engineering determined the tasks to be performed in minute detail, there was little evident need to "train and improve" the immigrants. The 20,000 workers at Goodyear Rubber, who applied themselves furiously to minute but often heavy tasks at the molds and ovens, were checked by one inspector for every ten producers. Almost all production workers were on piecework, so that failure to produce at a rapid pace brought immediate deprivation of income. A "flying squadron" of 800 men, largely recruited from outside the firm after the strike of 1913, was trained by a three-year course to cover any job in the plant. Hence the 600 to 700 employees who quit each month and had to be replaced were of little concern to the company, though it did find the daily average of 500 first-aid cases costly. Earlier Goodyear had tried to reduce turnover, but it concluded by 1919 that such efforts were futile and concentrated its attention on careful training of supervisory personnel.[9]

The general complex of oil, chemical, and rubber industries constituted the fastest-growing sector of nonfarm employment between 1870 and 1910, with a 1,900 percent increase in employment, and the Goodyear pattern prevailed throughout. Goodyear was remarkable only in that no more than a third of its workers were foreign-born. For these industries in general, two-thirds of the employees were immigrants, and in the New Jersey centers three-fourths. Steel, meat packing, and textiles also coupled minute tasks with detailed supervision, so that the intricate flow of operations needed to produce the final product confronted the immigrant as a self-motivating technological monster into which he might fit himself as best he could. Upton Sinclair's description of the awesome impact of a Chicago slaughterhouse on a Lithuanian peasant mirrored the sentiments of steelworkers, who sensed, quite consciously, that the mill had a life of its own.[10]

On the other hand, the experience of immigrants within these vast incarnations of science in the service of capital made a mockery of Taylor's appeals for scientific selection and training of workmen. In general, immigrants were assigned to their tasks, and even transferred

[8] Karl Marx, *Capital: A Critique of Political Economy* (Chicago, 1906) 1:396–97.

[9] Goodyear Tire and Rubber Co., Schedule B, Interviews, Saposs Papers, box 21.

[10] See "Occupations of Immigrants"; New Jersey, Department of Labor, *Thirty-Eighth Annual Report of the Bureau of Industrial Statistics* (Camden, 1916), pp. 210–46; Upton Sinclair, *The Jungle* (New York, 1906); John A. Fitch, *The Steel Workers* (New York, 1910), pp. 8–21.

from one work group to another, by the absolute authority of their foremen. They learned what to do and how to do it from their workmates. "I've had almost no instruction on any of my jobs from the bosses," noted Whiting Williams, the plant manager who lived for a year as a worker. They have "been too busy or else their bosses didn't think it was worth the time. But, Jiminy! I've had a lot of it from my buddies: Only most of that has been to help me get by with as little personal effort and discomfort as possible."[11]

In short, the immigrants' encounter with the factory impressed them not so much with system and rationality as with arbitrary, petty tyranny wielded by gang leaders, skilled workmen, and hiring bosses. "We went to the doors of one big slaughter house," recalled Antanas Kaztauskis. "There was a crowd of about 200 men waiting there for a job. They looked hungry and kept watching the door. At last a special policeman came out and began pointing to men, one by one. Each one jumped forward. Twenty-three were taken. Then they all went inside, and all the others turned their faces away and looked tired. I remember one boy sat down and cried, just next to me, on a pile of boards. Some policemen waved their clubs and we walked on."[12]

On the nine piers of Manhattan's Chelsea docks, there might have been twenty-five hundred jobs on a busy day. Invariably some five thousand men hung around the dockside, saloons, and Longshoremen's Rest in hopes of shaping up. Word spread through the ethnic neighborhoods behind each pier by the "Longshore Gazette" (that is, word of mouth) when a new ship was to be loaded or unloaded. Regular gangs were hired with some consistency, but even their members dared not leave a job once they had been hired. The man who could not "stick it" for twenty-eight hours or more of continuous work might lose his place on a "good gang." When one man left a ship, another was taken on in his place, and the first would rejoin the waiting throng if he returned another day. Aside from the fruit crates kept on hand to lift casualties out of the holds, there were no facilities for the workers' needs. So abundant was manual labor on the New York docks that not a single pier had even installed a moving crane before 1914. Mechanical hoists were found in Liverpool and Hamburg, where dockers' unions were strong. The winch, block and tackle, and muscular back were the hoists of New York. Safety precautions were correspondingly simple. If a rope looked dangerously frayed to a docker, he cut it.[13]

[11] Whiting Williams, *What's on the Worker's Mind, by One Who Put On Overalls to Find Out* (New York, 1921), pp. 132–83.

[12] Leon Stein and Philip taft, eds., *Workers Speak: Self-Portraits* (New York, 1971), p. 74.

[13] U.S., Congress, Senate, Commission on Industrial Relations, *Final Report and Testi-*

In stark contrast to the tenets of scientific management, the wages of hundreds of thousands of immigrants were fixed by common labor rates. For longshoremen in New York the rate was $0.33 an hour for day work in 1914, for packinghouse workers $0.18; at Republic Steel in Youngstown, $0.195; and in the New York building trades, where possibly two-thirds of the laborers were Italians, $3.00 a day. Fully 40 percent of the workers in each of these industries were paid the common labor rate, and in each case the irregularity of employment for this grade left most of them averaging $10.00 to $11.00 a week. Common-labor earnings turned out to be not only homogeneous among occupations but remarkably stable over the years, until the numerous laborers' strikes of 1915 and 1916. "Class wages," charged the scientific management apostle Henry Gantt, led to inefficiency, inequity, and a "low tone" in the factory.[14] But few employers heeded his advice when they hired laborers.

There was at the same time a widespread belief among employers that simple piecework, also at odds with scientific management principles, was the best pay-system for immigrants, and, above all, for immigrant women. Wherever workers spent the day on tasks that allowed measurement of the results of individual exertion, employers tended to pay them by the piece. That form of payment tempted newcomers, who were eager to maximize their earnings in what they anticipated would be a short career on the job, to strain themselves to the limit. In the clothing industry, where experience sufficed to teach a worker the technical mysteries of the trade, the piecework system easily lent itself to the subcontracting of work, both outside, through sweatshops, and within the modern factory. One worker, paid by the piece, employed others to work for him. But inside contracting was not confined to clothing. It also appeared in some eastern machinery works, like United Shoe Machinery and Baldwin Locomotive, where journeymen machinists directed the exertions of less skilled workmen in the fabrication of complex components for which bids were let.[15]

Piecework was often applied to workers who were gang leaders or setup men, as a means of increasing the output of their subordinates. In cotton textiles, for example, loom fixers, second hands, and menders were often paid premiums based on the output of the weavers in their rooms. The weavers exerted themselves to the limit of their endurance, tending eight to twelve looms apiece. Women fell ill and "asked out" with such

---

*mony,* 64th Cong., 1st sess., 1916, Document no 415, 3:2051, 2212. Hereinafter cited as C.I.R.

[14] The wage figures are from C.I.R.: 3:2053, 2056; 4:3465; 3:1757; *Iron Age* 98 (1916): 128; see also Robert Ozanne, *Wages in Practice and Theory* (Madison, Wis., 1968), pp. 83–107; Henry L. Gantt, *Work, Wages, and Profits,* 2d ed. (New York, 1919), p. 58.

frequency that the companies of Fall River kept a large crew of stand-by women for "sick weaving." "But that don't make no matter," said one woman who struck there in 1904. "There's plenty waitin' at the gates for our jobs, I guess. The Polaks learn weavin' quick, and they just as soon live on nothin' and work like that."[16]

Piecework and hourly rates not only tended to yield very similar weekly earnings for immigrants, they also placed on the worker the full burden of any inefficiency on either his part or his employer's. In shoe factories, where the highly competitive market and frequent style changes made workers shift frequently from one job lot to another, employers were notoriously lax about planning and routing work through their plants. "Go through any shift at any time of day," charged the Federated American Engineering Societies' study of the 1920s, "and you will find some operators in every department waiting for shoes."[17] The waiting pieceworkers were on the job but earning nothing.

Even worse was the evolution of New York's piano industry, where 90 percent of the workers were foreign-born by 1919. Piecework had become universal as the primarily Italian immigrants moved in. At the same time the manufacturers discontinued the practice of stocking parts when orders were slack, as they had formerly in order to retain their craftsmen. They began working only to fill orders, so that seemingly interminable working hours alternated with closings of whole departments or plants. Overabundant labor had induced a retrogression to the most primitive managerial methods.[18]

The sophisticated incentive-pay schemes promoted by the advocates of scientific management made little progress outside of the metalworking industries. A survey of factory wage plans undertaken by the National Industrial Conference Board in 1924 found 56 percent of the workers on hourly wages, 37 percent on piecework, and only 7 percent on premium or bonus plans.[19] But employers seemed to be convinced that simple piecework was especially effective in inducing high output from immigrant women. The sausage and canning departments of the Chicago packing-

[15] Lewis Lorwin, *The Women's Garment Workers: A History of the International Ladies' Garment Workers' Union* (New York, 1924), p. 12–23, 149–50; *Iron Age* 91 (1913): 334; *Machinists' Monthly Journal* 16 (1904):321, and 18 (1906):829–31.

[16] Stein and Taft, pp. 28–80. The quotation is on p. 30.

[17] Federated American Engineering Societies, Committee on the Elimination of Waste in Industry, *Waste in Industry* (New York, 1921), p. 143. On the comparability of hourly and piecework earnings, see David Brody, *Steelworkers in America: The Nonunion Era* (Cambridge, Mass. 1960), pp. 45–48; New Jersey, *Thirty-eighth Annual Report of the Bureau of Industrial Statistics,* pp. 227–28.

[18] Interview with Charles Dodd, president, Piano and Organ Makers Union, Dec. 18, 1918, Saposs Papers, box 21.

[19] Sumner H. Slichter, *Union Policies and Industrial Management* (Washington, D.C., 1941), p. 282n.

houses were the special domains of piecework and of Slavic women. The women stogie makers, cannery workers, candy dippers, clothing makers, laundry workers, core makers, coil winders, glass packers, hand-screw operators, and sheet mill openers studied by Elizabeth Butler were all on piecework.[20]

There is, in fact, some evidence to suggest that young, single women were less likely than male pieceworkers to hold their output down to a stint set by the peer group. When the union gospel swept through the packinghouses of Chicago between 1900 and 1904, women workers enrolled en masse, formed a local of their own to insure representation for themselves in the leadership, and waged an aggressive battle to raise their wage rates. Yet they alone of all the packinghouse workers made no effort to reduce their output. Similarly, in 1917, when women were introduced as metal polishers into the arms works of Bridgeport, the metal polishers' union quickly succeeded in equalizing the piece rates paid to women and to men (a demand unions often raised during the war in hopes of retarding the employment of women), only to find that employers ardently preferred women even without lower wage rates. The reason was that the women ignored the union's ceiling on a day's output, which was rigidly respected by all the men.[21]

The decisive variable in this response to piece rates, however, seems to have been age, not sex. Most of the women involved in the cases cited were in, or close to, their teen-age years, and young males were equally notorious for their proclivity to "rate busting." Furthermore, there is clear evidence, albeit from later years, of women bacon packers (a relatively good job that tended to be dominated by women with considerable seniority in the firm) rigidly policing output quotas of their own making.[22]

On the other hand, the responses of different groups of women workers to incentive plans suggest that variables other than age and nativity could influence the behavior of women workers. When Henry Gantt set task quotas for the bobbin winders at the Brighton Mills in New Jersey, where almost all the women were immigrants, he found that the older women quickly made the rates, while many young girls failed and quit. It is possible that in textiles, where married women often made

[20] John R. Commons, "Labor Conditions in Slaughtering and Meat Packing," in John R. Commons, ed., *Trade Unionism and Labor Problems* (Boston, 1905), pp. 238–41; Elizabeth Beardsley Butler, *Women and the Trades: Pittsburgh, 1907–1908* (New York, 1911).

[21] Commons, "Labor Conditions," pp. 240–41; Federal Mediation and Conciliation Service Reports, file 33/567, Records of the Department of Labor, Record Group 280, National Archives.

[22] See Stella Nowicki, "Back of the Yards," in Alice and Staughton Lynd, eds. *Rank and File: Personal Histories of Working-Class Organizers* (Boston, 1973), p. 79.

elaborate childcare arrangements in order to remain in the mills, they were especially anxious to hold their jobs. Similarly, when Joseph Feis tried to make his Clothcraft Shops in Cleveland a model of modern management, he found that the young women in his employ failed to increase their output in order to earn a bonus. In this case, however, Feis probed more deeply and learned that most of the women turned all of their earnings over to their parents. He tried the remedy of sending investigators to the homes of his employees to estimate their families' financial needs. Having determined for each woman a specific sum to be deducted from her pay and sent directly to her family, Feis had the rest of her earnings then paid separately to her. The scheme worked: output and incentive earnings shot up.[23] It may be that the traditional patterns of family relationships in a woman's nationality were as important as age and marital status in determining her reaction to piecework or incentive pay.

In any case, Feis was not the only employer to use sophisticated welfare plans in an effort to change the culture patterns of his employees. "Improved machines demand improved men to run them," William H. Tolman observed in 1914, and he found 2,000 firms that had already sought to promote such improvement through welfare plans for their 1,500,000 workers. Thereafter interest in professional personnel management, scientific management, and welfare programs increased as employers sought to counter what, from their perspective, was a disheartening tendency, especially on the part of immigrant labor, to thwart their expectations of high productivity. None of these companies outdid the Ford Motor Company, which sent 100 sociologists to check on the family cohesiveness, home cleanliness, civic participation, and spending habits of its workers, in order to determine which of them were worthy to participate in the company's "prosperity sharing" wage scale. Ford's plan was based on the assumption that "efficiency was to be a by-product of the clean and wholesome life."[24]

Henry Ford's approach was unusual, but his assumption was shared by other large employers. More than a decade before the Ludlow Massacre prompted John D. Rockefeller, Jr., to pioneer in the development of personnel management, the Colorado Fuel and Iron Company had established a sociological department, which looked into every aspect

[23] U.S., Congress, House, *Hearings before the Special Committee of the House of Representatives to Investigate the Taylor and Other Systems of Shop Management* (Washington, D.C., 1912), pp. 583–85; Robert T. Kent, "Employing Methods That Make Good Workers," *Iron Age* 98 (1916):244–47.

[24] William H. Tolman, *Social Engineering: A Record of Things Done by American Industrialists Employing Upwards of One and One-Half Million People* (New York, 1909), p. 2; John R. Commons *Industrial Government* (New York, 1921), pp. 13–25. The quotation is on p. 14.

of the workers' lives, from diet and drinking habits to public school curriculum. Its director, Dr. R. W. Corwin, explained that C.F.I.'s employees were "drawn from the lowest classes of foreign immigrants . . . whose primitive ideas of living and ignorance of hygienic laws render the department's work along the line of improved housing facilities and instruction in domestic economy of the utmost importance."[25]

The welfare secretary of the American Iron and Steel Institute expressed special concern with changing the habits of workers in matters that were beyond the direct control of the employers. He urged careful tutelage of the immigrant in "the regulation of his meals, the amount, the character and the mastication of them, the amount and character of drink, the hours of rest and sleep, the ventilation of rooms, . . . washing of hands before meals, daily washing of feet, proper fitting of shoes, amount and kind of clothing, care of the eye, ear and nose, brushing of the teeth, and regularity of the bowels. Cultivation of cheerful thoughts has much to do with the body." "Another thing that the workman should be taught," he concluded, "is that the first condition of health is fruitful toil. We are made to labor."[26]

As Herbert Gutman has pointed out, however, immigrant laborers were not passive clay to be molded by the requirements of American industry, but brought with them preindustrial work habits that shaped their responses to the environment they found here. On the other hand, the work pattern of "alternate bouts of intense labour and of idleness," which E. P. Thompson found to prevail "wherever men were in control of their own working lives," was but partially contested by the tasks to which immigrants were assigned. In steel, meat packing, chemicals, construction, longshore, and clothing, employment was extremely irregular, but the laborer himself had no control over the timing of the "alternate bouts" of toil and enforced idleness. The Chicago packinghouses, for example, slaughtered three-fourths of their cattle on Monday, Tuesday, and Wednesday. A small force sufficed for the remaining days of the week. Only when the workers were organized and aggressive did the companies request their commission buyers to stabilize the flow of cattle to the stockyards, so that employment in the packing houses might be less sporadic.[27]

Even at work the immigrant's exertion was often spasmodic, especially where the twelve-hour day prevailed. A study conducted by the steel

[25] Tolman, pp. 54–55. The quotation is on p. 55.

[26] Quoted in Gerd Korman, *Industrialization, Immigrants, and Americanizers: The View from Milwaukee, 1886–1921* (Madison, Wis., 1967), p. 122.

[27] Gutman, p. 553; Thompson, "Time, Work-Discipline, and Industrial Capitalism," *Past and Present* 38 (1967):73; C.I.R. 4:3490–91.

industry in 1912 to counter agitation against the seven-day week revealed that the idle time of an open-hearth crew ranged from 54 percent of the turn for a second helper to 70 percent for a steel pourer. Similarly hot-blast men at blast furnaces were found to toil furiously during 38 percent of the turn, moderately for 3 percent, and lightly, if at all, for 47 percent, and to spend the remaining 12 percent watching the furnace. Testimony of the workers themselves confirms this impression. At one moment an open-hearth laborer might hoist a hundred pound sack of coal on his shoulder, race toward a ladle of white hot steel and hurl the sack into it. Ten minutes later he might be sleeping, especially if it was the night turn.[28]

The immigrant laborer, furthermore, had one standard remedy for disgust with his job: he quit. Systematic studies of labor turnover were first undertaken during the economic boom of 1912–13 in the metal trades, where the cost to employers of breaking in new workers was especially burdensome. Annual turnover rates ranging from 100 percent to 250 percent of the original labor force were found to be commonplace. The Ford Motor Company hired 54,000 men between October 1912, and October 1913, to maintain an average work force of 13,000.[29] By far the greatest cause of separations was resignation, rather than discharge or layoff, and, understandably, the number of workers quitting spiraled upward in prosperous times.

Furthermore, though better-paid workers and those with several years' seniority or more were slow to quit, newcomers in laborers' or operatives' tasks moved through American factories as though they were revolving doors. Studies conducted in the meat packing and textile industries in the 1920s confirmed these patterns. Almost three-fourths of the separations found by Alma Herbst in Chicago packinghouses involved workers with less than three months' service. At Cheney Brothers silk mill in Paterson, N.J., the general turnover rate for 1922 was 30 percent, but among those with a tenure of six months to a year the rate was 239 percent.[30]

Much as they distressed employers, however, individual and traditional responses of immigrants, such as the high propensity to quit, celebration of national holidays in defiance of foremen's threats, Blue Mondays, and

[28] "Hours and Intensity of Steel Works Labor," *Iron Age* 89 (1912):312–13; interview with Slavish worker (Pittsburgh), B.C. O'Connell (Gary), Saposs Papers, box 26; Williams, pp. 15–27.

[29] Magnus Alexander, "Waste in Hiring and Discharging Men," *Iron Age* 94 (1914):1032–33; Paul H. Douglas, Curtice N. Hitchcock, and Willard E. Atkins, *The Worker in Modern Economic Society* (Chicago, 1923), pp. 310–13.

[30] Alma Herbst, *The Negro in the Slaughtering and Meat-Packing Industry in Chicago* (Boston, 1932), pp. 134–45; Horace B. Cheney, "What 86 Years Have Taught Us about Selecting Labor," *Monthly Labor Review* 18 (1925):9.

binges that, in fact, might easily last a week or two were not the only ways in which immigrants coped with the new industrial setting. The vastness and anonymity of the factory, mine, construction site, or pier should not blind us to the spontaneous formation of small informal groupings, which were the focal points of the immigrants' daily experience. In fact, the impersonal quality of the mill or dock itself made both sanity and survival depend on personal attachments to other workers. Older hands taught newcomers the techniques of survival and the covert forms of collective resistance—"lift it like this, lotsa time, slow down, there's the boss, here's where we hide, what the hell!"

Two aspects of this phenomenon deserve close attention. First, foremen and gang leaders themselves frequently organized their subordinates' deception of higher management. Anxious to protect their own performance records and bonuses, foremen were wise to keep their crews large, production standards sufficiently lax to make the group's output look good to higher authorities, and a sense of good will among the workers should some emergency call for special bursts of exertion. Many of the spontaneous strikes by immigrants in the second decade of this century were in protest against the discharge of a popular foreman. Conversely, in the needle trades many strikes were led by inside contractors, that is, by the "sweaters" themselves.[31]

Second, immigrants entering industrial society encountered not only the expectations and culture patterns of their employers but also the culture and techniques of survival and struggle of the American-born workers. There is considerable evidence from coal mines and railroad-car shops, where native or British-born workmen and new immigrants worked together in small, mixed groups, that the former initiated the latter into those attitudes toward work and employers which *they* considered socially acceptable. For example, the impulse of peasant immigrants to work furiously when an authority figure was present and loaf in his absence (a tendency that persisted strongly in steel mills) was soon exchanged in coal mines or car shops for the craftsman's ethic of refusing to work while a boss was watching. Similarly, greenhorns soon learned from veteran workers how to safeguard their piecework scales against reductions by systematically limiting their individual outputs and ostracizing the spoilers, who maximized their output. The manager of the American Can Company's Brooklyn plant was convinced that, though piecework was "best for foreigners," there was an evident "tendency on the part of

[31] See Stanley B. Mathewson, *Restriction of Output among Unorganized Workers* (New York, 1931), pp. 30–52; Lorwin, pp. 149–51; New Jersey, Bureau of Industrial Statistics, reports, 1911–16.

natives and Americanized immigrants to limit production" under the system.[32]

Neither the craftsman's bearing toward his boss nor the group-related stint of pieceworkers was preindustrial. Immigrants who adopted those behavior patterns had exchanged portions of their traditional culture, not for the values and habits welfare plans sought to inculcate, but for working-class mores.

Consequently, where immigrants encountered strong unions whose doors were open to them, as in the coal mines and the Chicago packinghouses before 1904, they adroitly made use of those unions to frustrate their employers' demands for a frenzied pace of work. John R. Commons's insightful study of the Chicago packinghouses before the 1904 strike revealed that each of the many amalgamated craft unions succeeded in establishing a "scale of work," except the women's local. Output per man-hour fell between 16 percent and 25 percent for the city's packinghouses as a whole.[33]

After 1910 each period of economic boom unleashed a rash of strikes by native craftsmen and immigrants alike, and the steady growth of unions in basic industries made them a part of the daily lives of millions of immigrants. Employers' complaints about the declining level of exertion among their employees then became almost universal. When the National Association of Credit Men surveyed 169 companies early in 1920, 70 percent of the respondents claimed that their workers were not as efficient as they had been in 1913–14. Full employment, high turnover, unrest, and unions were blamed for an alleged decline in individual output of roughly one-fourth, which was especially evident among immigrant workers.[34] On the New York docks, where no mechanical improvements offset the changing behavior of the unionized longshoremen, productivity per worker fell by one-half between 1914 and 1919, according to a Department of Labor study.[35]

As previously indicated, these developments spurred a new interest in time study, detailed supervision, systematization of work flow, and the other accoutrements of scientific management throughout American

[32] Carter Goodrich, *The Miner's Freedom: A Study of the Working Life in a Changing Industry* (Boston, 1925), p. 56; Williams, pp. 128–49; Mathewson, pp. 137–39; American Can Company, Schedule B, interviews, Saposs Papers, box 21.

[33] Commons, "Labor Conditions," pp. 227–28.

[34] Commons, *Industrial Government,* pp. 367–68. It is, unfortunately, impossible to test these claims, because the effects of workers' exertion cannot be isolated from those of technological improvement and economies of scale. The trend of output per man-hour was upward for the economy as a whole from 1913 to 1919. But the rate of growth for that period was remarkably uneven and consistently lower than the average rate for the period 1910–29 as a whole. See U.S., Department of Commerce, Bureau of the Census, *Historical Statistics of the United States, Colonial Times to 1957* (Washington, D.C., 1960), p. 599.

[35] *Monthly Labor Review* 18 (1924): 109–17.

industry after the war.[36] These reforms were diffused within the context of professional personnel management, which by then was well etablished. In 1911 fifty company officials had met to form the Employment Managers' Association. They were the pioneers of the new profession. By 1918 the association could gather 900 member at its convention. Harvard, Dartmouth, Rochester, and Columbia were all then offering university courses to train these executives, and Princeton was to be added to their number by means of a Rockefeller grant in 1922.[37]

Personnel managers by the war's end were asserting their importance by demanding salaries, deference, carpets, and office furnishings equal to those of the production superintendents. Their formulas for promoting higher productivity and reducing labor turnover, industrial strife, and the peril of unionization included systematic hiring procedures, a large staff to handle workers' grievances on and off the job, and employee representation plans to encourage a sense of participation by the workers in the execution of company policies. Scientific management and extensive welfare activity were easily grafted onto this core to create the American Plan.[38]

By 1923 the American Plan had succeeded in excluding unions from most industries and persuading union leaders to oppose their members' restrictive practices in others. Nevertheless, it had *not* realized the corporate executives' dream of enlisting the "support, loyalty and undivided effort" of immigrant workers.[39] Stanley B. Mathewson's study *Restriction of Output among Unorganized Workers* concluded in 1930 that American workers were frustrating their employers' efficiency schemes, even without the help of unions. His account of a Mexican immigrant in an automobile plant, who was assigned to the final tightening of nuts on cylinder heads, casts doubt on the efficacy of all management's efforts of the three previous decades to train and improve its new labor force:

[36] See *Waste in Industry;* Ozanne, pp. 175, 181–82; H. Dubreuil, *Robots or Men? A French Workman's Experience in American Industry* (New York, 1930); Sam A. Lewisohn, *The New Leadership in Industry* (New York, 1926); Solomon Blum, *Labor Economics* (New York, 1925), pp. 413–14.

[37] Meyer Bloomfield, "The New Profession of Handling Men," *Annals of the American Academy of Political and Social Science* 61 (Sept. 1915): 121–26; M. Bloomfield, "A New Profession in American Industry," in Daniel Bloomfield, ed., *Selected Articles on Employment Management* (New York, 1922), pp. 113–18; Clarence J. Hicks, *My Life in Industrial Relations: Fifty Years in the Growth of a Profession* (New York, 1941), pp.145–50.

[38] See Bloomfield, "New Profession"; Lewisohn; Hicks; Commons, *Industrial Government*; Leiserson, pp. 80–168.

[39] I am indebted to Professor Stephen Scheinberg for this quotation from *Report of the Special Conference Committee* (July 24, 1919).

The engines passed the Mexican rapidly on a conveyor. His instructions were to test all the nuts and if he found *one* or *two* loose to tighten them, but if three or more were loose he was not expected to have time to tighten that many. In such cases he marked the engine with chalk and it was later set aside from the conveyor and given special attention. The superintendent found that the number of engines so set aside reached an annoying total in the day's work. He made several unsuccessful attempts to locate the trouble. Finally, by carefully watching all the men on the conveyor line, he discovered that the Mexican was unscrewing a *third* tight nut whenever he found two already loose. It was easier to loosen *one* nut than to tighten *two.*[40]

[40] Mathewson, pp. 125–26.

# VII Irish Immigrant Culture and the Labor Boycott in New York City, 1880–1886

*Michael Gordon*

DURING THE SUMMER of 1882 a long and bitter freighthandlers' strike tied up the freight depots and sheds of all major railroads along the Hudson River in New York City and Jersey City. The strike began on June 12 after officials of the New York Central and Hudson River Railroad refused to grant some six hundred freighthandlers a wage increase of three cents an hour (from seventeen to twenty cents). Freighthandlers on other railroads soon quit their jobs when companies rejected identical wage demands. The strike eventually involved nearly three thousand men, most of whom were Irish immigrants.[1]

In spite of recurring nativist and antilabor sentiments, numerous businessmen, church and civic leaders, and newspapers joined with other labor organizations and Irish Land League branches in supporting the freighthandlers' modest demands. They denounced the greedy railroads, collected food and money for a strike fund, persuaded some landlords to delay workers' rent payments, and even sought legal ways to force the railroads to settle the dispute quickly and amicably.[2]

Nevertheless, by mid-August the strike collapsed. Unable to provide enough food for their families and fearful that Italian strikebreakers would permanently get their jobs, the freighthandlers began returning to work.[3] Efforts were made to deter the Italians, but strike leaders appeared even more concerned with preventing their own members from breaking ranks. As early as July 6, freighthandlers' president Jeremiah Murphy told the union's Executive Council of "five or six" such men, and said that "we propose to boycott them. We shall have circulars containing their names printed and distributed over the city, and sent home to Ireland, too. We will

I wish to thank the conference participants for their many helpful and cordial comments and the conference sponsors for their extraordinary kindness. More complete analysis and documentation of some of the points made in this paper can be found in my "The Labor Boycott in New York City, 1880–1886," *Labor History* 16 (1975):184–229.

[1] *New York Times,* June 15, 18, 20, 21, 1882; *Truth* (New York), June 21, 22, 1882. All newspapers cited are from New York unless noted otherwise.

[2] *New York Times,* June 24, 25, 27, 28, July 1, 7, 14–16, 18–20, 26, 29, 1882; *Truth*, June 24, July 14, 16, 1882; "The Freight-Handlers' Strike," *Harper's Weekly* 26 (1882): 427, 451.

[3] *New York Times,* June 21-31 and Aug. 1–10, 1882; *Truth,* Aug. 1–10, 1882.

march 1,000 men in front of their houses and let people know who the boycotted men are. We shall not speak to them on the street, and you will see that this system of boycotting will go much farther than using personal violence. We shall not harm them; they needn't fear that." By July 8 eighty-three men were named as boycott targets. Murphy delayed two weeks before having the blacklist printed and distributed to churchgoers as they left Sunday services.[4]

Murphy's understanding of the term *boycott* clearly differs from what it subsequently came to mean. Instead of advocating economic sanctions against the railroads, he sought to marshal family and community pressures against wayward freighthandlers. In fact, the word *boycott* had been adopted in 1880 by the Irish National Land League to describe a tactic used against landlords, their agents, and uncooperative peasants in rural Ireland. The term was borrowed by many immigrant workers in New York and elsewhere late that same year. For them, *boycott* meant the kind of social ostracism practiced by Irish peasants and advocated by figures like Jeremiah Murphy. However, very shortly it came to refer as well to the economic weapon used by labor organizations to force employers to comply with union demands.

The sudden explosion of both forms of boycotting behavior during that period drew the attention and frequent wrath of a broad segment of American society. A national survey conducted by *Bradstreet's* in late 1885, for example, uncovered 237 boycotts during the previous two years. In its four-page report the paper cited boycotts against manufacturers of hats, carpets, cigars, shoes, brooms, nails, bakery goods, beer, starch, and Chinese-made products. Boycotts also involved streetcars, newspapers, shipping lines, flour mills, theaters, and "a special beverage." New York State's Bureau of Labor Statistics began publishing boycotting statistics in 1886 when it recorded 165 boycotts; the following year 242 were listed. Because of the bureau's figures revealed the majority of boycotts accompanied strikes, its 1886 report concluded that workers adopted the practice when strikes either failed or were too costly to prolong.[5]

Many in New York City were concerned with more than just the incidence or rationale of the boycott. Irritated by immigrant pickets, and alarmed by the boycott's power, newspapers, employers, judges, and jurors attacked the boycott and its users in near hysterical language. The

[4] Quotation is from *New York Times,* June 29. See also ibid., July 6–8, 12, 13, 16, 27, 1882; *Truth*, July 9, 10, 12, 16, 17, 1882; *Sun*, July 24, 1882 (courtesy of Douglas V. Shaw).

[5] *Bradstreet's*, Dec. 19, 1885; New York, State Bureau of Labor Statistics, *Fourth Annual Report* (1886); New York, *Assembly Documents* 5, no. 27 (1887):713, 783–43, 420–57; the Bureau's *Fifth Annual Report* (1887); and *Assembly Documents* 5, no. 74 (1888):521–22.

*New York Times* called the tactic in all its manifestations "a foreign institution," a "savage and un-American mode of warfare." To one jury foreman it was like a "hydra-headed monster, dragging its loathsome length across this continent, sucking the very lifeblood from our trade and commerce." In his charge to a jury about to consider the fate of eighteen Bohemian boycotters in 1886, Judge George C. Barrett, long a nativist and city "reformer," reminded the jurors that the defendants "may have done unmanly things, things that seem unworthy of American citizenship and foreign to American methods, but they are not on trial for violations of good taste or the proprieties of civilized life." William Graham Sumner considered the social boycott's effects in even graver terms. He viewed it as "cutting a man out of the organization of society," and believed that it was "the severest trial to which our institutions have yet been put.[6]

Most labor historians have either uncritically supported the view that labor boycotts merely supplemented strikes, dismissed the tactic as a novel modification of the Land League's practice, or have simply ignored it. Studies by Leo Wolman in 1916 and Norman Ware in 1929 provided important insights by analyzing boycotts as the result of labor's inability to control labor supply and productivity and of the growth of a particular working-class consumer consciousness.[7] But, like other historians, they did not consider the experiences of the boycotters as immigrant workers or the concerns of the boycotters' critics. Jeremiah Murphy's proposal to the freighthandlers' community cannot be dismissed as an isolated and perhaps clever tactic. Nor was it merely an adaptation of previous practices used by Revolutionary mechanics and merchants, abolitionists, trade unionists, and others who issued "non-intercourse" proclamations or "do not buy" lists.[8] Such precedents may have influenced later practices. But Murphy's appeal for social ostracism was primarily derived from the Old World experiences of the freighthandlers, not from their participation in American labor affairs. His proposal evolved from related forms of protective behavior that were indigenous to nineteenth-century Irish rural culture and familiar to many Irish immigrants. Only the setting had changed.

[6] *New York Times,* Apr. 13, 15, 1886; *John Swinton's Paper,* May 9, 1886; *Fourth Annual Report,* p. 783; William Graham Sumner, "Industrial War," *Forum* 2 (Sept. 1886):7.

[7] Leo Wolman, *The Boycott in American Trade Unions* (Baltimore, 1916), pp. 17–20, 25–26; Norman Ware, *The Labor Movement in the United States, 1860–1895* (New York, 1929), chapt. 15.

[8] Lawrence H. Gipson, *The Coming of the American Revolution, 1763–1775* (New York, 1954), pp. 219–22; John B. Andrews, "Nationalisation (1860–1877)," in John R. Commons et al., eds., *History of the Labour Movement in the United States* (New York, 1918), 2:22–25 and Walter H. Merrill, *Against the Wind: A Biography of William Lloyd Garrison* (Cambridge, Mass., 1963), pp. 56, 80.

The freighthandlers' tactic can provide important insights into the adaptation of Irish immigrants to life in nineteenth-century industrializing America if the boycott is historically related to other aspects of Irish culture. *Adaptation* is used in this study to mean the responses made by immigrants to the acculturative pressures and new surroundings of life in America. This definition recognizes the importance of studying particular examples of adaptive behavior. Yet it shuns a too literal use of the term by suggesting that isolated behavioral responses were part of a broader process involving the transition of a unique culture. (*Culture* is understood here as the historical life experiences that shape attitudes and behavior.)

Considered within this conceptual framework, the boycott can be seen not only as an adaptation of a practice used in Ireland against affronts to Irish culture. It was also inseparably related to surviving Old World attitudes about land, work, the family, what some called "Anglo-Saxon civilization," and to other traditional forms of popular immigrant protest (such as mass demonstrations, parades, and rallies). Viewed in this way, the boycott represented an assertion of Irish cultural identity in Ireland *and* New York and revealed the tensions involved in the process of acculturation.

The culture from which the boycott emerged was rooted in the Irish countryside. For over a century before 1880, small villages and farmlands provided settings for the sporadic violence waged by agrarian secret societies. While the Whiteboys are perhaps best known, religious associations like the Ribbonmen and local kinship factions often shared with the Whiteboys common grievances, objects of attack, methods, and membership. Distinctions between these groups were not always clear, but all were firmly entrenched in a rural culture that dictated behavior and punished those who violated cultural norms.

Whiteboy violence, in particular, stemmed from changing landholding arrangements that caused thousands of evictions, and disregarded the traditional peasant assertion of the right to use rented land in perpetuity. Since their origins in the 1760s, the Whiteboys sought to defend by force what the British government and its courts would not recognize by law. Grievances differed from county to county, but the pattern of retaliation was similar. Peasant raiders, wearing white shirts and bound by secret oaths, destroyed fences and buildings belonging to landowners and their agents and intimidated tithe collectors. Whiteboys also attempted to prevent landlords from employing outside farm laborers, but reprisals were directed as much against such workers as their employers.[9]

[9] See especially Galen Broeker, *Rural Disorder and Police Reform in Ireland, 1812–36* (London, 1970); Gale E. Christianson, "Secret Societies and Agrarian Violence in

By the late 1870s Ireland was on the brink of another famine. Faced with starvation and eviction, bands of vigilantes again roamed the countryside maiming cattle, assaulting landlords, and threatening farmers who paid unjust rents or took the land of evicted tenants. In 1880 alone, 2,590 so-called agrarian outrages were reported. This crisis also sparked the formation of the Irish National Land League. Formed at a Dublin conference of nationalists and land reformers in October 1879, the league sought land reform legislation, reduced land rents, and supported those tenants who refused to pay all or part of their rents.

The league's principal weapon was the social boycott. Named after Capt. Charles Boycott, a county Mayo land agent, the boycott was, in Thomas N. Brown's words, a "legitimization of old Whiteboy techniques" by which the league "channeled traditional village hostilities into non-violent forms." It aimed at ostracising from rural society landowners or their agents, local government officials, and others who refused to acknowledge traditional peasant claims or to cooperate with league objectives. At a mass meeting in Ennis on August 29, 1880, Charles Stewart Parnell, leader of the Irish National Land League, gave specific instructions on how to apply the practice. An "enemy" should be shunned in the countryside, in village streets, in shops and the market-place, and even in church. "By leaving him severely alone," he concluded, "by isolating him from the rest of his fellow countrymen as if he were the leper of old, . . . there will be no man so full of avarice, so lost to shame as to dare the public opinion . . . and transgress your unwritten code of laws."[10]

The same culture from which Whiteboyism and the boycott derived strength in Ireland readily enabled its modification as a labor tactic in New York. For however much they may have differed over specific labor and nationalist issues, Irish immigrant workers had much in common. Their shared heritage combined actual life experiences with attitudes transmitted through oral and written history. It included the oppression of rack-renting landlords, the British government, and church officials; a hatred of Anglo-Saxons; decades of poverty; ancient communal and tribunal loyalties; a regulated way of life revolving around the seasons, marriages, and fairs; a religion intimately bound up with folklore; a tight family structure; and the clandestine traditions.

Irish workers shared this experience and hence the activities of the

---

Ireland, 1790–1840," *Agricultural History* 46 (1972):369–84; and Kevin B. Knowlan, "Agrarian Unrest in Ireland, 1800–1845," *University Review* (National University of Ireland) 2, no. 6 (1958):7–16.

[10] Thomas N. Brown, *Irish-American Nationalism, 1870–1890* (Philadelphia, 1966), pp. 101–3; *The Times* (London), Sept. 30, 1880. See also Joyce Marlow, *Captain Boycott and the Irish* (London, 1973).

freight handlers of New York and Jersey City were not isolated incidents. In local neighborhoods or small communities economic sanctions frequently and effectively supplemented social pressures. In April 1881, for example, many Brooklyn unions boycotted baker John Schultz, who had fired employees for joining a union. Twenty grocers refused to sell his bread, and some two hundred women, many of them Irish, visited his neighborhood customers telling them they should have nothing to do with him or his products.[11]

In South Norwalk, Conn., from twelve hundred to fifteen hundred hatters struck against four hat manufacturers for cutting wages and attempting to crush unions. "Our situation is becoming intolerable, and the whole community is influenced against us," a factory official reported in December, 1884. "We tried to board out [strikebreakers] . . . and not a boarding house would recluse them. Even the restaurant keeper at the depot refused to supply them with food." And the watchman's wife, who fed men at the factory, was warned that she would be unable to buy anything in town.[12] In March 1885 Knights of Labor hatters in Orange, N.J., boycotted the Berg hat factory as well as its strikebreakers. Curious about its effects, journalist John Swinton journeyed to Orange and later described what he saw as "the most striking exhibition of the power of the boycott yet seen in this country." Swinton told the tale of one strikebreaker's problems. The hatter's barber, grocer, saloon keeper, and baker all cried out "foul" when he entered their shops, and refused him service. His friends would not speak to him or sit with him in church.[13]

Meanwhile, some three thousand winders, setters, and weavers—most of them young women—employed at the Smith carpet mills in Yonkers were on strike over issues involving wage reductions and factory discipline. From February to May 1885 strikers tried to prevent outsiders from taking their jobs and old hands from returning to work. Swinton reported that they sometimes used "a father or mother, sister, brother or lover to help them." He quipped: "They never say that a man or store is *boycotted*—that is 'un-American' and they don't believe in it—but some tradesmen could tell a wonderful tale and the quiet 'ostracism' (that's an old word) will result in displacing capital."[14]

Nearby Orange, South Norwalk, and Yonkers were relatively small communities, but boycotts against goods intended strictly for working-class consumption could be effective even in a large city like New York. In March 1885, for example, the Central Labor Union ordered a boycott

[11] *Journal of United Labor,* Apr. 15, 1881.

[12] Quoted from the *World,* in *John Swinton's Paper,* Dec. 21, 1884.

[13] Ibid., Apr. 5, 1885.

[14] *New York Times,* Feb. 22, 1885; *Irish World,* Mar. 7, Apr. 4, May 23, 30, June 6, 1885; *John Swinton's Paper,* May 18, 24, June 7, 1885.

of Peter Doegler's beer after he fired all union members. By September over three hundred saloons refused to carry it, and Doegler conceded defeat by requiring employees to join a brewers' union. The dismissal of union members by Williamsburgh shoe manufacturers Brennan and White on April 25 elicited the same reaction. Shoe lasterer John Flynn told the Bureau of Labor Statistics how the resulting boycott against the company was organized in communities. He noted that the firm "made a very cheap shoe." Committees "go right into our neighborhood, where we live and tell our mothers and sisters; we even do it ourselves; I have sent my sister to one, my brother to one, and my father to others."[15]

By late spring 1886 widespread boycotting activity in New York City included bakers, cigar makers, printers, streetcar drivers and conductors, tailors, butchers, and even musicians. Day after day the nonlabor press, bolstered by a barrage of outraged letters from its readers, condemned boycott pickets as unruly foreigners who failed to appreciate the blessings of American freedom. Prompted by public pressure, police officials sent their squads scurrying about New York's streets making dozens of arrests. Nearly one hundred members of labor organizations eventually were indicted for conspiracy and related charges in connection with strikes and boycotts. Some went to prison. The mass arrests and trials of labor boycotters that year represent the beginning of concerted legal attempts to deprive workers of their new tactic. At the same time the boycotts of 1886 reveal that the boycott had become primarily an economic weapon that had spread rapidly to merchandisers and users of goods manufactured or sold by firms that failed to settle grievances with unions.[16]

Both economic and social forms of the boycott remained in use, however, and some Knights of Labor developed code words to distinguish between the two. During an 1889 hearing, ostensibly called to settle a dispute between rival factions within the Knights' District Assembly No. 49 over ownership of the assembly's Pythagoras Hall, Secretary Patrick Doody was asked to define the terms *let alone* and *let severely alone.* Doody said the latter meant "almost driving and starving a man to death, driving him out of the world, extermination." He understood the former as usually meaning "to buy no more of a man's goods."[17] Doody's definitions applied to the America of the 1880s, not to nineteenth-century Ireland, nor to an earlier period in the history of industrializing America. The distinctions are crucial, for immigrant workers in the late nineteenth

[15] *John Swinton's Paper,* Sept. 13, Oct. 11, 1885; *Journal of United Labor,* June 10, 1885; testimony of John Flynn, in the Bureau's *Third Annual Report* (for 1885); N.Y., *Senate Documents* 3, no. 23 (1886):140.

[16] See Gordon, "The Labor Boycott in New York City, 1880–1886."

[17] *New York Times,* Apr. 7, 1889.

century were confronted by an epochal shift in the nature of social relationships whereby the "industrial necessities" in earlier workshops and factories were far advanced toward becoming the "industrial ethos" of American society.[18]

The boycott as social ostracism could be effective in small communities or neighborhoods only as long as workers, small shopkeepers, and industrialists defined their existence by their place within those communities; they would suffer—even more socially and psychologically than economically—if they were "let severely alone" by their friends and neighbors. When considerations of the marketplace became more important in the lives of employers or merchants than the attitudes of the community, social ostracism could no longer speak to the social realities of their lives. The economic boycott is a significant indicator of that shift in consciousness created by the requirements of an increasingly industrialized society.[19]

The modification of Old World behavior from the social to the economic boycott may have also been related to the changed meaning of work which immigrants encountered in industrializing America. In *The Irish Countryman* anthropologist Conrad Arensberg analyzed the place of work in Irish rural culture during the 1930s. His observations have important implications for the study of work habits in nineteenth-century Ireland and New York, for he ascribes many of the attitudes toward work which he uncovered to long-established traditions. Arensberg described the family as a work unit—"a family economy" in which folklore and custom differentiated work tasks according to one's sex and determined the nature of rewards. Aside from the obvious survival motive, subsistence farm work contained other rewards that operated within Irish family relationships and the rural culture and hence added an even more important control on work habits than a pecuniary one. Bound with their education of work roles, boys and girls also learned related patterns of behavior and attitudes associated with their sex, and of the traditions which sanctioned them.

These tight family and kinship ties survived in America. In many ways the New World Irish immigrant family was still an economic unit, but the routines of work changed, as did the incentives and rewards. For some workers casual day labor became the primary source of income, where in Ireland it had been a necessary but nevertheless supplementary source. Wages, not crops, were needed for survival, and the family no longer

[18] Herbert G. Gutman, "Work, Culture, and Society in Industrializing America, 1815–1919," *American Historical Review* 78 (1973):531–88.

[19] David F. Noble's perceptive comments on this paper helped me (among other ways) to put Norman Ware's analysis of the boycott into this context.

worked together throughout the day on a parcel of land where work was central to the enculturation of children. Arensberg had observed, for example, that the child "learns not only his work but the whole code of conduct which constitutes the folkways of his class"; and specifically for the male child that "the boy learns work as he learns adulthood."[20]

Work was therefore not only important to physical survival. It was also integrally linked to cultural survival. Agrarian terror and social ostracism were directed against English and landlord threats to all the values of life on the land held for Irish peasants. Many of these same values regarding the meaning and importance of work, the family, and the land persisted among Irish immigrants in New York. But work occurred in a different relationship to the means of production and consumption, and it was a psychologically telling step from imposing social ostracism on fellow workers and strikebreakers to ordering economic pressures against employers and those who sold their wares. It was a step which simultaneously reflected the awareness that work had become a mere commodity independent of its Old World cultural meaning, and registered a protest against that deprivation.

There is another dimension to the boycott. In the matrix of attitudes toward land, work, and the family as revealed in poetry and song was a bitter hatred of Anglo Saxons. In "Defiant Still" (1874), William Collins included these lines in a poem written for the *Irish World*:

And bravely and long we battled
Through ages of wrong and woe,
And time has not quenched the hatred
We bear to the Saxon foe.[21]

Over a decade later the popular Irish-American songwriter Frank Harding expressed that sentiment another way in "Evicted":

Torn from the home that has shelter'd us, home of our joys and tears,
Thrust from the hearth where the laugh and songs gladden'd us many years,
Homeless we wander abroad to-night, under the moonlit sky.
England may break the Irish heart, but its spirit will never die.[22]

The hostility revealed in these and other lines stemmed from more than the resentment associated with English military victories. It resulted from the historical consequences calamitous battles entail for the victors and the defeated. Victory specifically required the English to conquer a culture which sustained Irish national identity by ridiculing Irish customs and

[20] Conrad Arensberg, *The Irish Countryman: An Anthropological Study* (1938; reprint ed., Garden City, N.Y., 1969), chap. 2.

[21] Collins, "Defiant Still," *Irish World,* Jan. 10, 1874.

[22] Frank Harding, "Evicted," in *Delaney's Irish Song Book No. 2* (song copyrighted 1887, n.p., n.d.), p. 6, box 271, Starr Music Collection, Lilly Library, Indiana University, Bloomington.

traditions and values. The English never succeeded in doing so. In *The Horn Book*, G. Legman argues that defeats such as expended by the Irish can have a "petrifying but protective" influence on the defeated. "The whole aspect of their culture," he writes, "has been . . . petrified in the form and image of the moment of that defeat." And yet that very "immobilization" has enabled them to preserve their "national and cultural identity."[23]

While that observation neglects to consider cultural change over time, it nevertheless provides further insight into the attitudes and behavior of New York's Irish immigrant workers. In the early 1880s there existed a symbiotic relationship between labor, land reform, and Irish nationalist activities. That alliance, however tenuous, is revealing, for it caused the distinctions separating some labor proposals from schemes for redressing Ireland's grievances to become blurred. This occurred for two principal reasons. First, important numbers of Irish immigrants believed that problems afflicting American workers and Irish peasants stemmed from identical sources. They viewed industrial and land monopoly as the aggrandizement of natural resources which God had intended to be shared by all. Relatedly, the monopolists in both countries were viewed by Irish immigrants as attempting to destroy their cultural identity; hence attacks on Anglo-Saxon civilization assumed a central place in their demands for land reform.

During the 1882 freighthandlers' strike, for example, tailor Robert Blissert, a founder of New York's Central Labor Union and an ardent Irish nationalist, spoke to a gathering of strikers at New York's Temperance Hall. Blissert was particularly critical of those politicians who were influenced by English money. "English power," he said, "is as much felt in this City as in Ireland. English money owns the Erie, which has been grinding you down." He derided political parties for financing their campaigns with "English gold," and then selling out workers "to the capitalist who controls the politician." Four days later—on July 7—Blissert spoke to another strike meeting at St. Michael's Institute in Jersey City and made the crucial connection between English power and the need for land reform in America. The *Irish World* paraphrased Blissert's remarks: "The cause of all your troubles is the private ownership of land. . . . From the land comes everything. It is the great storehouse from which all things are drawn, and while a few men are allowed to own it, *they own you*. . . . Until the Land Question is settled there is no hope." To great cheering, Blissert closed by urging workers to "build up a true Republic where all

[23] Legman, *The Horn Book: Studies in Erotic Folklore and Bibliography* (Hyde Park, N.Y., 1964), p. 365.

men shall enjoy the rights and benefits that a merciful God intended for us."[24]

Blissert's concerns for the future of the Republic were shared by many other Irish immigrant workers. Boycotters frequently justified their use of the boycott by citing similar practices used against the English in Revolutionary times. They did so not because they were resurrecting a practice used with great effect by the Revolutionary generation, but rather to legitimize their claim that the boycott in America was linked with efforts to win independence from the British empire and to establish a nation based upon Jeffersonian principles.[25] Coupled with demands for land reform, these claims reflected an Irish immigrant faith in republicanism and a determination to prevent America from falling victim to the evils of Anglo-Saxon civilization. Within this context, the labor boycott and kindred social ostracism were seen as customary and proper tactics against unscrupulous employers and other workers who violated their "unwritten code of laws" and their rights to share God's bounty—just as they had been used in Ireland against landlords and others for similar reasons.

The *Times* and Sumner were correct in stating that the boycott was "a foreign institution" aimed at ostracising people from society. Their unstated fears stemmed from what the perpetuation of such behavior meant for industrializing America. It was not just the labor boycott which had to be stopped. The preindustrial ethnic subcultures which nourished it had to be broken to conform to the requirements of industrial culture.

As the trials of labor boycotters in 1886 well demonstrate, boycotts were conducted by immigrants other than the Irish—a fact suggesting that similar forms of behavior may have been common to the Old World experiences of many New York workers. It also suggests the need to study those backgrounds and what happened when those particular ways of life were transplanted in America. We need to know much more, for example, about the customs, traditions, beliefs, work habits, and folklore of preemigrant peoples, and how and what people learned from them. Studies of the graphic and plastic arts, of songs and poetry, may also reveal much about immigrant values and perceptions. There is also a need to explore the private and tender relationships between males and females, and to examine the ways in which conventional immigrant sexual behavior in general differed (if at all) from that encountered in America.

The conceptual framework sketched earlier suggests only one way of

[24] *New York Times,* July 4, 1882; *Irish World,* July 15, 1882 (ellipses and italics mine).

[25] See, for example, letters from T. Dwight Stow and George A. Schilling to *John Swinton's Paper,* Jan. 17, Apr. 25, 1886, and articles in May 2, June 13, 1886; *Irish World,* Dec. 25, 1880, Jan. 22, 1882; and *Progress,* Mar. 25, 1884.

analyzing these and other aspects of immigrant peoples' lives and the worlds they knew. Yet whatever the model, the study of cultural transitions must proceed from a broad historical vision that recognizes, as Melville Herskovits wrote long ago, that people order their behavior according to the traditions of their groups, "that these traditions are historically, not biologically, derived, and that each society has modes of conduct that differ from those of other societies."[26]

[26] Melville J. Herskovits, *Cultural Anthropology,* rev. ed. (New York, 1955), p. 75.

# VIII Immigrants and Industry: The Philadelphia Experience, 1850–1880

*Bruce Laurie, Theodore Hershberg, and George Alter*

Shortly after Stephan Thernstrom published *Poverty and Progress* (1964), the first study by an American historian of social mobility in an urban setting, interest in the mobility patterns of the past century mushroomed. "Nowhere, perhaps," was "there a more obvious fit between national ideology and scholarly preoccupation," Michael Katz reminds us, than with "this American concern with making it."[1] In our haste to get on with it, however, historians turned to the sociological literature. And, in being "more attentive initially to the sociologists who developed this field than to economic and labor historians pursuing changes in the composition and experience of the workforce in particular occupations or in the economy as a whole," we were guilty of a serious and time-consuming false start.[2]

Studies of occupational mobility, in particular studies that attempt to describe social mobility, require the construction of vertical stratification schema for the classification of occupations according to skill, income, status, and so forth. Mobility is frequently thought of as connoting improvement, but movement among strata can be in three directions: from lower to higher, from higher to lower, or horizontally between two positions on the same level. The role assumed by the stratification scheme in such studies is crucial. The empirical findings will be seriously flawed if the strata *at each point in time* do not reflect the accurate ranking of occupations.

Sociologists who study social mobility concentrate primarily on status.

This study was prepared for the Immigrants in Industry Conference and was also published in essentially the same form in the December 1975 issue of the *Journal of Social History*. The data presented were collected by the Philadelphia Social History Project, directed by Dr. Theodore Hershberg, and are part of a larger study of the relationships among social mobility, family structure, neighborhood, industrialization, urbanization, and transportation. The authors wish to express their appreciation to the Center for the Study of Metropolitan Problems of the National Institute of Mental Health, whose financial support has made this research possible. Bruce Laurie wished to thank the National Endowment for the Humanities for supporting his research with a postdoctoral fellowship.

[1] Michael B. Katz, *The People of Hamilton, Canada West: Family and Class in a Mid-Nineteenth-Century City* (Cambridge, Mass., 1976), chap. 4.

[2] Clyde Griffen, "Occupational Mobility in Nineteenth-Century America: Problems and Possibilities," *Journal of Social History* 5 (1972): 310–30.

They are able to construct classification schema which are justifiable empirically. "Some individual titles apparently have shifted their relative position," surveys of public opinion have shown, "but the overall transformation of the hierarchy in the last fifty years has been glacial in nature."[3] Unfortunately, historians do not have comparably firm data about occupational status for the nineteenth century. Extrapolating the current trend backward in time to a period that was dissimilar in important respects (such as income, education, skill levels, and industrial structure) would be dubious at best and fundamentally ahistorical. The occupational stratification schema used by sociologists scrutinizing the twentieth century cannot simply be appropriated by historians who wish to understand the nineteenth.

In retrospect this should not be surprising. Industrialization in the nineteenth century had a significant impact on the occupational universe; it altered occupational patterns perhaps more fundamentally, and certainly differently, than it did in the twentieth century. Radical changes were brought about through the reorganization of work and the introduction of labor-saving technologies. The problem of constructing occupational stratification schema in such an environment should not be underestimated or ignored.

If, for example, both the shoemaker who worked with his hands to fashion a pair of shoes in 1850 and the shoemaker who worked with the aid of a pegging machine to complete only part of the work required to make a pair of shoes in 1880 were classified in the same stratum (vertical category), no change would be recorded by the historian. Yet significant change would have occurred. There was a clear dilution of skill, a drop in income, and probably a decline in status as well. Classification schema based on skill, income, and status, therefore, would consider the change in the work done by the shoemaker as downward mobility, regardless of the fact that the occupational designation "shoemaker" remained the same in both years. A useful occupational classification scheme must take all of these factors into account.

Where does one acquire such detailed knowledge about nineteenth-century occupations? Even for those occupations about which we know a great deal, such as shoemaking, the required information seems almost impossible to find. General studies are available that describe the industry in England and Massachusetts, but are of limited value. Like most industries, shoemaking varied greatly from place to place, and knowledge of how the industry or occupation generally operated will not suffice when it is necessary to know the state of the industry or occupation for a *specific*

[3] David L. Featherman and Robert M. Hauser, "On the Measurement of Occupation in Social Surveys," *Sociological Methods and Research*, 2, no. 2 (Nov. 1973): 241.

*locale at a given time*. And if this is true for the few occupations and fewer industries about which we know relatively much, what about those of which we know little or nothing at all?

A considerable body of recent scholarship has produced important refinements in our understanding of the occupational structure by using the now familiar sources of the "new" social history—manuscript population censuses, city directories, and tax lists. Clyde Griffen argues, for example, that the line separating skilled craftsmen from proprietors is a blurred line, movement across which connotes as much downward as upward mobility.[4] Michael Katz suggests that the division between manual and nonmanual work was not as "firm or noticeable" as has been assumed.[5] Furthermore, it is now apparent that the category of "semiskilled" worker has rested on too little knowledge of work-content to make it analytically useful. While these insights are valuable, the sources of the new social history suffer from several limitations: they cannot be employed systematically to devise strata sensitive to industrial changes in specific settings at specific dates; they can *describe*, but not *explain* the changing occupational patterns observed.

There is a source of information, however, which provides the requisite data. The manuscript schedules of the U.S. Census of Manufactures report wage rates, number and sex ratios of employees, mechanization, capital investment, and values of raw materials and finished products. This detailed information for each firm makes possible the differentiation of industries and their ranking by *desirability* for the working man. When used in conjunction with the population manuscripts and impressionistic sources, they permit the description of the impact of industrialization on the occupational universe.

Systematic use of these data reveals how industrialization affected incomes, working conditions, and opportunities for career advancement. Specifically, the data point to further shortcomings in traditional occupational ranking schema. They reveal a considerable amount of variation in the objective conditions of skilled occupations which are usually assigned to a *single* category and indicate that the line separating skilled from unskilled workers blurs when one considers firm size and industry type. Above all, they demonstrate that industrialization shuffled the distribution of occupations within the occupational hierarchy. Traditional occupational ranking schema are static and, therefore, unable to capture the subtle changes in the occupational universe wrought by the process of industrialization.

[4] Griffen, pp. 324–27.

[5] Michael B. Katz, "Four Propositions about Social and Family Structure in Preindustrial Society," paper presented at the International Conference on Comparative Social Mobility, Institute for Advanced Study, Princeton, N.J., June 15–17, 1972, pp. 10–14.

What began for us as an attempt to improve the occupational stratification schema borrowed from sociologists has resulted in the determination that such schema are inappropriate to the tasks we have assigned them and that it makes sense to abandon the practice of using a priori occupational stratification schema as the *means* to the study of social mobility. For the time being we should concern ourselves with understanding the ways in which nineteenth-century occupations were actually stratified. Our new *means* might include socioeconomic and demographic profiles of individual occupations over time and sophisticated techniques of record linkage in order to reconstitute the actual careers of individuals. Our new *end* should be the accurate stratification of the nineteenth-century occupational universe.

To demonstrate both the opportunities and pitfalls inherent in such a reorientation of scholarly efforts, we focus in this paper on changes in the fourteen largest manufacturing industries in Philadelphia between 1850 and 1880. We will seek to explain both how the industrial and occupational hierarchy changed and how this change affected the distribution of selected ethnic groups in the manual labor force.[6]

## Patterns of Industrial Change

The fourteen industries under examination have been divided into manufacturers of consumer goods and manufacturers of producer goods.[7] The first group encompasses industries important in Philadelphia since the

[6] Our discussion focuses on three distinct groups of males above the age of 18: (1) the Irish and Germans, foreign-born immigrants identified by their place of birth; (2) second-generation Irish and Germans, American-born sons of Irish and German fathers; and (3) native white Americans, American-born sons of native white parents. Second-generation males can be differentiated from native whites only for the year 1880. The 1850 census identified the place of birth for the individual *only*, while the 1880 census reported the place of birth for the father and mother as well as for the individual. The 1850 figures for native white Americans, then, include all native-born whites regardless of parental birth (see Table 17).

Although we have data available for all black males above the ages of 18 as well, they have not been included in this analysis. Blacks were so excluded from the industrial sector of the economy that discussing their occupational patterns within the context of this paper would be counterproductive. Their occupational patterns are treated in Theodore Hershberg, "Free Blacks in Antebellum Philadelphia: A Study of Ex-slave, Freeborn, and Socioeconomic Decline," *Journal of Social History* 5 (1972): 191–92, 198–200. The occupational distribution of Philadelphia's Negro community is discussed in Theodore Hershberg, "Mulattoes and Blacks: Intra-Group Color Differences and Social Stratification," *Journal of American History* (in press, 1976).

[7] It should be added that these are crude categories, constructed to facilitate our discussion. As will become evident, there are exceptions in each group, the most conspicuous of which are printing and building construction in the consumer group and textiles in the producer group.

days of Dr. Franklin, namely, shoemaking, clothing, baking, building construction, blacksmithing, printing, and traditional metal crafts. Included in the second group are textiles, hardware, machine tools, and iron and steel. With the exception of textiles, which appeared in colonial times but showed little growth before the Jacksonian period, these industries were new to the city. They emerged in the 1820s and 1830s when entrepreneur-inventors like Samuel Merrick, Matthias Baldwin, and Alfred Jenks opened foundries and machine shops and pioneered in the production of metal and metal products.

Though they were newer than the consumer industries, the producer industries developed more quickly and displayed greater industrial maturity in 1880. As Table 15 demonstrates, they were far more mechanized than the older industries both in 1850 and 1880. By 1880 nearly four-fifths of the firms in iron and steel and two-thirds of the firms in textiles and machine tools produced wares with the aid of steam or waterpower. Firms in the older industries were primitive by comparison. Printing and publishing houses showed the most advancement, but only 38.8 percent of them in 1880 boasted power-driven presses. Furniture makers rank a distant second: less than 12 percent of them were equipped with steam or waterpower, while less than 10 percent of the firms in each of the remaining industries used steam engines or waterwheels.

The predominance of steam power in the newer industries helps account for the striking disparity in capitalization between them and the older industries (see Table 16). Median capitalization of these firms surpassed consumer industries in 1850 and 1880, and median capitalization in each producer-goods industry increased dramatically. Capitalization also increased in printing and furniture making, but they are exceptional. Capital costs of most consumer industries either remained constant between 1850 and 1880 or actually declined, as in clothing, blacksmithing, harness making, shoemaking and metal crafts.[8]

Firms in the newer industries not only required more capital and used more power-driven machinery, they also employed more workers than firms turning out consumer goods. As Table 17 shows, the rank order did not change appreciably between 1850 and 1880. Table 18 analyzes shop size another way; it distinguishes firms with one to five employees, firms with six to fifty employees, and firms with more than fifty employees. The

[8] Because of an undercounting of small firms in the 1850 manufacturing census, the figures for median capitalization presented in Table 16 may be somewhat inflated, masking a slight increase in capitalization by 1880. Any increase that might have occurred, however, remains small by comparison with the increases observed in the producer industries.

*Table 15.* Percentage of firms using steam or waterpower

| Rank | 1850 Industry | % | 1880 Industry | % |
|---|---|---|---|---|
| 1 | Iron and steel | 76.3 | Iron and steel | 79.1 |
| 2 | Textiles | 50.6 | Machines and tools | 67.4 |
| 3 | Machines and tools | 47.8 | Textiles | 66.3 |
| 4 | Hardware | 17.6 | Hardware | 39.2 |
| 5 | Printing | 15.1 | Printing | 38.8 |
| 6 | Metal | 7.4 | Furniture | 12.3 |
| 7 | Building construction | 5.5 | Metal | 8.7 |
| 8 | Furniture | 4.6 | Clothing | 6.2 |
| 9 | Clothing | 2.2 | Meat processing | 4.6 |
| 10 | Baking | 1.2 | Blacksmithing | 4.0 |
| 11 | Shoes | 0.2 | Baking | 3.2 |
| 12 | Harnesses | 0 | Building construction | 2.6 |
| 13 | Meat processing | 0 | Harnesses | 2.5 |
| 14 | Blacksmithing | 0 | Shoes | 2.4 |

SOURCES: U.S., Census Office, Census of the United States, Manufacturing Schedule, County of Philadelphia, 1850 and 1880 (Microfilm MSS, National Archives).

*Table 16.* Median capitalization (in $)

| Rank | 1850 Industry | Median capitalization | 1880 Industry | Median capitalization |
|---|---|---|---|---|
| 1 | Iron and steel | $10,867 | Iron and steel | $29,750 |
| 2 | Textiles | 4,833 | Textiles | 9,194 |
| 3 | Hardware | 4,500 | Hardware | 5,461 |
| 4 | Machines and tools | 3,250 | Machines and tools | 5,250 |
| 5 | Printing | 3,125 | Printing | 5,232 |
| 6 | Clothing | 2,958 | Clothing | 2,487 |
| 7 | Furniture | 1,538 | Furniture | 2,200 |
| 8 | Metal | 1,375 | Meat | 1,479 |
| 9 | Meat | 1,350 | Metal | 1,288 |
| 10 | Harness | 1,030 | Baking | 1,036 |
| 11 | Building construction | 948 | Building construction | 975 |
| 12 | Baking | 839 | Harness | 780 |
| 13 | Shoes | 690 | Shoes | 681 |
| 14 | Blacksmith | 582 | Blacksmith | 492 |

SOURCES: Census of the U.S., 1850 and 1880.

*Table 17.* Median number of employees per firm

| Rank | 1850 Industry | 1850 Median no. of employees | 1880 Industry | 1880 Median no. of employees |
|---|---|---|---|---|
| 1 | Textiles | 19.50 | Iron and steel | 31.88 |
| 2 | Iron and steel | 13.00 | Printing | 9.75 |
| 3 | Clothing | 9.69 | Textiles | 9.50 |
| 4 | Printing | 9.50 | Hardware | 6.92 |
| 5 | Machines and tools | 6.08 | Machines and tools | 6.86 |
| 6 | Furniture | 4.96 | Clothing | 6.06 |
| 7 | Building construction | 4.92 | Furniture | 3.98 |
| 8 | Hardware | 4.71 | Building construction | 3.39 |
| 9 | Shoes | 4.55 | Metal | 2.52 |
| 10 | Harness | 3.75 | Shoes | 2.14 |
| 11 | Metal | 2.73 | Blacksmith | 1.92 |
| 12 | Blacksmith | 2.65 | Baking | 1.61 |
| 13 | Baking | 2.05 | Harness | 1.46 |
| 14 | Meat | 1.41 | Meat | 1.39 |

Sources: Census of the U.S., 1850 and 1880.

*Table 18.* Percentage of work force by number of employees per firm

| Industry | % of work force 1850 No. of employees 1–5 | 6–50 | 50+ | 1880 No. of employees 1–5 | 6–50 | 50+ |
|---|---|---|---|---|---|---|
| Iron and steel | 1.7 | 34.1 | 64.2 | 0.7 | 16.9 | 82.4 |
| Textiles | 1.8 | 20.2 | 78.0 | 2.4 | 39.6 | 58.0 |
| Hardware | 11.8 | 23.9 | 64.3 | 3.9 | 35.9 | 60.2 |
| Machines and tools | 6.2 | 38.2 | 55.6 | 4.8 | 38.2 | 57.0 |
| Printing | 5.0 | 51.2 | 43.8 | 3.6 | 37.7 | 58.7 |
| Building construction | 22.6 | 54.0 | 23.4 | 24.0 | 45.7 | 30.2 |
| Clothing | 4.8 | 44.3 | 50.9 | 2.8 | 17.3 | 79.9 |
| Furniture | 17.9 | 62.1 | 20.0 | 11.7 | 45.5 | 42.8 |
| Metal | 48.6 | 33.0 | 18.3 | 22.2 | 41.3 | 36.5 |
| Meat | 67.2 | 32.8 | – | 59.7 | 27.3 | 12.9 |
| Harness | 15.8 | 41.0 | 43.2 | 15.3 | 30.5 | 54.2 |
| Baking | 71.1 | 28.9 | – | 45.2 | 34.8 | 19.9 |
| Shoes | 16.9 | 46.6 | 36.5 | 8.5 | 28.6 | 62.8 |
| Blacksmith | 61.0 | 28.4 | 10.6 | 78.3 | 21.7 | 0 |
| All 14 industries | 11.2 | 37.7 | 51.1 | 9.5 | 29.6 | 60.8 |

Sources: Census of the U.S., 1850 and 1880.

aggregate picture conforms to our expectations in that categories 1 and 2 lost ground to category 3. Where in 1850 the largest firms employed 51 percent of the labor force, in 1880 they employed 61 percent. Exceptions to this pattern are apparent in textiles and hardware, where the largest firms gave way to middle-sized ones, but in these industries the largest firms still employed 58.0 percent and 60.2 percent of their labor force in 1880. In the consumer industries the trend toward larger firms is unmistakable, but even more striking is the persistence of small shops, especially in meat, baking, and blacksmithing. Even in shoes and clothing, where most of the labor force was located in large firms, there were still large numbers of small shops in 1880 (see Table 19).

Data contained in the industrial census of 1800 confirm the suspicion that firms with less than five employees were not the proverbial handicraft shops of bygone days whose journeymen and masters produced custom goods on flexible work schedules and enjoyed relatively cordial relations. Instead, they were sweatshops characterized by frequent layoffs, the division of labor, and long hours under the rigid hand of severe taskmasters. Table 20 offers some insight into the abysmal working conditions in "sweated" industries—meat, baking, clothing, and shoemaking. The table shows that they were among the most flagrant violators of the standard ten-hour day, operating in excess of ten hours as well as running on "short time" and capriciously shutting down in the middle of the day.

We are also skeptical of the view put forth by some historians that large firms and heavy industry were the bane of the skilled worker. It is misleading to equate nineteenth-century foundries and iron and steel mills with modern factories and to envisage those who labored in such settings as an undifferentiated mass of semiskilled workers. The production of iron, steel, and heavy machinery entailed a range of intricate processes. The various craftsmen, semiskilled workers, and unskilled workers who performed this labor were linked in an elaborate occupational hierarchy. The work environment could be disagreeable and the work itself was often dangerous, but skilled workers in large firms were well compensated for their endeavors. Cross tabulations of the wages of skilled workers by size of firm demonstrate that there was a direct relationship between firm size and average daily wage, so that *by 1800 the larger firm, the higher the wage* (see Table 21). Some skilled workers, no doubt, objected to what one historian calls the "impersonal and mechanical" relations with employers.[9] Yet it is not entirely clear that factory work in heavy industry was as degrading in the eyes of the skilled worker as many historians believe. The perceptions of workers obviously deserve more treatment than is possible

[9] Edward C. Kirkland, *Industry Comes of Age: Business, Labor, and Public Policy, 1860–1897* (Chicago, 1967), p. 351.

*Table 19.* Number of firms by number of employees per firm

| Industry | Number of firms 1850 No. of employees 0–5 | 6–50 | 50+ | Total | 1880 No. of employees 0–5 | 6–50 | 50+ | Total |
|---|---|---|---|---|---|---|---|---|
| Iron and steel | 6 | 13 | 3 | 22 | 6 | 20 | 17 | 43 |
| Textiles | 46 | 87 | 53 | 186 | 25 | 59 | 8 | 92 |
| Hardware | 76 | 42 | 7 | 125 | 114 | 122 | 27 | 263 |
| Machines and tools | 42 | 44 | 6 | 92 | 96 | 113 | 19 | 228 |
| Printing | 36 | 60 | 10 | 106 | 105 | 148 | 36 | 289 |
| Building construction | 83 | 59 | 3 | 145 | 588 | 227 | 18 | 833 |
| Clothing | 165 | 294 | 43 | 502 | 301 | 255 | 93 | 649 |
| Furniture | 84 | 66 | 3 | 153 | 185 | 105 | 20 | 310 |
| Metal | 83 | 11 | 1 | 95 | 166 | 47 | 5 | 218 |
| Meat | 81 | 3 | 0 | 84 | 458 | 23 | 2 | 483 |
| Harness | 32 | 15 | 3 | 50 | 96 | 21 | 2 | 119 |
| Baking | 384 | 29 | 0 | 413 | 910 | 73 | 8 | 991 |
| Shoes | 339 | 224 | 20 | 583 | 441 | 139 | 34 | 614 |
| Blacksmith | 141 | 18 | 1 | 160 | 187 | 12 | 0 | 199 |

SOURCES: Census of the U.S., 1850 and 1880.
NOTE: Due to the fact that the census only recorded firms producing more than $500 per year, there may be serious undercounting of firms with one or no employees.

*Table 20.* Percentage of firms by hours worked per day, May to November

| Industry | % of firms working -10 hrs. | 10 hrs. | +10 hrs. |
|---|---|---|---|
| Iron and steel | 2.3 | 97.7 | 0 |
| Textiles | 14.1 | 81.5 | 4.4 |
| Hardware | 3.0 | 94.7 | 2.3 |
| Machines and tools | 3.9 | 94.7 | 1.3 |
| Printing | 18.3 | 81.0 | 0.7 |
| Building construction | 4.3 | 95.0 | 0.7 |
| Clothing | 14.8 | 81.4 | 4.0 |
| Furniture | 4.8 | 93.9 | 1.2 |
| Metal | 3.2 | 95.4 | 1.5 |
| Meat | 21.9 | 38.5 | 39.5 |
| Harness | 1.7 | 95.8 | 2.5 |
| Baking | 10.3 | 36.4 | 53.3 |
| Shoes | 8.4 | 85.4 | 6.4 |
| Blacksmith | 1.5 | 93.5 | 5.0 |

SOURCES: Census of the U.S., 1850 and 1880.

*Table 21.* Average daily wages paid by number of male employees per firm, 1880

| Industry | Average daily wages: Skilled mechanic, No. of employees 1–5 | 6–50 | 51+ | Ordinary mechanic, No. of employees 1–5 | 6–50 | 51+ |
|---|---|---|---|---|---|---|
| Iron and steel | $1.97 | $2.30 | $2.48 | $1.25 | $1.35 | $1.42 |
| Textiles | 1.84 | 1.99 | 2.00 | 1.24 | 1.31 | 1.31 |
| Hardware | 2.04 | 2.25 | 2.44 | 1.24 | 1.28 | 1.39 |
| Machines and tools | 2.09 | 2.29 | 2.47 | 1.15 | 1.40 | 1.34 |
| Printing | 2.03 | 2.45 | 2.70 | 1.14 | 1.27 | 1.48 |
| Building construction | 2.07 | 2.18 | 2.29 | 1.39 | 1.93 | 1.45 |
| Clothing | 1.90 | 2.14 | 2.55 | 1.10 | 1.19 | 1.30 |
| Furniture | 2.08 | 2.18 | 2.27 | 1.23 | 1.42 | 1.34 |
| Metal | 2.00 | 2.18 | 2.40 | 1.25 | 1.28 | 1.27 |
| Meat | 1.57 | 1.80 | 2.00 | 0.99 | 1.31 | 1.38 |
| Harness | 1.78 | 2.07 | 2.00 | 1.16 | 1.23 | — |
| Baking | 1.65 | 2.20 | 2.50 | 1.20 | 1.26 | 1.30 |
| Shoes | 1.65 | 2.06 | 2.54 | 0.93 | 1.32 | 1.67 |
| Blacksmith | 1.86 | 2.38 | — | 1.14 | 1.38 | — |

SOURCE: Census of the U.S., 1880.
NOTE: Entries in this table have been weighted by number of male employees per firm.

here, but it appears that some skilled workers found decided advantages in working for large employers, quite apart from the fact that they earned higher wages. One such worker, a machinist by trade though not a Philadelphian, tells us that

> large firms can hire help to better advantage than small ones. The mass of workingmen like to feel that their situations are as permanent as possible, and this they cannot do when employed in a small shop. For one of the limited means to secure the services of an expert and really valuable assistant, extra considerations must be offered, and even these will not retain such labor if the work seems likely to fail. The highly paid assistant hired in this small way, must be frequently employed upon a class of work which in a large shop would be done by the most unskilled inexperienced and, of course, poorly paid labor."[10]

When we translate daily wages into average yearly earnings, we begin to appreciate the plight of the small master craftsman and his journeymen under the stress of industrialization. Calculations of average yearly earn-

[10] Massachusetts, Bureau of the Statistics of Labor, *Report* (Boston, 1870), pp. 338–39.

*Table 22*. Average yearly wages paid to males by number of male employees per firm, 1850 and 1880

| Industry | Average yearly wages | | | | | | | |
|---|---|---|---|---|---|---|---|---|
| | 1850 | | | | 1880 | | | |
| | No. of male employees | | | | No. of male employees | | | |
| | 1–5 | 6–50 | 50+ | Total | 1–5 | 6–50 | 50+ | Total |
| Boots and shoes | $272 | $274 | $263 | $270 | $378 | $462 | $492 | $469 |
| Harness | 322 | 339 | 378 | 353 | 440 | 484 | n.a. | 469 |
| Textiles | 268 | 226 | 197 | 206 | 436 | 491 | 436 | 468 |
| Clothing | 319 | 333 | 236 | 287 | 409 | 449 | 329 | 359 |
| Baking | 271 | 281 | – | 273 | 393 | 526 | 400 | 435 |
| Meat | 305 | 336 | – | 306 | 385 | 440 | 422 | 405 |
| Furniture | 373 | 335 | 374 | 351 | 457 | 489 | 433 | 462 |
| Blacksmith | 300 | 268 | – | 300 | 448 | 466 | – | 452 |
| Printing | 355 | 370 | 372 | 370 | 398 | 445 | 578 | 518 |
| Building | 375 | 340 | 159 | 307 | 453 | 446 | 508 | 467 |
| Hardware | 391 | 329 | 320 | 330 | 498 | 418 | 609 | 534 |
| Metal | 383 | 319 | 330 | 352 | 414 | 466 | 444 | 446 |
| Machines and tools | 354 | 326 | 328 | 329 | 469 | 464 | 544 | 509 |
| Iron and steel | 319 | 394 | 345 | 361 | 474 | 454 | 670 | 631 |

SOURCES: Census of the U.S., 1850 and 1880.
NOTE: All entries in this table have been weighted by number of male employees per firm. Because only *total* wages for all employees were reported for 1880 firms, male earnings in that year were estimated using the following procedure: Average male wages = total wages paid/number of males +0.4 number of females +0.3 number of youths.

ings of each industry are presented in Table 22. The table suggests that in 1850 handicraft producers enjoyed an enviable position in the marketplace since their journeymen earned the highest incomes. And while there was a considerable gap between industries, the range within industries was nominal. Thirty years later, however, industrialization undermined the small producer, who could not compete with larger, more efficient firms and whose workers therefore held the least remunerative jobs. Workers employed by the largest and medium-sized employers, whether they were in the consumer or the producer group, secured the best incomes. In the consumer industries, for example, workingmen employed by the *largest* printers and publishers, boot and shoe manufacturers, and construction bosses earned the highest incomes, as did workers in the remaining industries who found employment in the medium-sized firms. In the producer industries, workers employed in the largest firms (with the exception of textiles) garnered the best incomes.

In this thirty-year period, moreover, the disparity in earnings within industries increased considerably. To take a few examples, the range in incomes between wage earners in small and medium-sized shoemaking shops in 1850 was only $2, but widened to $84 in 1880. In the meat packing and baking firms, the disparity between incomes was $31 and $10, respectively, in 1850, $55 and $133 thirty years later. The same pattern holds for the new metal trades in which the margin between the smallest and largest iron and steel mills and machine shops was $26 in both in 1850, $196 and $75 in 1880. This period also witnessed the development of major differentials between the incomes of workers in the producer and consumer groups. Table 23, which ranks each industry by average yearly income, shows that in 1850 neither group dominated; representatives of each were dispersed randomly in the rank order. But in 1880 the producer industries achieved superiority and occupied three of the top four positions in the ranking. The average yearly income of manual workers in these industries ranged between $468 and $631, while the range within the consumer groups, if we exclude printing for the moment, was between $359 and $469. Or, to put it another way, by 1880 the highest average earning in the consumer group was the lowest in the producer group.

These developments in industrial Philadelphia closely parallel the findings of Eric Hobsbawm in his brilliant study of the "Labour Aristocracy" in nineteenth-century Britain.[11] In both countries metal trades developed rapidly. Iron and steel mills, foundries, and machine shops proliferated and employed a highly diversified labor force comprised partly of iron puddlers, rollers, machinists, and other skilled workers who formed the aristocracy of labor, partly of semiskilled workers who toiled alongside the aristocrats, and partly of unskilled workers who performed menial tasks.[12]

Puddlers, rollers, machinists, and other skilled metalworkers earned the highest incomes of all tradesmen, though superior earnings alone did not distinguish them from other workers. As Hobsbawm notes, a number of nonwage factors—conditions of work, relations with other workers and other social classes, styles of life—also figure in the equation. Historians are only beginning to treat these complex matters, but some evidence suggests that skilled metalworkers occupied a more advantageous position in the workshop than most handicraft workers. Not the least of their advantages was considerable autonomy, despite the impressive advances in technology. They often combined managerial functions with manual

[11] Erik J. Hobsbawm, *Labouring Men* (New York, 1964), pp. 272–315.

[12] For an example of the range of wage rates and occupations in the metal industries, see Pennsylvania, *Annual Report of the Secretary of Internal Affairs of the Commonwealth of Pennsylvania, Part III, Industrial Statistics* 4, 1875–76 (Harrisburg, 1877): 546, 621 ff. See also ibid., 6 (1877–78).

*Table 23.* Average yearly wages paid to males

| 1850 | Wages paid to males | 1880 | Wages paid to males |
|---|---|---|---|
| Printing | $370 | Iron and steel | $631 |
| Iron and steel | 361 | Hardware | 534 |
| Harness | 353 | Printing | 518 |
| Metal | 352 | Machine and tools | 509 |
| Furniture | 351 | Boots and shoes | 469 |
| Hardware | 330 | Harness | 469 |
| Machines and tools | 329 | Textiles | 468 |
| Building construction | 307 | Building construction | 467 |
| Meat | 306 | *All 14 industries* | 464 |
| Blacksmith | 300 | Furniture | 462 |
| *All 14 industries* | 288 | Blacksmith | 452 |
| Clothing | 287 | Metal | 446 |
| Baking | 273 | Baking | 435 |
| Boots and shoes | 270 | Meat | 405 |
| Textiles | 206 | Clothing | 359 |

SOURCES: Census of the U.S., 1850 and 1880.
NOTE: Entries have been weighted by number of male employees.

skills, hiring their own crews and frequently determining the quantity and quality of outputs. It was precisely such autonomy that would inspire a determined effort by large employers and scientific managers to wrest control of the workplace from skilled workers in the 1890s and at the turn of the century. But in the third quarter of the nineteenth century, as David Montgomery demonstrates, skilled metalworkers were the vanguard of tradesmen who exercised "control over the actual use of . . . implements in the productive process."[13] Few if any of them could realistically aspire to become employers because of the enormous capital requirements, but they commanded considerable status and respect, both from employers, who relied heavily on their skill and judgment, and from wage earners below them in the occupational hierarchy.

Workers performing semiskilled tasks and ordinary labor in the new metal trades, moreover, were better off than their counterparts in the older industries. They earned slightly more per day than most ordinary workers in consumer industries, and had more access to skilled jobs atop the

[13] David Montgomery, "Trade Union Practice and the Origins of Syndicalist Theory in the United States," paper read at the Sorbonne, 1968, p. 3., U.S., Congress, Senate, *Report of the Committee of the Senate upon the Relations between Capital and Labor* (Washington, D.C., 1885), 2:2–3; David Brody, *Steelworkers in America: The Non-Union Era* (Cambridge, Mass., 1960), p. 52.

occupational hierarchy because these industries had a greater ratio of skilled to unskilled jobs than did the old crafts. In the crafts, on the other hand, the division of labor diluted skills, and mobility held less promise for the ordinary workers who competed for a diminishing number of "skilled" jobs.

Within the consumer group certain industries expanded, namely, printing and to a lesser extent building construction. These industries contained their own occupational hierarchy with a sizable labor aristocracy, paid relatively high wages, and offered skilled workers considerable job satisfaction and prestige.[14] In fact, "aristocrats" could be found in most older industries, as in cabinetmaking, where a select few fashioned expensive furniture, or in clothing where garment cutters whose ability to ruin employers with a fatal slip of the knife earned them prestige, respect, and high wages.[15]

In the main, however, working people found consumer industries less rewarding and less desirable between 1850 and 1880. These pursuits lacked the elaborate occupational hierarchy of the newer industries, which provided a career ladder for workers withing a given firm. The alternative to rising within a firm was opening a small shop, which was still possible in many industries whose capital costs were not prohibitively high. Such was the case in meat processing, clothing, shoemaking, and baking, where shops capitalized at $500 were still common as late as 1880.

Yet it is improbable that journeymen bettered themselves by opening small shops. Small producers usually operated on the fringe of their industry as subcontractors producing specialized goods for large manufacturers.[16] The intense competition of subcontracting forced small employers to "sweat" journeymen and even to work alongside them in the hope of cutting costs. This arrangement necessarily blurred the functional line between employer and employee in the shop, but the risk remained squarely on the shoulders of the employer, who operated on a thin profit margin and was constantly haunted by the specter of ruin. Many, and perhaps most of them, did fail, and those who succeeded earned little more than the people they hired and less than many factory foremen (see Table 24).[17]

[14] Seymour M. Lipset, Martin Trow, and James S. Coleman, *Union Democracy* (Glencoe, Ill., 1956), pp. 1–76, and Robert Christie, *Empire in Wood* (Ithaca, N.Y., 1956), pp. 25–28.

[15] See Montgomery, "Trade Union Practice," and Edwin T. Freedley, *Philadelphia and Its Manufactures* (Philadelphia, 1858), p. 221.

[16] Blanche E. Hazard, *The Organization of the Boot and Shoe Industry in Massachusetts before 1875* (Cambridge, Mass., 1921), pp. 87–126. See also Charles Booth, *Labor and Life of the People* (New York, 1970), 1st ser. 4:37–156 and 2d ser. 3:9–50.

[17] A foreman blacksmith from Philadelphia reported to Pennsylvania's secretary

*Table 24.* Average gross profits of firms reporting capital of $500 or less

| Industry | 1850 No. of firms | 1850 Average profits ($) | 1880 No. of firms | 1880 Average profits ($) |
|---|---|---|---|---|
| Boots and shoes | 261 | 427 | 287 | 520 |
| Harness | 15 | 341 | 50 | 482 |
| Textiles | 14 | 428 | 5 | 818 |
| Clothing | 73 | 529 | 148 | 674 |
| Baking | 147 | 552 | 308 | 914 |
| Meat | 15 | 650 | 154 | 1,665 |
| Furniture | 34 | 477 | 82 | 637 |
| Blacksmith | 75 | 413 | 116 | 744 |
| Printing | 15 | 816 | 18 | 1,058 |
| Building construction | 50 | 780 | 333 | 877 |
| Hardware | 11 | 638 | 41 | 620 |
| Metal | 21 | 323 | 70 | 631 |
| Machines and tools | 10 | 283 | 21 | 687 |
| Iron and steel | 0 | — | 0 | — |
| All 14 industries | 741 | 482 | 1,633 | 907 |

SOURCES: Census of the U.S., 1850 and 1880.

## Patterns of Occupational Change

Changes in the ethnic composition and occupational distribution of the male labor force accompanied the transformation of Philadelphia's industrial activity.[18] Population doubled between 1850 and 1880, but the city's principal nativity groups–Irish and German immigrants and native-born whites–did not contribute equally to the population growth. Table 25 shows that Philadelphia's male work force grew from 100,404 in 1850 to 215,686 in 1880, an increase of over 100 percent. During this period the Irish maintained their standing as the city's largest immigrant group with 27,152 adult males in 1850 and 39,428 in 1880. But Irish immigration failed to keep pace with the city's expansion, and the Irish fell from 27 percent of the male work force in 1850 to 18

of internal affairs that his yearly income for 1880 was $900 (*Industrial Statistics* 8 [1879–80]:247). This compares favorably with the average profit of small blacksmith firms, which was $744 in 1880 (see Table 24). The same source indicates that foremen in various industries earned daily wages ranging from $2.25 to $6, annual incomes of $675 to $1,800 (ibid., 4 [1875–76]: 546–49 and 9 [1880–81]: 163–65).

[18] Although we have collected data on the occupational patterns of women, they were not available for use in this paper. The discussion in this section, therefore, is based on the male work force above the age of 18.

*Table 25.* Male work force by ethnicity

| | Adult male work force | | | | | | | |
|---|---|---|---|---|---|---|---|---|
| | Black | Irish | Irish 2† | German | German 2† | NWA* | Other 2† | Total |
| 1850 | | | | | | | | |
| Number | 5,071 | 27,152 | – | 11,427 | – | 56,754 | – | 100,404 |
| % of total | 5.1 | 27.0 | – | 11.4 | – | 56.5 | – | 100.0 |
| 1880 | | | | | | | | |
| Number | 9,443 | 39,428 | 24,399 | 27,099 | 13,860 | 87,930 | 13,527 | 215,686 |
| % of total | 4.4 | 18.3 | 11.3 | 12.6 | 6.4 | 40.8 | 6.3 | 100.0 |
| % increase | 86.2 | 45.2 | – | 137.1 | – | 54.9 | – | 114.8 |

SOURCES: Census of the U.S., 1850 and 1880.
NOTE: Only males 18 years and older are included.
*NWA = native white American.
† Irish 2, German 2, and Other 2 identify American-born sons of parent(s) born in Ireland, Germany or other foreign states, respectively.

percent in 1880. German immigrants, on the other hand, increased at the rate of 137 percent, from 11,427 in 1850 to 27,099 in 1880. The number of native white males in Philadelphia increased from 56,754 to 87,930, a rate of increase of 55 percent. Less than half of the native white entrants into the labor force in this period, however, were of native-born parentage. In 1880 there were 24,399 native-born sons of Irish immigrants and 13,860 native-born sons of German immigrants. (The columns headed "Irish 2", "German 2", and "Other 2" in Table 25 give the number of native-born sons with foreign-born parents.)

The proportion of each group which found employment in manufacturing declined between both census years. The Germans showed the smallest decrease (64.1 percent to 61.1 percent) followed by the Irish (40.7 percent to 33.8 percent) and the native whites (53.7 percent to 44.0 percent). The sons of German immigrants were just about as heavily concentrated in manufacturing as their fathers in 1880 (59.7 percent). The sons of Irish immigrants, however, reversed the trend of their fathers and entered manufacturing, so that 47.3 percent of them worked in that sector of the economy in 1880.

What concerns us here are the skilled and unskilled workers employed in our fourteen industries.[19] Occupations in these industries account for slightly less than half the skilled labor force in 1850, slightly more than half of it in 1880. Occupations in the consumer industries–shoemaker, tailor, butcher, and the like–represent a much larger segment of the skilled labor force in both census years than those in the producer industries. In the ensuing three decades, however, they declined from 25.3 percent of the labor force to 23.2 percent, while the occupations in the producer industries increased from 6.9 percent to 8.2 percent of the labor force. And there is every reason to believe that this trend continued, since the metal trades and other producer industries expanded dramatically in the following three decades.

Four consumer industries–meat, baking, printing, and the old metal crafts–increased their share of the labor force. All others lost ground, usually in the neighborhood of 0.5 percent of the total male work force. The most dramatic declines occurred in shoes, whose share of the laboring population fell from 6.2 percent to 3.4 percent, and in clothing, which declined from 3.4 percent to 2.7 percent in 1880 (see Tables 26 and 27). Conversely, the producer industries grew, the only loss coming in

[19] Unskilled labor is of two types: *specified* occupations, such as "watchman," and *unspecified* occupations, such as "laborer," "day labor," "laboring man," etc. Our discussion here focuses on the *unspecified* category "laborer"; that is, occupations whose designation in the population manuscripts do not allow for categorization into an industry category.

*Table 26.* Percentage of ethnic group by industry

| Industry | Irish | Irish 2† | German | German 2† | NWA* | Total |
|---|---|---|---|---|---|---|
| | % of adult male labor force | | | | | |
| Iron & steel | | | | | | |
| 1850 | 0.3 | — | 0.3 | — | 0.9 | 0.6 |
| 1880 | 1.4 | 2.2 | 0.6 | 1.3 | 1.6 | 1.4 |
| Textiles | | | | | | |
| 1850 | 13.0 | — | 2.9 | — | 0.8 | 4.3 |
| 1880 | 4.0 | 6.4 | 3.2 | 2.6 | 1.9 | 3.3 |
| Hardware | | | | | | |
| 1850 | 0.4 | — | 0.7 | — | 0.9 | 0.7 |
| 1880 | 1.1 | 1.6 | 0.8 | 1.8 | 1.2 | 1.2 |
| Machines & tools | | | | | | |
| 1850 | 0.6 | — | 1.4 | — | 1.8 | 1.3 |
| 1880 | 1.1 | 2.4 | 2.3 | 2.4 | 2.9 | 2.3 |
| Printing | | | | | | |
| 1850 | 0.6 | — | 0.9 | — | 2.3 | 1.6 |
| 1880 | 0.7 | 3.2 | 1.3 | 3.1 | 3.3 | 2.4 |
| Bldg. construction | | | | | | |
| 1850 | 4.2 | — | 2.6 | — | 10.2 | 7.4 |
| 1880 | 4.4 | 6.7 | 3.0 | 5.7 | 11.0 | 7.3 |
| Clothing | | | | | | |
| 1850 | 2.9 | — | 8.6 | — | 2.9 | 3.4 |
| 1880 | 1.9 | 1.3 | 8.3 | 3.9 | 1.6 | 2.7 |
| Furniture | | | | | | |
| 1850 | 0.5 | — | 4.7 | — | 1.7 | 1.7 |
| 1880 | 0.4 | 0.6 | 3.7 | 1.7 | 1.3 | 1.4 |
| Metal | | | | | | |
| 1850 | 0.3 | — | 0.5 | — | 0.8 | 0.6 |
| 1880 | 0.4 | 1.4 | 0.9 | 1.3 | 0.9 | 0.9 |
| Harness | | | | | | |
| 1850 | 0.3 | — | 0.5 | — | 0.7 | 0.5 |
| 1880 | 0.3 | 0.1 | 0.4 | 0.1 | 0.3 | 0.3 |
| Baking | | | | | | |
| 1850 | 0.9 | — | 7.8 | — | 1.0 | 1.7 |
| 1880 | 0.6 | 0.3 | 7.7 | 5.1 | 0.7 | 1.8 |
| Boots & shoes | | | | | | |
| 1850 | 5.2 | — | 11.6 | — | 5.9 | 6.2 |
| 1880 | 4.2 | 2.1 | 8.1 | 3.1 | 2.4 | 3.4 |
| Blacksmith | | | | | | |
| 1850 | 1.4 | — | 1.7 | — | 2.0 | 1.7 |
| 1880 | 2.1 | 1.8 | 1.4 | 1.5 | 1.1 | 1.4 |
| Medical/Legal | | | | | | |
| 1850 | 0.3 | — | 0.4 | — | 2.0 | 1.3 |
| 1880 | 0.3 | 1.4 | 0.5 | 1.3 | 2.9 | 1.7 |
| Street trades | | | | | | |
| 1850 | 4.3 | — | 1.0 | — | 1.2 | 2.1 |
| 1880 | 5.1 | 6.4 | 1.6 | 3.1 | 2.7 | 3.5 |

SOURCES: Census of the U.S., 1850 and 1880.
NOTE: Only males 18 years and older are included.
*NWA = native white American
†Irish 2 and German 2 identify American-born sons of parent(s) born in Ireland and Germany, respectively.

textiles, which dropped 1 percent of the labor force between 1850 and 1880 when the hand-loom weaving industry virtually disappeared.

Table 27 displays the occupational distribution of the Irish, German, and native-born groups, and it reveals few surprises. Even by a crude occupational rank order the Irish fare the worst of the three groups in 1850, for nearly half of them were located in day labor (30.3 percent), hand-loom weaving (11.6 percent), and carting (3.3 percent). Less than a third of them worked at skilled trades (excluding hand-loom weavers). The Germans also fulfill our expectations. We know that many of them arrived in America as skilled workers, and it is not surprising to find them less dependent upon unskilled labor and more heavily represented in the skilled trades than the Irish. In 1850 only 11.6 percent of them toiled as day laborers, and nearly two-thirds worked at skilled trades. They were especially prevalent in shoemaking, tailoring, and baking, which together account for one-fifth of the German male labor force (Table 27). The occupational superiority of the native-born whites requires little elaboration. Suffice it to note that they were much less involved in unskilled labor than the other groups, less evident than the Germans in clothing and shoemaking, but more concentrated in the prestigious building trades and printing, and disproportionately represented in commerce and the professions.

Thus at mid-century native-white Americans and German immigrants dominated the most desirable skilled occupations. Heavily involved in printing, building, clothing, and shoemaking, they plied trades which promised fairly high wages and whose skills were just beginning to be diluted by segmentation of task or by machinery. Many of them were extremely articulate, a talent they often parlayed into leadership positions in social organizations, trade unions, and local political parties. Local leaders of some prestige, they easily qualified as the labor aristocracy of their day.[20]

The occupational distribution of the immigrants in 1880 looks much as it did in 1850. Only two changes stand out. About 10 percent of the Irish ceased operating hand looms as weaving finally moved into the factory, and the proportion of German day laborers fell from 11.6 percent to 6.4 percent, an impressive change by any measure. Otherwise there were not striking changes. The Irish were still mired in unskilled labor, the Germans still employed chiefly in traditional crafts.

Upon closer examination, however, Table 27 indicates a trend barely perceptible among the immigrants but apparent in the native whites and native-born sons of immigrants. These groups began to abandon traditional trades in the consumer industries (excluding printing and

[20] See Bruce Laurie, "The Working People of Philadelphia, 1827–1853," Diss. Pittsburgh 1971, chaps. 7, 8, and app. C.

*Table 27.* Percentage of ethnic group by occupation

| | % of adult male labor force | | | | | |
|---|---|---|---|---|---|---|
| Occupation | Irish | Irish 2† | German | German 2† | NWA* | Total |
| Laborer | | | | | | |
| 1850 | 30.3 | – | 11.6 | – | 3.7 | 13.0 |
| 1880 | 30.0 | 14.7 | 6.4 | 6.1 | 5.8 | 12.6 |
| Weaver | | | | | | |
| 1850 | 11.6 | – | 2.4 | – | 0.4 | 3.6 |
| 1880 | 1.6 | 1.7 | 1.1 | 0.9 | 0.2 | 0.9 |
| Dyer | | | | | | |
| 1850 | 0.7 | – | 0.5 | – | 0.2 | 0.4 |
| 1880 | 0.4 | 1.1 | 0.6 | 0.3 | 0.3 | 0.5 |
| Molder | | | | | | |
| 1850 | 0.2 | – | 0.1 | – | 0.5 | 0.4 |
| 1880 | 0.4 | 1.2 | 0.1 | 0.6 | 0.6 | 0.5 |
| Iron molder | | | | | | |
| 1850 | 0.0 | – | 0.0 | – | 0.0 | 0.0 |
| 1880 | 0.2 | 0.4 | 0.1 | 0.3 | 0.3 | 0.3 |
| Boiler maker | | | | | | |
| 1850 | 0.1 | – | 0.1 | – | 0.1 | 0.1 |
| 1880 | 0.5 | 0.3 | 0.2 | 0.2 | 0.2 | 0.2 |
| Machinist | | | | | | |
| 1850 | 1.5 | – | 3.3 | – | 2.7 | 2.3 |
| 1880 | 1.0 | 2.2 | 2.0 | 1.8 | 2.4 | 2.0 |
| Printer | | | | | | |
| 1850 | 0.3 | – | 0.3 | – | 1.2 | 0.8 |
| 1880 | 0.3 | 1.5 | 0.4 | 1.3 | 1.5 | 1.1 |
| Stone mason | | | | | | |
| 1850 | 0.7 | – | 0.3 | – | 0.3 | 0.4 |
| 1880 | 0.8 | 0.2 | 0.6 | 0.2 | 0.2 | 0.4 |
| Plumber | | | | | | |
| 1850 | 0.1 | – | 0.0 | – | 0.2 | 0.1 |
| 1880 | 0.3 | 1.1 | 0.1 | 0.3 | 0.8 | 0.6 |
| Carpenter | | | | | | |
| 1850 | 2.7 | – | 1.6 | – | 6.5 | 4.6 |
| 1880 | 1.9 | 1.7 | 1.6 | 2.1 | 4.3 | 2.8 |
| Painter | | | | | | |
| 1850 | 0.6 | – | 0.7 | – | 1.6 | 1.1 |
| 1880 | 0.6 | 1.2 | 0.6 | 1.3 | 2.0 | 1.3 |
| Bricklayer | | | | | | |
| 1850 | 0.4 | – | 0.1 | – | 1.6 | 1.1 |
| 1880 | 0.4 | 1.2 | 0.2 | 0.3 | 0.9 | 0.7 |

*Table 27. (cont.)*

| | % of adult male labor force | | | | | |
|---|---|---|---|---|---|---|
| Occupation | Irish | Irish 2† | German | German 2† | NWA* | Total |
| Plasterer | | | | | | |
| 1850 | 0.3 | — | 0.0 | — | 0.9 | 0.6 |
| 1880 | 0.4 | 0.6 | 0.0 | 0.3 | 0.7 | 0.5 |
| Tailor | | | | | | |
| 1850 | 2.4 | — | 7.4 | — | 1.9 | 2.6 |
| 1880 | 1.3 | 0.2 | 6.4 | 2.0 | 0.5 | 1.5 |
| Turner | | | | | | |
| 1850 | 0.1 | — | 0.7 | — | 0.3 | 0.3 |
| 1880 | 0.0 | — | 0.1 | 0.2 | 0.1 | 0.1 |
| Varnisher | | | | | | |
| 1850 | 0.1 | — | 0.1 | — | 0.1 | 0.1 |
| 1880 | 0.1 | 0.2 | 0.2 | 0.4 | 0.1 | 0.1 |
| Cabinetmaker | | | | | | |
| 1850 | 0.4 | — | 4.0 | — | 1.1 | 1.2 |
| 1880 | 0.1 | 0.2 | 2.9 | 1.2 | 0.6 | 0.8 |
| Locksmith | | | | | | |
| 1850 | 0.1 | — | 0.6 | — | 0.1 | 0.2 |
| 1880 | 0.0 | — | 0.4 | 0.2 | 0.1 | 0.1 |
| Tinsmith | | | | | | |
| 1850 | 0.1 | — | 0.3 | — | 0.2 | 0.2 |
| 1880 | 0.3 | 1.0 | 0.6 | 0.5 | 0.6 | 0.6 |
| Butcher | | | | | | |
| 1850 | 0.1 | — | 1.0 | — | 0.7 | 0.5 |
| 1880 | 0.3 | 0.7 | 3.5 | 3.5 | 1.5 | 1.5 |
| Harness maker | | | | | | |
| 1850 | 0.1 | — | 0.1 | — | 0.1 | 0.1 |
| 1880 | 0.2 | 0.1 | 0.3 | — | 0.2 | 0.2 |
| Saddler | | | | | | |
| 1850 | 0.2 | — | 0.4 | — | 0.6 | 0.4 |
| 1880 | 0.1 | — | 0.1 | 0.1 | 0.1 | 0.1 |
| Baker | | | | | | |
| 1850 | 0.8 | — | 6.3 | — | 0.5 | 1.2 |
| 1880 | 0.5 | 0.3 | 5.4 | 3.5 | 0.3 | 1.2 |
| Shoemaker | | | | | | |
| 1850 | 3.5 | — | 7.4 | — | 4.2 | 4.2 |
| 1880 | 3.2 | 1.3 | 6.5 | 2.2 | 1.4 | 2.4 |
| Blacksmith | | | | | | |
| 1850 | 1.4 | — | 1.8 | — | 2.0 | 1.7 |
| 1880 | 2.0 | 1.8 | 1.4 | 1.4 | 1.1 | 1.3 |

*Table 27. (cont.)*

| | % of adult male labor force | | | | | |
|---|---|---|---|---|---|---|
| Occupation | Irish | Irish 2† | German | German 2† | NWA* | Total |
| Lawyer | | | | | | |
| 1850 | 0.1 | — | 0.0 | — | 0.9 | 0.6 |
| 1880 | 0.1 | 0.6 | 0.0 | 0.3 | 1.0 | 0.5 |
| Doctor | | | | | | |
| 1850 | 0.1 | — | 0.3 | — | 1.1 | 0.7 |
| 1880 | 0.1 | 0.3 | 0.4 | 0.6 | 1.5 | 0.8 |
| Clerk | | | | | | |
| 1850 | 1.5 | — | 1.2 | — | 5.0 | 3.4 |
| 1880 | 0.3 | 2.3 | 0.4 | 2.4 | 3.8 | 2.2 |
| Drayman | | | | | | |
| 1850 | 1.0 | — | 0.4 | — | 0.1 | 0.4 |
| 1880 | 0.3 | 0.1 | 0.0 | — | 0.0 | 0.1 |
| Ostler | | | | | | |
| 1850 | 0.6 | — | 0.7 | — | 0.2 | 0.4 |
| 1880 | 0.6 | 0.0 | 1.0 | 0.2 | 0.2 | 0.4 |
| Carter | | | | | | |
| 1850 | 3.3 | — | 1.4 | — | 0.9 | 1.6 |
| 1880 | 1.0 | 0.6 | 0.2 | 0.6 | 0.2 | 0.5 |
| Teamster | | | | | | |
| 1850 | 0.0 | — | 0.0 | — | 0.1 | 0.0 |
| 1880 | 1.2 | 1.6 | 0.4 | 1.3 | 0.9 | 1.0 |

SOURCES: Census of the U.S., 1850 and 1880.
NOTE: Only males 18 years and older are included.
*NWA = native white American
† Irish 2 and German 2 identify American-born sons of parent(s) born in Ireland and Germany, respectively

building trades), though they did so at slightly different rates. The desertion of sons of Germans is most impressive, for only 15.7 percent of them plied these trades compared to 30.1 percent of the 1850 immigrant cohort, a shift of 52.7 percent. The sons of Irish immigrants and native-born whites followed close behind and displayed shifts of 47.5 percent and 29.4 percent, respectively. In 1880 only 5.7 percent of the sons of Irish immigrants and 6.6 percent of the native whites worked at these trades. It is perhaps ironic, but in the occupations of the consumer industries, the Irish sons and the native whites resemble one another more than the Germans. German immigrants were so concentrated in these crafts in 1850 and 1880 that their native-born sons constituted a sizable residual force despite the alacrity with which they abandoned the handicrafts.

An even broader parallel between the occupational distributions of the sons of immigrants and native whites emerges when we examine the ethnic composition of printing and the building trades. Unlike other older crafts, these trades still commanded relatively high wages in 1880. All of the groups entered the expanding printing industry in this period, but setting type was more of a magnet for the immigrant sons. The proportion of printers in the native white population increased by only 0.3 percent (from 1.2 percent to 1.5 percent, see Table 27), and the immigrant proportions hardly changed at all. The sons of immigrants, however, entered printing more rapidly than the native whites and more easily than their fathers, and achieved parity with the native whites by 1880. In building construction the three native-born groups began to converge. The percentage of native whites declined from 11.1 percent in 1850 to 8.9 percent in 1880, while large numbers of immigrant sons became building tradesmen. Six percent of the Irish sons, for example, worked at skilled construction trades compared to 4.8 percent of the 1850 Irish cohort; the proportion of German sons in building was 4.6 percent, almost two percentage points higher than the Germans in 1850.

The sons of Irish immigrants also gained access to the prestigious jobs in the new metal industries. Slightly over 4 percent of them, compared to 1.8 percent of the 1850 cohort, plied skilled trades in machine shops, iron foundries, and rolling mills. Indeed, they had a higher proportion in these trades in 1880 than both the native whites (3.5 percent) and the sons of German immigrants (2.9 percent).

By 1880 German immigrants and their sons had as low a proportion of their numbers in casual labor as the native whites (roughly 6 percent). The percentage of native white day laborers actually increased between 1850 and 1880 (from 3.7 percent to 5.8 percent), probably as a result of in-migration from rural areas. A sizable share of Irish-born Philadelphians (30.0 percent) still worked as unskilled laborers in 1880, but casual labor was not as appealing to their sons. Only 14.7 percent of them were so employed in 1880. It appears, then, that the position of unskilled Irish sons paralleled that of skilled German sons in the traditional consumer crafts. Each group rapidly deserted the sphere of its fathers, but Irish immigrants were so dependent upon casual labor and German immigrants so concentrated in the older crafts that their sons could not help but remain heavily represented in those occupations.

## Conclusion

The evidence presented here warrants two concluding observations and invites speculation about the relationship between immigrants, occupations, and industrial change. First, it is evident that the occupational distribution of Irish and German immigrants did not change significantly between 1850 and 1880. Aside from the Irish retreat from hand-loom weaving, which was not a matter of choice but a necessity since the industry disappeared, and the German shift out of day labor, each group clustered in the same occupations in 1850 and 1880.

The occupational distribution of these immigrants had less to do with the conditions in America than with prior experience in the Old World. Rural, underdeveloped Ireland bequeathed her sons very little in the way of industrial experience or skill, which forced Irish immigrants in Philadelphia to assume positions at the bottom of the occupational hierarchy. They entered either day labor, occupations easily learned such as hand-loom weaving or shoebinding, or street trades that required no skill and small capital investment. Germans who left their country in the midst of the Industrial Revolution brought skills with them, and it is fitting that we find the majority of them in skilled trades, especially in shoemaking, tailoring, and baking in 1850 and 1880.

A combination of factors made it difficult for immigrants to take advantage of opportunities and shift into more rewarding occupations. Nativist feelings, which ran high in Philadelphia after the anti-Catholic riots of 1844 and which were directed chiefly against the Irish, probably inspired some employers to reserve the most remunerative jobs for native-born Americans. Germans could have been victimized by nativism to some extent as well, though one suspects that they had peculiar reasons not to seek new opportunities. Many of them left for America expressly to practice trades which were threatened by technology in the homeland. Wedded to the traditional crafts by habit and custom, they were not especially disposed to forsake the trades they valued so highly.[21] Shifting into new occupations also necessitated acquiring skills, which took time and commitment, and German and Irish immigrants were much older than the native-born population in 1880. Well into their careers, they could not easily shift into more desirable jobs.

Second, our analysis of industrial change runs counter to the view held by many historians, who see this period as an "age of industrialization," animated by the rapid and wholesale application of steam power and technological improvements.[22] This essential misunderstanding derives from equating industrialization with mechanization. The use of

[21] Mack Walker, *Germany and the Emigration, 1816–1885* (Cambridge, Mass., 1964), p. 69.

[22] See, for example, Thomas C. Cochran and William Miller, *The Age of Enterprise*, rev. ed. (New York, 1961), p. 223; Ray Ginger, *Age of Excess* (New York, 1965), pp. 35–36; and Carl N. Degler, *The Age of the Economic Revolution, 1876–1900* (Glenview, Ill., 1967), p. 34.

mechanized production techniques constitutes only a single *stage* (with greater import for the economics than the sociology of industrialization), which occurred relatively late in the process of industrialization. John R. Commons's classic study of the shoe industry made clear that significant changes in the organization of work, authority relationships, and production techniques transformed the role of the craftsman long before mechanization was introduced.[23]

Towns like Fall River, Mass., or Johnstown, Pa., which housed textile factories and iron and steel mills, shifted to mechanization early and rapidly. Perhaps the dramatic nature of the industrial change experienced by towns dominated by a single industry explains why some historians have mistakenly equated industrialization and mechanization. But in a large city with a diversified economy like Philadelphia, which produced everything from silk hankerchiefs to iron rails, the complexity and unevenness of industrial development precludes such a view.

In Philadelphia mechanization did not reach much beyond heavy industry and textiles, which we referred to earlier as producer industries. Modern though they were, these pursuits employed a relatively small proportion of the manual labor force. Most of the city's male manual workers were located in the consumer industries, which were not as mechanized as we have been led to believe. Still, significant changes did occur. Between 1850 and 1880 these industries underwent considerable division of labor, used the latest handtools, employed larger numbers of workers per firm, and produced their goods in factories, even though they did not rely upon independent power supplies. It was not unusual in the 1870s, for example, for 150 shoemakers to be working under one roof without steam power.

Such transformations in the premechanized stages of work occurred at different times in different industries in different cities. A host of factors influenced these changes: the state and cost of local technology and the expertise of local craftsmen in fashioning new tools and machines; the strength of organized labor; the level of skills, availability, and ethnic composition of the labor force. In some industries innovations were so gradual that workers experienced no great or abrupt changes in procedures and work methods. Other industries changed more rapidly, which forced workingmen to make major adjustments to new methods. Whatever the case, it seems that the most important developments in authority relationships and work-roles occurred before mechanization. The independent craftsman or skilled worker, in other words, was not reduced to the factory operative in one fell swoop. A major challenge

[23] John R. Commons, "American Shoemakers, 1848–1895," *Quarterly Journal of Economics* 24 (1910): 39–84.

facing historians will be to comprehend the socioeconomic consequences of such incremental changes for those who worked in this period of premechanized industrialization.

The nature of industrial change in Philadelphia, coupled with the occupational careers of its immigrants, sheds some light on our limited understanding of occupations and job mobility. All too often we treat skill as an absolute and assume that an occupation is either skilled or it is not, that a man who calls himself a tailor, carpenter, or butcher is a skilled worker. It should be clear, however, that skill is relative in that one skilled occupation may require more skill than another, though we hasten to add that measuring the differences is extremely difficult. It should also be evident that the skill level of an occupation changes over time as do wage rates and the immediate environment of the workplace. We know, for example, that occupations such as butchering, tailoring, and shoemaking changed considerably relative to newer occupations in Philadelphia between 1850 and 1880. Division of labor diluted skills, sweatshops with rigorous work routines emerged, wages declined, and career opportunities for workingmen were limited because these operations lacked an articulate occupational hierarchy. The reverse occurred in the new metal trades, where both skilled and unskilled workers commanded relatively high wages, skill was at a premium, and career opportunities were probably good because of the developed occupational hierarchy.

All of which is to say that we must not assume that all skilled occupations were equally desirable or inherently *better* than unskilled occupations. Skilled jobs generally commanded higher wages in the period under discussion, but the wage differential between skilled and unskilled labor is not so great as we have been led to believe. The line between these occupational groups blurs when we introduce the variable of shop size, for we find that wages of "skilled" workers in small shops in select consumer industries were hardly better than wages of "ordinary" workers in the largest shops in the new metal trades. Judging from wage rates presented in Table 21, moreover, it appears that there was as great a differential among rates paid to skilled workers as there was between the wages of the lowest paid skilled workers and unskilled laborers. Jobs in the consumer industries were even less desirable from the standpoint of career potential. Many of them were a dead end, and no one realized this more than the sons of immigrants.

If we regard career potential as an important component of occupation, then it behooves us to rethink our stereotype of unskilled labor. We might consider the possibility that German immigrants were not that much better off than their Irish counterparts simply because they were more likely to be skilled workers.[24] German immigrants were locked into declining crafts. Just as large numbers of Irish sons remained in day labor where their fathers were so heavily concentrated, the sons of German immigrants were still located principally in the crafts in 1880. But many of these first-generation Americans perceived that better opportunities lay in the developing industries and assumed skilled jobs in printing, building construction, and heavy industry.

The means by which the sons of immigrants moved into these occupations is not known since we have not yet traced the careers of individuals. But we cannot resist the temptation to speculate that the Irish immigrant's lack of skills was not so great a disadvantage to their sons as has been thought.[25] It seems that the crucial occupation designation is "laborer," which we normally associate with deprivation—low status, low wages, and limited career potential—and usually locate at the bottom of the occupational rank order. The problem with this assessment is that it fails to consider the career potential of some day laborers employed in building construction and the metal trades.[26] These laborers may have been

[24] If the ownership of real property is considered as a measure of well-being, this possibility gains support. Although the proportion of Germans who were skilled workers was *twice* that of the Irish, the Germans were only 20 percent more likely to own real property. In 1870, 16.2 percent of the Germans and 13.6 percent of the Irish owned real property (these figures are age-standardized).

[25] Stephan Thernstrom, *Poverty and Progress* (Cambridge, Mass., 1964), pp. 99–102, 109–11, 155–57.

[26] The problem, of course, is how operationally to differentiate among this large group of workers. The population census manuscripts do not provide any information beyond the designation "laborer" that can be used to resolve this problem. Although the manufacturing census manuscripts contain information which explicitly and implicitly describes the work environment, they do not list by name the individuals employed by each firm. Taken alone, neither of these two sources of information is useful in overcoming the problem at hand. But if they can be combined in some fashion, it may be possible to differentiate among laborers.

The Philadelphia Social History Project has worked out a method ("industrial geography") which links the residence of the individual worker to the location of the individual firm in which he may have worked (this method is not limited to laborers but can be used in the linkage of any worker to any firm). Laborers who lived within roughly a two-block radius (empirically derived) of the firm are identified as likely to have worked in the firm, and their careers are treated separately in analysis. A profile of their well-being, including ownership of real and personal property, whether wives worked and children attended school, can be constructed and compared to profiles of other groups of laborers. The profiles of laborers who are identified as employed by firms paying high wages, for example, should be better than those of laborers who were linked to firms paying low wages or to undifferentiated laborers who probably were employed on a very casual basis. This method of linking individuals to the firms in which they may have worked will be most successful in the outlying areas of the city where heavy industry was located and where identification of potential employees will not be complicated by the dense concentration of people and firms at the city's center. "Industrial geography" is discussed in greater detail in Theodore Hershberg, "The Philadelphia Social History Project: A Methodological History," Diss. Stanford 1973.

engaged in on-the-job training, or what we should like to call "informal apprenticeship."[27] Toiling beside skilled workers on construction sites and in foundries and machine shops, they probably learned how to perform highly skilled jobs, which they later practiced as skilled workers. German sons followed a similar career pattern, but did so more slowly, partly because they did not have as much access as their Irish counterparts to the informal training ground of unskilled labor.[28]

By 1880, then, we find that the sons of Irish and German immigrants have begun to abandon occupations in the consumer industries and have gained a foothold in skilled occupations in printing, building construction, and the new metal industries. By entering these trades, they established themselves as labor aristocrats, an honor previously held by native-born Americans and some German immigrants. In abandoning the older crafts, they made room for the new immigrants who flocked to meat packing, the needle trades, and to unskilled positions in the iron and steel industry at the turn of the century.

[27] See, for example, Robert Tressel, *The Ragged Trousered Philanthropists* (London, 1971), p. 15, and Sidney Pollard, *A History of Labour in Sheffield* (Liverpool, 1959), p. 84.

[28] See the proportion of Irish and German sons with occupations in building construction, new metal trades and printing (Tables 26 and 27).

# IX Ethnicity and Occupation in the Mid-Nineteenth Century: Irish, Germans, and Native-born Whites in Buffalo, New York

*Laurence Glasco*

WE ARE INCREASINGLY well informed about the rates and patterns of occupational mobility in nineteenth-century America, and even of some of the ethnic factors underlying that mobility. We know relatively little, however, about the ethnic and demographic characteristics of the occupational *structure* through which such individuals were moving, and we know even less about how ethnic occupational differences affected other areas of life—property ownership and family structure, for example.

The present paper, using the Irish, Germans, and native-born whites of Buffalo as a case study, will examine three aspects of the relationship between ethnicity and occupation in the mid-nineteenth century. First, it will describe how the city's occupations were divided along ethnic lines and will suggest the operation of a mechanism of ethnic dominance/ exclusion in the labor market. The second part of the paper, after grouping occupations into broad levels of skill, will examine the ways in which the occupational skill level of each group was related to two demographic factors—age and persistence. The third part of the paper will demonstrate the degree to which ethnic differences in three areas—property ownership, family structure, and fertility rates—transcended rather than simply reflected ethnic differences in occupation and socioeconomic status.

## The City: An Overview

Like many other northern cities in the middle of the nineteenth century, Buffalo was undergoing extraordinarily rapid growth. Between 1845 and 1855 its population more than doubled, from fewer than 30,000 to more than 70,000 inhabitants in just a decade, making it one of the fastest growing cities in the nation.

Buffalo's growth depended on two basic factors. The first derived from its strategic position at the western terminus of the nation's major inland transportation route. The Erie Canal, that fabulous waterway along which flowed an ever-increasing volume of goods, transected the state of New York and served as the link between America's seaboard cities and its vast agricultural hinterland. As the newly opened regions of Ohio, Michigan, Indiana, Illinois, and Wisconsin developed in the late 1830s, 1840s, and 1850s, Buffalo became the breakpoint for their goods, the point at which they were transferred from lake boats to canal barges for shipment further east. By 1854 the city's papers were boasting that Buffalo had surpassed Chicago, Odessa, Galatz, and Saint Petersburg as the leading grain port in the world.

During the late 1840s and 1850s Buffalo's economy began to diversify, and by 1855 it included a substantial and rapidly growing manufacturing component. The development of the city's manufacturing sector had been retarded earlier by a lack of cheap power—the surrounding region lacked coal and sufficient waterpower. However, the completion of a rail link with the bituminous coal region of Pennsylvania assured the rapid development of the city's iron industry, supplementing its earlier tanning and shipbuilding industries.

As one of the nation's leading commercial centers and with a healthy and rapidly expanding manufacturing sector, Buffalo's economy generated an enormous demand for labor, both manual and nonmanual. The commercial houses, operated by wealthy commission merchants—the men who contracted for the output of western grain producers—employed numerous clerks and other white-collar workers who handled the voluminous paperwork. The grain elevators, which stored the produce, and the canal barges and lake ships, which carried it, provided jobs for a small army of unskilled and semiskilled laborers. Finally, the rapid population growth itself provided a demand for a wide range of secondary occupations—from carpenters to build houses to grocers to supply food to tailors to make clothing.

Shortly after 1845 the pace of Buffalo's growth and the character of its population changed dramatically. Up to that time Buffalo had experienced a rather steady flow of in-migrants, primarily native-born New Yorkers and a few Germans. Severe economic dislocations in Europe, culminating in the disastrous potato harvests of the 1840s, uprooted millions of Europeans, particularly in Ireland and Germany. As these dislodged peasants and artisans took flight to America, they hit the east coast of the United States in a wave that spilled westward across a wide swath of the northeast. Located directly in the path of that great population flow, Buffalo saw its already sizable foreign-born population skyrocket. By 1855, when the flow subsided, Buffalo was no longer an "American" city. In that year three-fourths of its adult population was foreign-born. Native-born whites made up less than a quarter of the adult population;

the Irish comprised a fifth; and both were overshadowed by the German-speaking element, which comprised almost half of the city's adults. These three populations formed over 80 percent of the family heads and together constituted the principal cleavages within the city's trisected occupational structure.[1]

## Occupational Structure and Ethnicity

The New York State manuscript census provides a detailed picture of the occupational structure of Buffalo in 1855. A display of the occupational distribution of the city's family heads shows that about 21 percent had no occupation at the time (or the census taker failed to record the occupation), while another 50 percent were distributed among only 32 occupations (see Table 28).[2] The percentage of family heads for each ethnic group having no listed occupation ranged from 30 percent of the Germans to 33 percent of the native-born to nearly half (45 percent) of the Irish (see Table 29). My first suspicion, that these might have represented something of an "underclass," without occupation or means of support, was not borne out in subsequent analysis.[3]

Ethnic differences in skill level reflected the fact that occupations were not distributed evenly among the groups (see Table 30). Usually one of the three major ethnic groups was either overrepresented or severely underrepresented in a given occupation. The native-born, perhaps not surprisingly, dominated the white-collar and professional occupations, comprising over half of the clerks, two-thirds of the retail merchants, wholesalers, commission merchants, and physicians, as well as over four-fifths of the lawyers. This domination of white-collar occupations did not carry over into the crafts, however; of the skilled trades the native-born were overrepresented only among the mechanics. Only among a handful

[1] English and Canadians made up most of the rest; blacks comprised less than 1 percent. The vast majority of the city's Irish were Catholics from southern Ireland; very few Ulster Irish came to Buffalo. For every German coming from the northern Protestant regions, there were two from southern, predominantly Catholic regions. See Glasco, "Ethnicity and Social Structure: Irish, Germans, and Native-born of Buffalo, N.Y., 1850–1860," Diss. Buffalo 1973.

[2] The following analysis is based on family heads, not on the total male work force of the city. A family was defined as two or more persons related by blood or marriage and living in the same household. It was possible to identify such family units because the census specified the relationship of each person to the head of the household. There were 15,392 family heads in the city, most of whom were household heads. This figure excludes wives, children, and most of the following: unmarried relatives living in the household, servants (most of whom were young girls), and some 4,300 of the 4,700 boarders (most of whom were native-born males).

[3] See Glasco, chap. 2.

*Table 28.* Major occupations of family heads

| Occupation | Family head No. | Family head % | Assigned skill level* |
|---|---|---|---|
| None or not given | 3,220 | 20.9 | — |
| Laborer | 2,105 | 13.7 | Unskilled |
| Carpenter | 1,042 | 6.8 | Skilled |
| Tailor | 560 | 3.6 | Skilled |
| Shoemaker | 405 | 2.6 | Skilled |
| Grocer | 327 | 2.1 | Entrepreneur |
| Merchant (unspecified) | 292 | 1.9 | Entrepreneur |
| Sailor | 226 | 1.5 | Semiskilled |
| Farmer | 225 | 1.5 | Entrepreneur |
| Painter | 225 | 1.5 | Skilled |
| Clerk | 212 | 1.4 | Nonmanual |
| Smelter | 176 | 1.1 | Semiskilled |
| Butcher | 163 | 1.1 | Skilled |
| Cooper | 161 | 1.1 | Skilled |
| Blacksmith | 151 | 1.0 | Skilled |
| Ship carpenter | 151 | 1.0 | Skilled |
| Teamster | 140 | 1.0 | Semiskilled |
| Mechanic | 132 | 0.9 | Skilled |
| Lawyer | 124 | 0.8 | Nonmanual |
| Engineer | 124 | 0.8 | Nonmanual |
| Gardener | 100 | 0.7 | Unskilled |
| Physician | 95 | 0.6 | Nonmanual |
| Commission merchant | 94 | 0.6 | Nonmanual |
| Cabinetmaker | 93 | 0.6 | Skilled |
| Boardinghouse keeper | 85 | 0.6 | Nonmanual |
| Baker | 82 | 0.5 | Skilled |
| Servant | 80 | 0.5 | Unskilled |
| Tanner | 72 | 0.5 | Skilled |
| Bookkeeper | 70 | 0.5 | Nonmanual |
| Molder | 69 | 0.5 | Skilled |
| Wagon man | 67 | 0.4 | Semiskilled |
| Others; misc. | 4,324 | 28.1 | — |
| Total | 15,392 | 100.0 | |

SOURCE: Data compiled from the New York State Manuscript Census for 1855.

* Persons listed in the 1855 Buffalo City Directory as having their own shops are categorized as entrepreneurs in this table.

*Table 29.* Occupational skill level

| Level | % of Family Heads Native-born | Irish | German |
|---|---|---|---|
| Not given | 33.3 | 44.9 | 30.0 |
| Unskilled | 2.3 | 22.5 | 22.5 |
| Semiskilled | 8.8 | 8.6 | 12.3 |
| Skilled | 21.7 | 16.4 | 36.9 |
| Master craftsman | 0.1 | 0.0 | 0.0 |
| Foreman | 0.6 | 0.1 | 0.0 |
| Nonmanual | 12.9 | 2.3 | 2.4 |
| Clerk | 5.8 | 1.2 | 0.7 |
| Sales | 3.2 | 0.8 | 0.9 |
| Entrepreneur | 9.8 | 2.7 | 2.9 |
| Manager | 0.5 | 0.0 | 0.0 |
| Total | 100.0 | 100.0 | 100.0 |

Source: N.Y. Manuscript Census, 1855.

of other manual occupations were the native-born even represented proportionate to their numbers in the city.

Virtually all of the crafts were dominated by the Germans, who comprised at least 70 percent of the masons, coopers, and shoemakers, and at least 60 percent of the cabinetmakers, tailors, butchers, and ironworkers. Because the Germans made up almost 40 percent of the city's population, one could expect them to form nearly half of any occupation, but in many crafts their dominance went even further, constituting something approaching a monopoly. The Irish, on the other hand, dominated no single occupation but formed a disproportionate percentage of the unskilled laborers, domestics, sailors, and ship carpenters, and comprised 45 percent of the teamsters.[4]

An ethnic group that did not dominate a given occupation often was severely underrepresented. The Germans and Irish were almost totally missing from the white-collar and professional occupations. Germans were virtually unrepresented among the sailors and ship carpenters; the Irish were missing from among the farm laborers and gardeners. The native-born were missing among the unskilled laborers, servants, gardeners, and most of the skilled crafts, except for the painters and machinists.

Some occupations were dominated not by one ethnic group but by two. In such cases usually the native-born were combined with one of the

[4] Unless otherwise specified, "German" refers to persons born in Germany or in one of the provinces that later were incorporated into the German nation. It excludes the French, most of whom were German-speaking Alsatians.

*Table 30.* Occupation by ethnicity

| Occupation | % of family heads Native-born | Irish | German | Other Imm. | Un-known | Total |
|---|---|---|---|---|---|---|
| Farmer/farm laborer | 25.8 | 6.7 | 33.8 | 12.9 | 20.8 | 100 |
| Laborer (unspecified) | 2.5 | 25.9 | 58.8 | 7.3 | 5.5 | 100 |
| Servant/domestic | 10.1 | 34.2 | 36.7 | 12.7 | 6.3 | 100 |
| Gardener | 6.0 | 7.0 | 48.0 | 33.0 | 6.0 | 100 |
| Teamster | 19.3 | 45.0 | 19.3 | 12.9 | 3.5 | 100 |
| Sailor | 27.2 | 30.4 | 10.3 | 26.8 | 5.3 | 100 |
| Ship carpenter | 22.5 | 37.1 | 8.6 | 30.5 | 1.3 | 100 |
| Carpenter | 16.9 | 9.4 | 50.0 | 16.7 | 7.0 | 100 |
| Brickmason | 4.1 | 8.7 | 70.0 | 8.4 | 8.8 | 100 |
| Painter | 25.3 | 8.4 | 40.0 | 21.3 | 5.0 | 100 |
| Cabinetmaker | 11.8 | 5.4 | 65.6 | 10.8 | 6.4 | 100 |
| Cooper | 6.3 | 8.1 | 74.4 | 3.8 | 7.4 | 100 |
| Tailor | 7.2 | 6.4 | 68.0 | 11.3 | 7.1 | 100 |
| Shoemaker | 4.2 | 6.9 | 76.7 | 7.9 | 4.3 | 100 |
| Butcher | 6.9 | 3.1 | 66.3 | 18.8 | 4.9 | 100 |
| Blacksmith | 13.2 | 21.2 | 37.1 | 23.8 | 4.7 | 100 |
| Mechanic | 31.8 | 10.9 | 28.7 | 23.3 | 5.3 | 100 |
| Smelter | 7.4 | 11.4 | 59.7 | 13.1 | 8.4 | 100 |
| Grocer | 20.2 | 18.3 | 41.4 | 8.0 | 12.1 | 100 |
| Merchant (retail) | 66.1 | 3.8 | 8.9 | 14.0 | 7.2 | 100 |
| Clerk | 52.8 | 9.4 | 13.7 | 18.9 | 5.2 | 100 |
| Lawyer | 86.3 | 1.6 | 2.4 | 9.7 | 0.0 | 100 |
| Engineer (unspecified) | 45.2 | 10.5 | 10.5 | 31.5 | 2.3 | 100 |
| Physician | 66.3 | 5.3 | 13.7 | 11.6 | 3.1 | 100 |
| Merchant (wholesale) | 67.0 | 5.3 | 5.3 | 22.3 | 0.1 | 100 |

SOURCE: N.Y. Manuscript Census, 1855.

major immigrant groups, with the other immigrant group largely excluded. Thus, the native-born and Irish dominated among sailors and ship carpenters; the native-born and other immigrants (mainly English) dominated among the clerks, engineers, and commission merchants. Foreign-born groups together dominated only in the menial occupations; the Irish and Germans constituted a clear preponderance among unskilled laborers and servants.

These ethnic patterns of dominance / avoidance produced corresponding differences in the occupational structure of each group (Table 29). Not surprisingly, a much higher proportion of the native-born were in professional and white-collar occupations than the others. Nearly a third of the native-born were so classified, compared to less than ten percent of the Irish and Germans. Similarly, a much smaller percentage of the native-born were in the lowest occupational range; less than 12 percent were unskilled and semiskilled, compared to about one-third of the Irish and Germans. An astoundingly low percentage of the native-born family heads (about 2 percent) were unskilled, compared to one-fourth of the Irish and Germans. Among skilled workers the native-born (with 22 percent) were significantly below the Germans (37 percent) and had only a moderately higher percentage than the Irish, with only 16 percent.

This description of the ethnic distribution of occupations and levels of skill presents a basically static picture. It can take on dynamic qualities, however, if we examine how such patterns were related to demographic factors, in particular to age and length of residence in the city. We need to know, for example, whether there were changes in occupational structure such that the young and those recently arrived in the city concentrated in unskilled occupations, while those who were older or present longer had made a move upward into skilled or white-collar occupations. In the following analysis, therefore, we will examine the effects of age and length of residence separately, and then in combination for each ethnic group. The aim will be to see what effects these two demographic factors had on the degree of occupational variation within each group and what effects it had on modifying ethnic differences in occupational level of skill.[5]

## The Effects of Age and Persistence

Except for the Germans, age had only a marginal effect on the level of skill distribution. Thus, a native-born white worker was neither more nor less likely than his older counterpart to be either an unskilled, semiskilled, or skilled worker. Only among white-collar occupations was there a difference: younger native-born family heads (in their twenties, thirties, and forties) were somewhat more likely to be clerks and nonmanual workers, while older family heads (men in their fifties and sixties) were more likely to be clerks and nonmanual workers, while older family heads (men in their fifties and sixties) were more likely to be entrepreneurs (see Table 31 and Fig. 1).

There were so few Irish in nonmanual occupations that age differences were unimportant. Age, moreover, did not make any difference among the semiskilled or skilled occupational categories. For the Irish only among unskilled workers and among those without any listed occupation do we find age differences—and even there the differences are incon-

[5] The occupations were classified as shown in Table 28.

*Table 31.* Level of skill by age of family head

| | % of family heads | | | | | | No. of family heads |
|---|---|---|---|---|---|---|---|
| | Age | | | | | | |
| Skill Level | 10–19 | 20–29 | 30–39 | 40–49 | 50–59 | 60–69 | |
| Native-born | | | | | | | |
| Level not given | 78.4 | 22.7 | 24.6 | 27.8 | 28.7 | 45.5 | 845 |
| Unskilled | – | 4.2 | 2.7 | 0.5 | 2.9 | 0.6 | 72 |
| Semiskilled | 3.9 | 13.6 | 10.8 | 8.2 | 6.8 | 5.8 | 302 |
| Skilled | 3.9 | 24.5 | 22.7 | 24.8 | 24.7 | 16.9 | 715 |
| Master craftsman | 2.0 | 1.0 | 0.8 | 0.5 | 1.8 | – | 27 |
| Undetermined* | 2.0 | 1.3 | 0.6 | 0.5 | 1.3 | – | 25 |
| Clerk; nonmanual | 7.8 | 24.8 | 26.5 | 26.3 | 19.2 | 18.8 | 754 |
| Entrepreneur | 2.0 | 7.8 | 11.3 | 11.4 | 14.5 | 12.3 | 336 |
| Total | 100.0 | 100.0 | 100.0 | 100.0 | 100.0 | 100.0 | 3,076 |
| Irish | | | | | | | |
| Level not given | 73.9 | 38.4 | 39.5 | 32.4 | 36.0 | 44.1 | 873 |
| Unskilled | 13.0 | 21.0 | 22.4 | 31.3 | 32.4 | 26.9 | 575 |
| Semiskilled | – | 12.4 | 9.5 | 8.5 | 7.7 | 7.5 | 224 |
| Skilled | 8.7 | 19.9 | 20.1 | 16.9 | 18.0 | 16.1 | 435 |
| Master craftsman | – | 0.2 | 0.1 | 0.4 | – | – | 4 |
| Undetermined* | – | 0.5 | 0.2 | 1.2 | – | 1.1 | 12 |
| Clerk; nonmanual | 4.3 | 5.7 | 5.8 | 5.8 | 3.2 | 3.2 | 110 |
| Entrepreneur | – | 1.9 | 3.8 | 3.5 | 2.7 | 1.1 | 69 |
| Total | 100.0 | 100.0 | 100.0 | 100.0 | 100.0 | 100.0 | 2,302 |
| Germans | | | | | | | |
| Level not given | 43.5 | 15.9 | 15.5 | 15.8 | 21.1 | 35.5 | 958 |
| Unskilled | 13.0 | 18.4 | 21.2 | 29.2 | 31.6 | 28.5 | 1,310 |
| Semiskilled | 13.0 | 15.3 | 13.3 | 11.7 | 12.2 | 5.7 | 730 |
| Skilled | 26.1 | 43.9 | 41.9 | 34.9 | 29.6 | 24.1 | 2,178 |
| Master craftsman | – | – | 0.1 | – | – | – | 2 |
| Undetermined* | 4.3 | 0.4 | 0.2 | 0.5 | – | – | 17 |
| Clerk; nonmanual | – | 4.4 | 4.3 | 4.1 | 2.5 | 2.6 | 224 |
| Entrepreneur | – | 1.8 | 3.5 | 3.7 | 3.1 | 3.5 | 171 |
| Total | 100.0 | 100.0 | 100.0 | 100.0 | 100.0 | 100.0 | 5,590 |

SOURCE: N.Y. Manuscript Census, 1855.
* Census description too vague to assign a skill level.

Fig. 1: Occupational skill level by age of family head

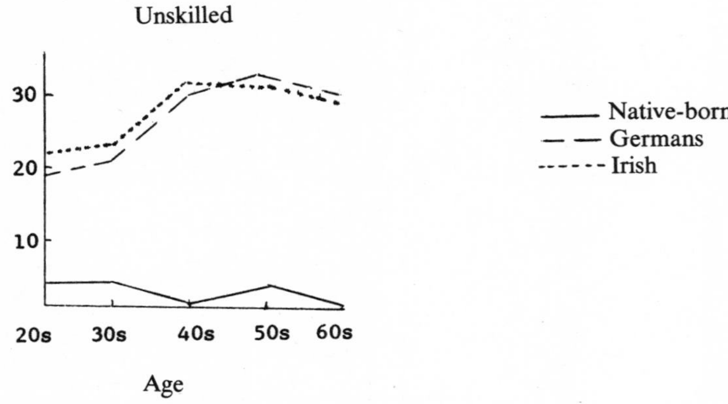

Fig. 1. *(cont.)*

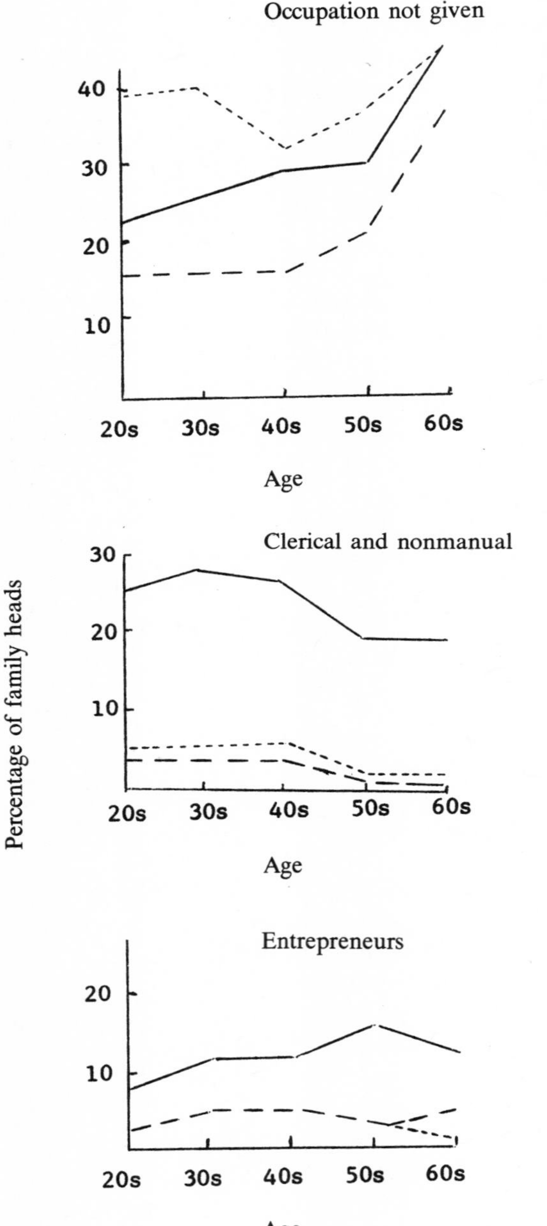

Occupation not given
40
30
20
10
20s
30s
40s
50s
60s
Age
Native-bor
Germans
Irish
Clerical and nonmanual
30
20
10
Percentage of family heads
20s
30s
40s
50s
60s
Age
Entrepreneurs
20
10
20s
30s
40s
50s
60s
Age

clusive. Thus, older men constituted a substantially greater proportion of unskilled workers, but a correspondingly *lower* proportion of workers without any listed occupation at all.

Only among the German manual workers did age make a substantial impact on the occupational structure. Not only was an older German substantially more likely to be unskilled than his younger counterpart, he was also less likely to be a skilled worker. The reasons for this are not altogether clear, but several possibilities come to mind. Could it have been that advancing age brought a decline in health and strength, causing older Germans to lose their perhaps tenuous grip on a particular niche in the occupational structure and fall downward into the unskilled, day laboring class? Did age differences reflect the greater ability of younger, more flexible workers to move upward into skilled work? Or had the *type* of emigrant changed, such that earlier (older) immigrants had come to the country largely unskilled, while more recent (younger) immigrants had left Germany with a greater assortment of skills?

The fact that the Irish display no corresponding drop in the proportion of skilled workers with increasing age casts doubt on the "declining strength" thesis. The percentage of skilled workers among the Irish varied between 15 percent and 20 percent for all age groups from those in their twenties to those in their sixties, and it is difficult to conceive of the age / health relationship being markedly different among the Germans.

An examination of persistence—the length of residence in the city—adds insight to the situation, however (see Figs. 2–4). Among native-born whites length of residence in the city made only a moderate impact on the occupational distribution by age, and then primarily among the clerical / white-collar and entrepreneurial types of occupation. Similarly for the Irish, length of residence did little to modify the age distribution of occupational skills.

It was among the Germans, again, that persistence had the greatest interrelationship with age in affecting level of occupational skill. This is most dramatically seen among skilled workers. Younger family heads, in their twenties and thirties, showed no consistent, substantial change in percentage of skilled workers *regardless* of when they arrived in the city.[6] Older family heads, however, present less than 10 years, had a much lower percentage of skilled workers than did their more early-arrived counterparts. This reveals a sharp break in the pre- and post-blight migration. Only among the latter was there a sharp age difference in the skill level of German immigrants. This age difference was not the result of a greater

[6] There is a sharp drop in the percentage of skilled workers among the twenty-year-olds living in Buffalo 15 to 19 years, which may be a function of small cell sizes.

Fig. 2: Native-born: Occupational skill level by persistence, controlling for age

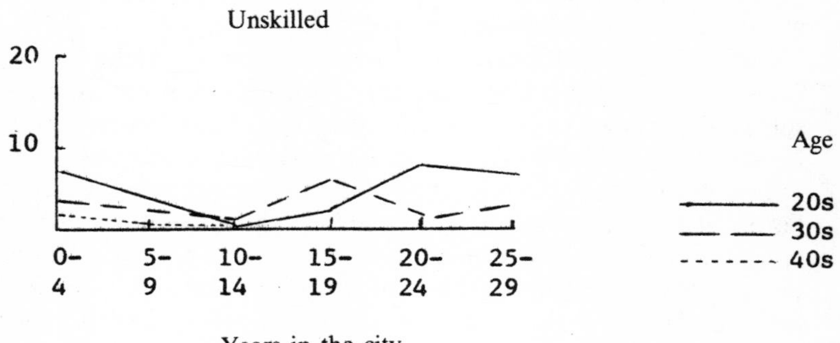


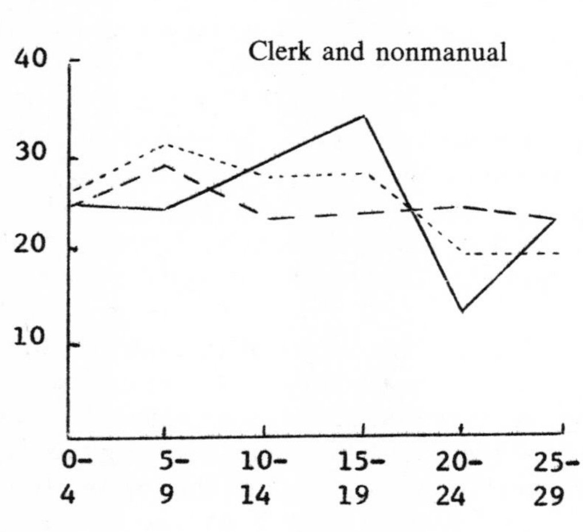


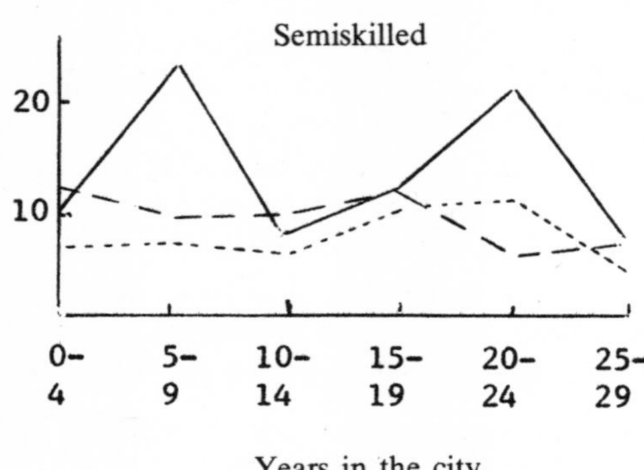

Fig. 2. *(cont.)*

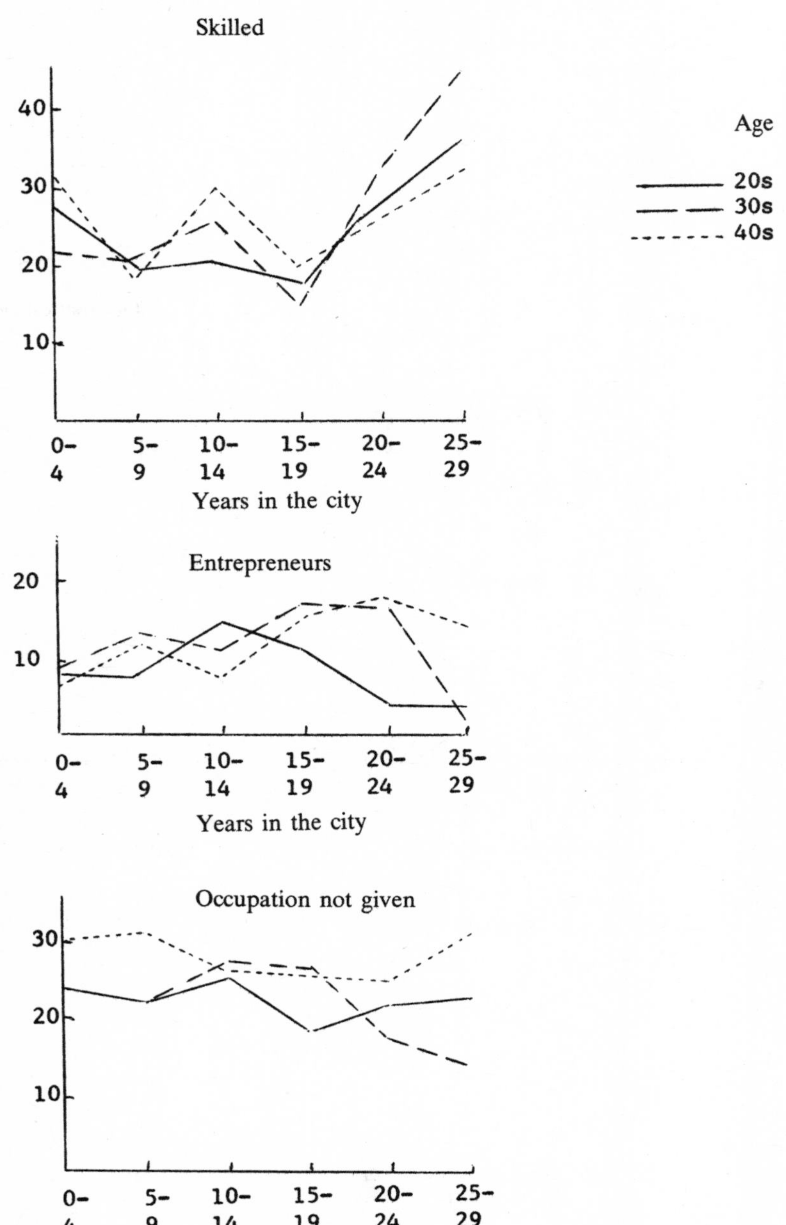
Skilled
40
30
20
10
0-
4
5-
9
10-
14
15-
19
20-
24
25-
29
Years in the city
Age
20s
30s
40s
Percentage of family heads: Native-born
Entrepreneurs
20
10
0-
4
5-
9
10-
14
15-
19
20-
24
25-
29
Years in the city
Occupation not given
30
20
10
0-
4
5-
9
10-
14
15-
19
20-
24
25-
29
Years in the city

Fig. 3: Irish: Occupational skill level by persistence, controlling for age

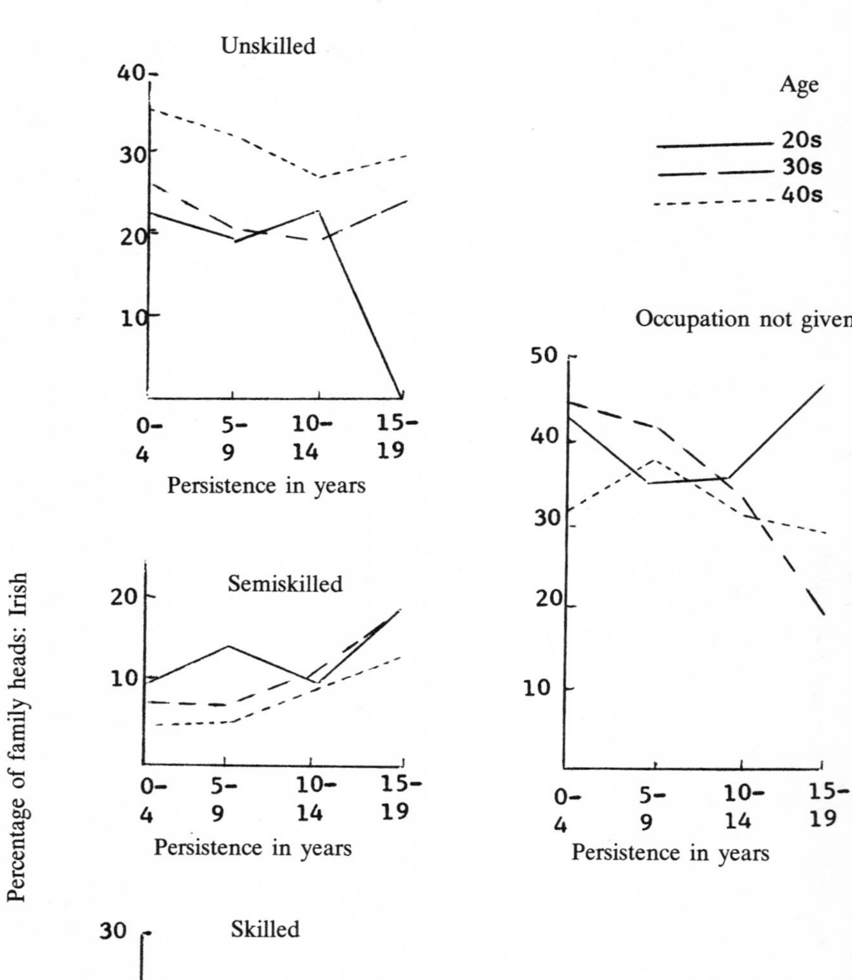

Fig. 4: Germans: Occupational skill level by persistence, controlling for age

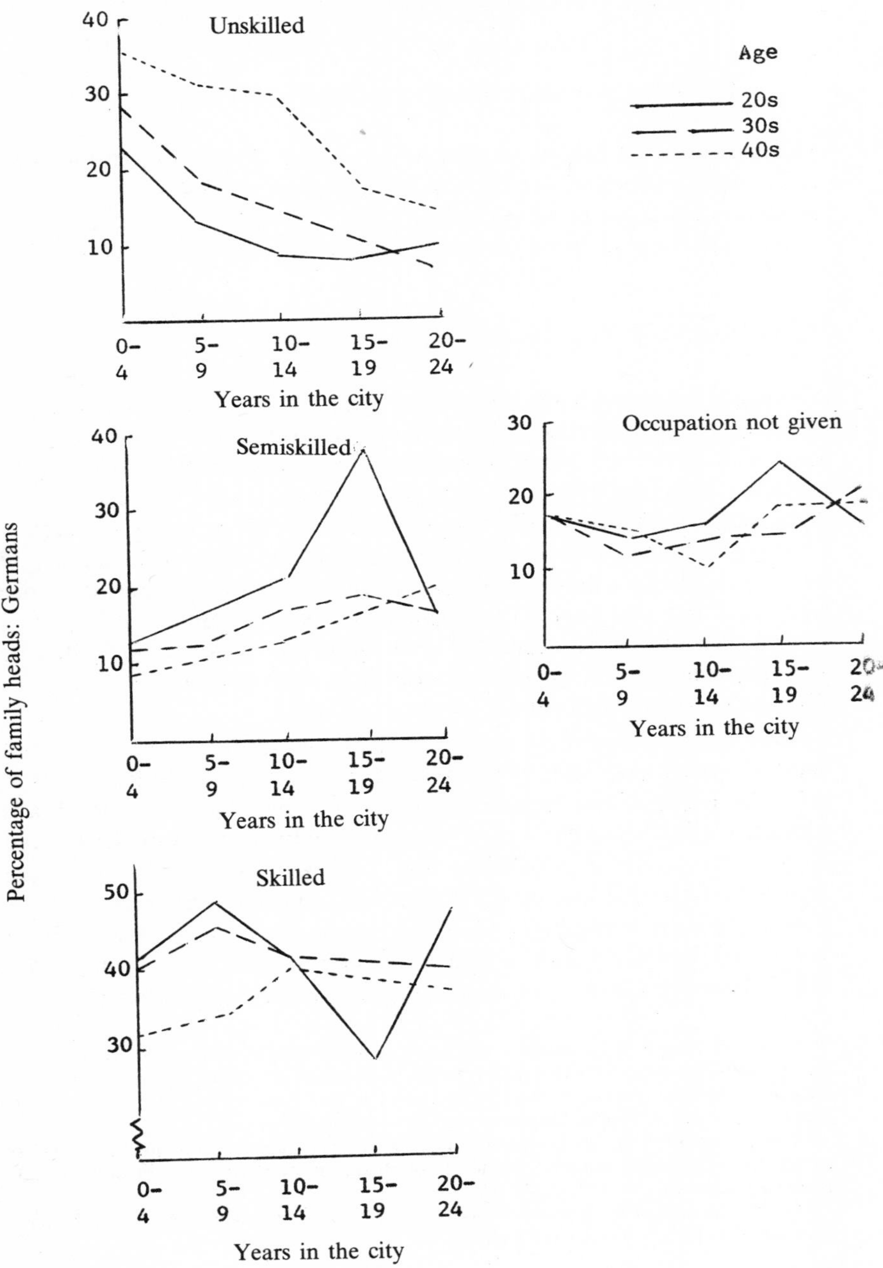

influx of young family heads arriving *with* skills, but rather of a sharp increase in the proportion of older family heads migrating *without* skills.[7]

## Property Ownership, Family Structure, and Fertility Rates

Having examined the ethnic and demographic dimensions to the city's occupational structure, let us now turn to an investigation of the consequences of those occupational patterns, specifically their impact on ethnic patterns of property ownership, family structure, and childbearing.

### Level of Skill and Property Ownership

Obviously, an individual's level of skill greatly influenced his chances of owning property. The assumption that a craftsman, for example, would have a much better chance of earning the income to purchase a house than, say, an unskilled worker, held true for Buffalo (see Table 32). However, increasing skill level did not uniformly increase property ownership. The largest increase in property ownership occurred between unskilled and semiskilled workers. Between semiskilled and skilled workers the difference was much less pronounced; the percentage of nonmanual workers who owned property was considerably lower than that of skilled ones; finally, entrepreneurs showed the highest percentage of property owners, between 50 percent and 60 percent for all three groups.[8]

Even allowing for differences in age, length of residence in the city and level of occupational skill by no means eliminate all ethnic differences in terms of patterns and degree of property ownership. Thus, Germans almost invariably had the highest proportion of property owners, followed by the native-born and Irish (see Figs. 5, 6, and 7).[9] If we try to locate factors that affected interethnic differences, additional patterns emerge. First, differences between the Irish and the other groups (the Germans in particular) increased with length of residence and level of skill and diminished with age. This becomes clear when one compares the property-

[7] Of course, length of residence in the city was not the same as length of residence in the country. However, an examination of the birthplaces of immigrant children shows virtually all to have been born either in Europe or in Erie County (Buffalo). This suggests that most families arrived in Buffalo soon after coming to America.

[8] Those without a listed occupation had either the same percentage of property owners as did unskilled workers (Germans), or slightly more (Irish), or even substantially more (native-born).

[9] Graphs have not been prepared for white-collar workers among the immigrants because their numbers were too small for analysis.

*Table 32.* Property ownership by skill level

| Skill level | % of family heads Native-born | Irish | Germans |
|---|---|---|---|
| Not given | 36.1 | 18.5 | 31.1 |
| Unskilled | 26.4 | 17.0 | 32.2 |
| Semiskilled | 38.3 | 33.0 | 40.9 |
| Skilled | 43.2 | 33.1 | 45.7 |
| Clerk; nonmanual | 36.0 | 31.6 | 36.0 |
| Retail merchant | 57.6 | 58.0 | 53.2 |

SOURCE: N.Y. Manuscript Census, 1855.

owning curves for unskilled family heads in their thirties and forties with semiskilled family heads in their twenties and thirties. Differences for the native-born were not quite so sharp, but again, in comparison with the Germans, differences tended to increase with age and persistence, but not so much with increasing level of skill.

## Socio-Economic Status and Household Structure

With these observations in mind, we can now turn to an examination of ethnic family and household structure, testing the relative effects of these class / occupational differences on such cultural patterns. Such an examination shows that although the nuclear household was the typical living arrangement for all of Buffalo's ethnic groups, the native-born were much more likely to take in both relatives and boarders than were the foreign-born. Thus, some twenty-five percent of native-born households had at least one relative living with them, compared to only 15 percent of Irish and 6 percent of German households. Similarly, 22 percent of native-born households had boarders living with them, compared to less than 3 percent of Irish and German households. Finally, some 40 percent of native-born households had a servant living in, compared to 10 percent and 7 percent of Irish and German households.[10]

The question naturally arises as to what extent these ethnic differences in household structure stemmed from class factors. Taking occupational level of skill as a readily available, although imperfect, indicator of class levels, Table 33 addresses this question. The occupations have been arranged roughly in order of skill and status, from unskilled to skilled to clerical to entrepreneurial and professional. Although the cell sizes are too

[10] Glasco, pp . 152–59.

Fig. 5: Property ownership by persistence, controlling for age: Unskilled

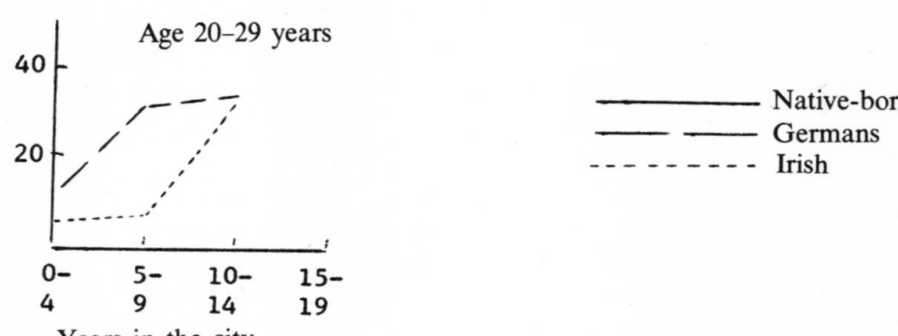


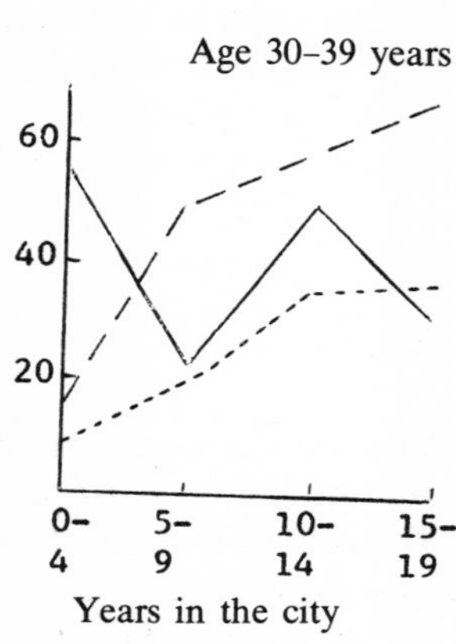


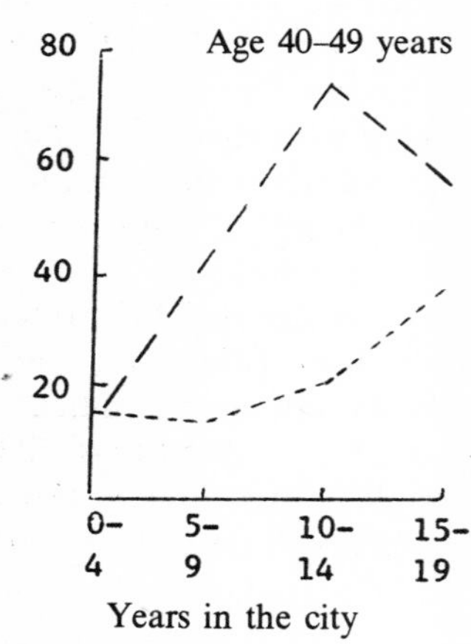

Fig. 6: Property ownership by persistence, controlling for age: Semiskilled

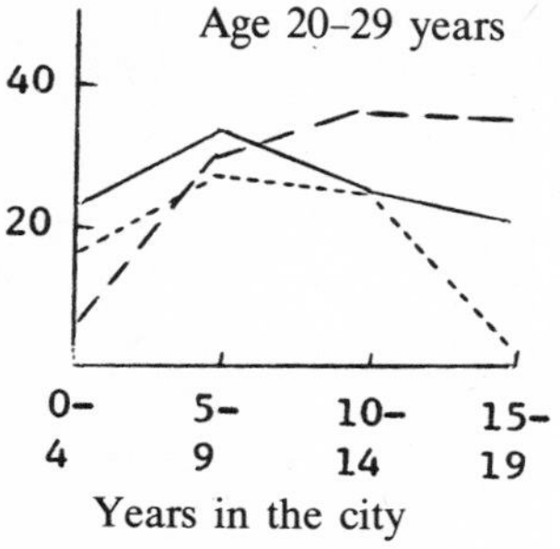


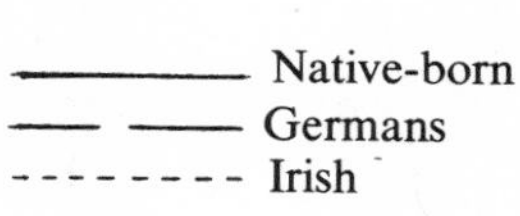


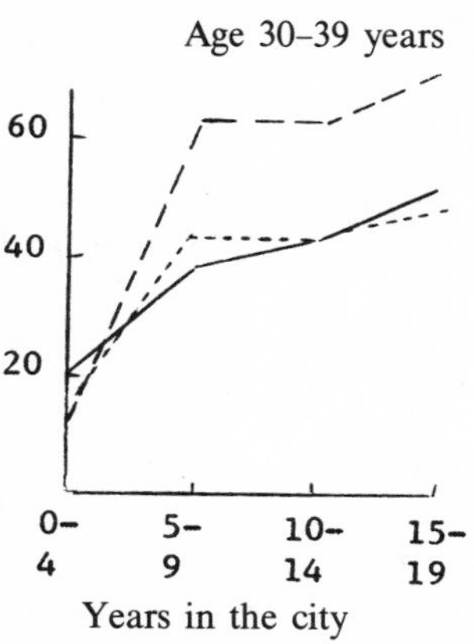


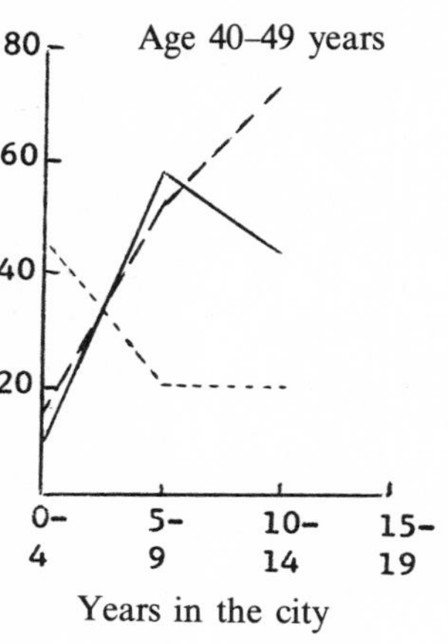

Fig. 7: Property ownership by persistence, controlling for age: Skilled

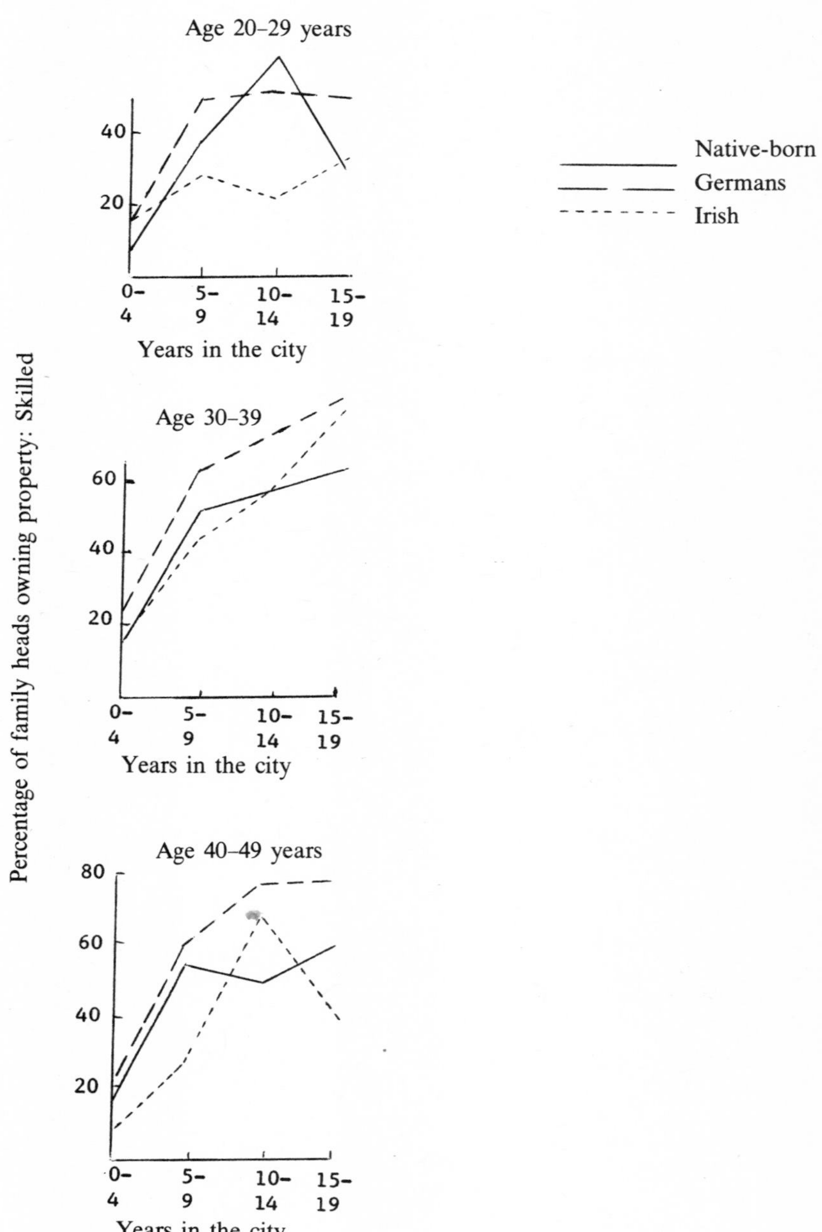

*Table 33.* Family type by occupation of family head

| | % of families | | | | | | | | | | | |
|---|---|---|---|---|---|---|---|---|---|---|---|---|
| Occupation | Native-born | | | | Irish | | | | Germans | | | |
| of family head | Nucl. | Extn. | Aug. | No. | Nucl. | Extn. | Aug. | No. | Nucl. | Extn. | Aug. | No. |
| Laborer | 80.0 | 0.0 | 20.0 | 5 | 67.3 | 21.5 | 8.4 | 105 | 93.9 | 4.6 | 1.5 | 131 |
| Sailor | 53.8 | 23.1 | 23.1 | 13 | 66.7 | 19.0 | 14.3 | 21 | — | — | — | — |
| Carpenter | 74.2 | 6.5 | 16.1 | 31 | 78.6 | 7.1 | 14.3 | 14 | 85.3 | 2.9 | 11.8 | 68 |
| Painter | 61.5 | 7.7 | 30.8 | 13 | 66.7 | 16.7 | 16.7 | 6 | 77.8 | 11.1 | 11.1 | 9 |
| Machinist | 44.4 | 11.1 | 44.4 | 9 | 75.0 | — | 25.0 | 4 | — | — | — | — |
| Clerk | 40.8 | 22.2 | 37.0 | 27 | 33.3 | 66.7 | — | 6 | 60.0 | — | 40.0 | 5 |
| Grocer | 60.0 | 26.7 | 13.3 | 15 | 78.6 | 21.4 | — | 14 | 64.6 | 5.9 | 29.4 | 17 |
| Retail merchant | 41.8 | 32.6 | 25.6 | 43 | 60.0 | 20.0 | 20.0 | 5 | 83.3 | — | 16.7 | 6 |
| Commission merchant | 35.3 | 17.6 | 47.0 | 17 | — | — | — | — | — | — | — | — |
| Lawyer | 31.6 | 31.6 | 31.6 | 19 | — | — | — | — | — | — | — | — |
| Physician | 66.7 | — | 33.3 | 9 | — | — | — | — | — | — | — | — |

SOURCE: N.Y. Manuscript Census, 1855.

small to be more than suggestive, they reveal that, for the native-born, class made a significant difference. Persons in white-collar occupations generally were more likely to live in an extended household than those in bluecollar occupations. The exceptions were sailors, who had an unusually high percentage of extended households, and commission merchants, who had an unusually low percentage.

So few Irish and Germans had white-collar employment that only one occupation, grocers, occurred in our sample with enough frequency to permit analysis, yet even here we find interesting differences. Table 33 shows that for the Irish and Germans the pattern we observed for the native-born dissolves: grocers were no more likely to have an extended family situation than were unskilled or skilled workers, and in a number of cases for the Germans they had considerably fewer. Thus, whereas for the native-born the extended family was a middle-class phenomenon, this was not so for the immigrants, among whom class and family structure were not related.

Unfortunately, these figures do not permit us to say whether these household characteristics were simply a consequence of migration; whether, regardless of the socioeconomic status of the immigrants, the fact that they had recently been uprooted and transported over a long distance meant that they simply had not had time to reestablish their kin network. There are certain clues that can help us to decide, however: in particular, the fact that a substantially greater percentage of Irish households had relatives present (15 percent) than did German households (6 percent). Moreover, on the average the Irish had been in the city for a shorter period (7 years) than the Germans (8 years). These figures suggest that immigrant household patterns reflect something more than just class and migration factors.

## Fertility and Occupation

Just as there were substantial ethnic differences in household structure, so with the rate of reproduction. The fertility rate—the number of children aged 0-4 years per 1,000 women aged 15-44 years—for the Irish and Germans, at 1,000, was almost double the rate for the native-born whites (585).[11]

Such differences were not simply a function of age differences. We do not have the ages of the spouses, but among the family heads, less than two years separated the Irish and Germans (36.2 and 37.3 years, respectively) from the native-born (38.5 years). It is possible, however, that they reflected

[11] Ibid., p. 167.

class differences. After all, the native-born predominated in the white-collar occupations, the Germans in the crafts, and the Irish in unskilled labor. Moreover, there is a popular notion today that the fertility rates of middle-class families is lower than that of the lower classes.[12] Table 34 is designed to probe that question. In it the fertility rate is calculated for each ethnic group while controlling for the occupational level of skill of the family head. The table shows two remarkable patterns. First, among the native-born, class indeed was related to fertility. Wives of unskilled native-born workers had the highest rate of any group, and blue-collar occupations in general had a higher rate than white-collar groups. This is what we might expect. When we turn to the foreign-born, however, the pattern is *reversed*. Among the Irish, wives of salesmen and agents had the highest rate; among the Germans, wives of entrepreneurs and retail merchants shared that honor. Among the foreign-born, then, white-collar families displayed a higher rate than blue-collar. Differences among the ethnic groups transcended class lines; within each occupational level of skill the Irish and Germans displayed a higher fertility rate than the native-born. This demonstrates two things: class differentials among the immigrants were not related to infant mortality, and in all of this we are dealing with cultural as well as class differences.

*Table 34.* Number of children aged 0–4 years per 1,000 women aged 14–55 years, according to husband's level of skill

| Skill level | Native-born | Irish | Germans |
|---|---|---|---|
| Unskilled | 793 | 1,000 | 947 |
| Semiskilled | 691 | 891 | 1,060 |
| Skilled | 721 | 1,030 | 1,047 |
| Nonmanual | 630 | 866 | 873 |
| Clerk | 673 | 1,300 | 1,085 |
| Agent | 560 | 1,250 | 1,091 |
| Entrepreneur | 685 | 931 | 1,129 |

Source: N.Y. Manuscript Census, 1855.

[12] Wilson H. Grabill, Clyde V. Kiser, and Pascall H. Whelpton, *The Fertility of American Women* (New York, 1958), pp. 127–29, 155–65; E. A. Wrigley, *Population and History* (New York, 1969), pp. 186–87.

## Conclusions and Implications

These patterns of occupation and property structure show that although commerce, manufacturing, and construction determined the range of occupations, ethnicity clearly affected their allocation. Each ethnic group had a niche carved out of the city's occupational pyramid, producing a pattern in which a group either dominated or was severely underrepresented in an occupation. The native-born dominated the professional, clerical, and entrepreneurial occupations, the Germans dominated the crafts, and the Germans and Irish together dominated the unskilled occupations. Similarly, the native-born had relatively few skilled workers, except among the sailors, painters, and mechanics, and almost no unskilled laborers; the Irish and Germans had very few clerks and retail merchants, and almost no professionals. These ethnic occupational distributions were largely unaffected by age or length of residence in the city, with the substantial exception of the Germans.

Property ownership, like occupational distribution, showed sharp ethnic differences. In this case, however, the Germans and native-born stood apart from the Irish. The former two groups had an astonishingly high percentage of property owners, 40 percent compared to the 20 percent or so for the Irish. If the occupational structure was closed so that changes in age or length of residence only slightly affected one's occupational chances, the reverse was true of property ownership. The paths to ownership were varied. Occupation vitally affected the patterns, with a clearly increasing percentage of ownership among unskilled, semi-skilled, and skilled workers, culminating not surprisingly among entrepreneurs. Similarly, age and length of residence had a positive relationship. It is important to note, however, that such factors reduced, but by no means eliminated, ethnic differences in ownership. That is, differences in age, occupation, and length of residence in the city did not eliminate the consistent hierarchy in percentage ownership, starting with the Germans, descending to the native-born and ending with the Irish.

The broader implications of these patterns of occupational and property structure are several. First, the fact that the occupational distribution was generally unaffected by age or length of residence in the city meant that recent migrants were not particularly a depressed class; occupationally they may not have been better off than their older, more settled counterparts, but neither were they particularly worse off. Second, the pattern of ethnic occupational niches implies that, as with residential patterns, most ethnic displacement and succession had been completed by 1855, simply because immigration was off and there were so few still to be displaced. Similarly, overt job competition would have been minimized among the groups. Third, property ownership was quite accessible and, given its positive relationship to age, persistence, and skill level, a highly desired goal for all ethnic groups.

The different ethnic patterns of household structure and fertility rates serve as a useful counterpoint to the patterns of property ownership. That is, with increasing occupational skill, each group demonstrated a higher degree of property ownership, even though overall ethnic differences in degree of ownership were not always reduced or eliminated—even allowing for age and persistence factors as well as occupation. When we look at household structure and fertility rates, we see that ethnic differences existed not just in degree but in direction as well. Thus, among the native-born whites, household structure responded to socioeconomic status; among the foreign-born it did not. Fertility rates of the native-born declined among families of higher socioeconomic status; among the foreign-born the trend was either inconclusive or just the opposite. All of this serves to highlight the complexity of both the cause and the consequences of ethnic occupational structures in the mid-nineteenth-century city.

# X The "Old" Immigration and Industrialization: A Case Study

*Clyde Griffen*

THE COINCIDENCE OF heavy immigration with increasing scale and specialization in manufacturing has long encouraged an oversimplified view of immigrant adaptation in American cities during the middle decades of the nineteenth century. Viewing the artisan shop as obsolete and the big factory as the wave of the future, historians have emphasized the stimulus abundant unskilled immigrant labor gave to capital intensification.[1] This emphasis has seemed appropriate because so many foreigners reported no skilled occupation upon arrival and because some of them soon found employment in the nation's biggest factories. The Irish presence in New England manufacturing, especially in mill towns like Lowell and Lawrence, captured the attention of contemporaries and historians.

Unfortunately, the traditional analyses are predicated on an exaggerated notion of the dominance of the factory before 1870, a notion that obscures the role of immigrant labor in the early stages of industrial development. In the 1850s, for example, Edward Everett Hale anticipated the focus of subsequent interpretations of the relationship between immigration and industrialization when he described the famine refugees as providing cheap labor to extend the factory system, thereby increasing opportunities for natives as inventors, superintendents, foremen, machinists, and other more highly skilled workers.[2] From the beginning, however, this focus has coexisted with a mass of evidence indicating a much more complex

I am indebted to Sally Griffen, my collaborator on the Poughkeepsie project, for assistance with both analysis and presentation; our forthcoming book (Harvard University Press) is entitled *Natives and Newcomers: The Ordering of Opportunity in Poughkeepsie, New york, 1850–1880.* I have benefited from the criticism of members of the Columbia University Seminar on the City as well as of participants in the Immigrants in Industrial America conference, who heard earlier and quite different versions. A National Science Foundation Grant supported the project.

[1] See Brinley Thomas, *Migration and Economic Growth* (Cambridge, Eng., 1954), pp. 166–67, and George Rogers Taylor's remarks on immigration, in David T. Gilchrist and W. David Lewis, eds., *Economic Change in the Civil War Era* (Greenville, Del., 1965), pp. 16–17.

[2] Oscar Handlin, *Boston's Immigrants; A Study in Acculturation,* rev. ed. (New York, 1968), p. 84.

relationship. Native artisans in the big cities protested bitterly during the forties against competition from immigrants in their trades; indeed, the surplus of artisans resulting from immigration encouraged division of labor even in the absence of mechanization. That this competition endured after the Civil War is evidenced by an 1869 report to the British parliament which observed that "the foreign is everyday replacing native skilled labor" in the United States.[3]

Not all of the Irish who engaged in manufacturing here came without skills or entered factories; more important, German and British immigrants comprised a higher proportion of industrial workers than the Irish in many cities during the middle decades. They predominated most frequently in the Middle Atlantic States, which consistently exceeded New England in value of manufacturing product, total number of hands employed, and also prevalence of small shop manufacturing as judged by average number of employees per firm.[4] Worthington Ford of the State Department's Bureau of Statistics was only one among many contemporaries who commented on "the remarkable predominance of the United Kingdon and Germany in supplying the United States with skilled labor."[5] Ford identified the English with the rapidly expanding and technologically sophisticated producer-goods industries and the Germans with the consumer-goods industries, especially the traditional handicrafts.

Recent research adds new evidence of complexity in the process of industrialization and in the relationship of immigration to it. It has demonstrated that factories remained decidedly atypical in manufacturing before 1870. It has also emphasized the persistence of an artisan culture in the United States, especially among immigrants; it has documented the coexistence of old and new methods and of small shops and factories within the same manufacturing industries.[6] But we have yet to refine adequately the usual scenario in which cheap immigrant labor extends the

[3] Edith Abbott, ed., *Historical Aspects of the Immigration Problem: Select Documents* (Chicago, 1926), p. 383.

[4] In the 1870 census, the average number of hands per manufacturing establishment in the five Middle Atlantic states was less than three-fifths of the average in the six New England states; average capital and product value were about two-thirds (computation from Table 96: Manufactures by Totals of States and Territories, 1870, in *Compendium of the Ninth Census* [Washington, D.C., 1872], pp. 796–97).

[5] Abbott, *Documents*, p. 389.

[6] See, for example, David S. Landes, *The Unbound Prometheus: Technological Change and Industrial Development in Western Europe from 1750 to the Present* (Cambridge, Eng., 1969); W. Paul Strassmann, *Risk and Technological Innovation: American Manufacturing Methods during the Nineteenth Century* (Ithaca, N.Y., 1959); Richard L. Ehrlich, "The Development of Manufacturing in Selected Counties in the Erie Canal Corridor, 1815–1860," Diss. Buffalo 1972, pp. 111–12; Herbert G. Gutman, "Work, Culture, and Society in Industrializing America, 1815–1919," *American Historical Review* 78 (1973): 541–71.

factory system, hastens the destruction of the older system of artisan manufacture, and results fairly quickly in a new industrial stratification along ethnic lines. Moreover, we have not progressed much beyond Worthington Ford in exploring what the variations in occupational concentration between immigrant groups reveal about their adaptation to an industrializing society.

However, the basis for an improved understanding of these matters has been established in the past decade by social mobility studies for individual communities that have pointed up one major methodological limitation of all previous investigations of how American workers adapted to a changing economy.[7] Even the best earlier community studies, including those that focused upon immigrants, relied upon aggregate analysis of population enumerations at one point in time. Lacking any systematic tracking of individuals through successive enumerations, they could not describe the *process* of change in individual occupations and industries and in the labor force as a whole. As recent studies focusing on mobility suggest, this shortcoming can be eliminated by the technique of tracing, which permits the measurement of change over time.

Tracing allows us to determine the loss of workers in any occupation due to retirement, death, emigration, and shifts to other jobs within the city. It allows us to measure the recruitment of new workers in any occupation and to determine the relative contribution of foreign and native-born workers new to the city, young residents new to the labor market, and old residents new to the occupation. Tracing also permits comparison of fathers' and sons' careers to find out when major differences between generations begin.[8]

The initial association of tracing as a method of investigation with the study of residential and vertical social mobility is only the beginning of its potential usefulness to historians. Those who start with a primary interest in social fluidity soon find that the results of their tracing force them to ask new questions which lead beyond that interest. Thus, my own discovery that foreign artisans who appeared in Poughkeepsie, New York, initially as journeymen were, in many trades, more likely to open their

[7] Stephan Thernstrom, "Reflections on the New Urban History," *Daedalus* 100 (1971): 359–75, especially p. 364; for a comparison of some results of occupational mobility studies thus far, see Thernstrom's *The Other Bostonians: Poverty and Progress in the American Metropolis, 1880–1970* (Cambridge, Mass., 1973), chap. 9.

[8] The meaning of occupational continuity or change is neither self-evident nor stable over time; adequate interpretation still depends upon the quality of evidence available in manufacturing censuses, newspapers, firm histories, credit reports, and other sources of information on the wages, skills, and working conditions associated with particular occupations at particular times and places. The more the historian can identify workers with individual firms through payrolls or city directories, the more useful specific information on an occupation in any community becomes.

own shops than natives made me wonder about the significance of this self-employment. What kind of adaptation did it represent in an age of increasing scale and specialization in manufacturing? Did it promise prosperity in either the short or the long run, or was it economically marginal and anachronistic?

Similarly, the frequency of both sons and daughters of native craftsmen and of Irish laborers in new factories opened in the seventies made me wonder whether factory employment leveled up or down. Discovery that skilled craftsmen, regardless of national origin, rarely entered these new factories made me wonder further whether the transition from artisan to factory manufacture was accomplished largely by a shift between generations in type of employment. Questions like these forced me to ask whether we might not learn more about the economic adaptation of immigrants by focusing on the circumstances of specific kinds of employment rather than dwelling on frequencies of mobility between occupational strata that may have been defined on the basis of perceptions of both status and financial return which do not adequately represent nineteenth-century realities.[9]

The purpose of the present essay is to show how tracing the male labor force of one city, Poughkeepsie, N.Y., can help provide answers to the queries posed above and in so doing can help refine our picture of the relationships between immigration and industrialization at mid-century. Tracing for this small city confirmed many, but not all, of the impressions gained from previous snapshots by statisticians and historians, especially tabulations of the occupational distribution of ethnic groups at successive censuses.[10] Thus, men of native parentage began and remained at professional, financial, and clerical jobs and became owners of the larger enterprises in commerce and manufacturing more often than either immigrants or their children. Furthermore, that natives of foreign parentage did become clerical and sales workers far more often than the immigrant generation corroborates the common theory that social mobility for the newcomers came with assimilation in the second generation (see Table 35).

The one apparent exception to that theory in Poughkeepsie, the superior record of foreign compared to native artisans in achieving self-employment, represented a remarkably successful economic adaptaton for many

[9] For a fuller development of this questioning, see my "Occupational Mobility in Nineteenth-Century America: Problems and Possibilities," *Journal of Social History* 5 (1972): 310–30.

[10] To document properly the general quantitative results summarized in this and the next two paragraphs would require tables excessive in number and length for this paper. These tables will appear in our book. Preliminary tables describing the general dimensions of intra- and inter-generational occupational mobility, including comparison by national origin, can be found in my "Making It in America: Social Mobility in Mid-Nineteenth-Century Poughkeepsie," *New York History* 51 (1970): 479–99.

*Table 35.* Index of ethnic concentration by occupation

| Skill level | Native-born, native parent | British | Native-born, British parent | German | Native-born, German parent | Irish | Native-born, Irish parent |
|---|---|---|---|---|---|---|---|
| | Index number | | | | | | |
| Professional | | | | | | | |
| 1850 | 144 | 56 | — | 45 | — | 10 | — |
| 1860 | 149 | 97 | — | 50 | — | 6 | — |
| 1870 | 163 | 80 | 89 | 36 | 13 | 17 | 16 |
| 1880 | 158 | 103 | 129 | 39 | 6 | 15 | 23 |
| Proprietorial | | | | | | | |
| 1850 | 135 | 73 | — | 98 | — | 30 | — |
| 1860 | 130 | 124 | — | 95 | — | 39 | — |
| 1870 | 135 | 125 | 40 | 138 | 48 | 44 | 18 |
| 1880 | 119 | 133 | 97 | 174 | 64 | 54 | 39 |
| Clerical and sales | | | | | | | |
| 1850 | 145 | 54 | — | 9 | — | 26 | — |
| 1860 | 157 | 18 | — | 24 | — | 15 | — |
| 1870 | 148 | 27 | 184 | 35 | 197 | 7 | 115 |
| 1880 | 148 | 51 | 134 | 18 | 144 | 8 | 76 |
| Skilled | | | | | | | |
| 1850 | 108 | 151 | — | 148 | — | 52 | — |
| 1860 | 101 | 126 | — | 133 | — | 74 | — |
| 1870 | 99 | 121 | 159 | 119 | 160 | 72 | 124 |
| 1880 | 96 | 147 | 146 | 1,133 | 158 | 63 | 87 |
| Semiskilled | | | | | | | |
| 1850 | 85 | 203 | — | 52 | — | 80 | — |
| 1860 | 84 | 155 | — | 82 | — | 106 | — |
| 1870 | 80 | 157 | 104 | 73 | 55 | 131 | 118 |
| 1880 | 84 | 85 | 62 | 78 | 113 | 107 | 160 |
| Unskilled | | | | | | | |
| 1850 | 70 | 58 | — | 89 | — | 197 | — |
| 1860 | 58 | 47 | — | 91 | — | 225 | — |
| 1870 | 55 | 61 | 32 | 89 | 61 | 228 | 140 |
| 1880 | 68 | 56 | 28 | 69 | 45 | 236 | 148 |

SOURCES: The data for 1850, 1860, 1870, and 1880 in Tables 35–39 come from the manuscript population schedules of the federal censuses for Poughkeepsie. Data for 1856, 1879, and 1890 come from J. I. Underhill, *Poughkeepsie City Directory for 1856–57*; Lawrence and Company, *Dutchess County Directory for 1879–80*; and R. V. LeRoy, *Poughkeepsie City Directory for 1890–91*.

NOTE: The index number is computed by dividing the percentage the nativity group comprises of the skill level by the percentage it comprises of the city's labor force and multiplying it by 100. A score of more than 100 means that the group is overrepresented at the occupational level; less than 100 shows underrepresentation.

Before 1870 the native-born of German, Irish, and British parentage who can be identified are too small a percentage of the labor force for comparison. The overrepresentation of these three groups among clerical and sales workers and their underrepresentation among proprietors is due in part to their relative youthfulness in 1870; similarly, the overrepresentation of the foreign-born among proprietors partly reflects the aging by 1870 of the great antebellum immigrant influx. But the differences between nativity groups remain marked within birth cohorts.

immigrants during the fifties and even the sixties; however, in many industries thereafter, self-employment seems increasingly a dead end as the market for custom manufacture dwindled. Decline in artisan manufacture and increase in small retail and service ventures by the seventies also narrowed substantially the earlier sharp gap between artisans and less skilled workers in frequency of achieving proprietorship, a shift that gave no advantage to the immigrant. Proportionate to their numbers in the city, native laborers, factory operatives, and service workers opened small businesses outside of manufacturing as often as the foreign-born of their native children.

Tracing did not show immigrants and their children becoming the primary source of unskilled or semi-skilled factory operatives in every industry during this period. Rather, it disclosed marked differences among the city's largest, most mechanized enterprises in the ethnic composition of their work forces. These differences do generally support the conventional impression that immigrants, especially the Irish, were most likely to find employment in factories where dirty, arduous, or otherwise unpleasant tasks predominated. However, in several Poughkeepsie factories men of native parentage comprised a majority of the unskilled workers, and in all factories dominated by natives an important minority of immigrants shared the more skilled tasks and appear to equal advantage when they and their children took jobs out of the factories. The kind of industry and even the specific place of employment seem more important in shaping the future prospects of some groups of factory operatives than their national origin or even their initial level of skill. The significance of these and other variations is the concern of the following, more detailed description of immigrant employment in Poughkeepsie's manufacturing.

Textile factories had been operating in the city more than three decades before the famine immigration. The Irish who came to construct the Hudson River Railroad in the late forties and the Germans arriving in the fifties did swell a village of less than 8,000 in 1840 into the small municipality of 12,000 incorporated in 1854. But the size of the village before the influx of foreign newcomers had not meant either commercial isolation or backwardness in manufacturing. Poughkeepsie enjoyed good river transportation and so participated in the regional market that by the beginning of the nineteenth century extended from Albany to Long Island. Its role as central place and especially as point of transshipment for an agricultural hinterland had been supplemented very early by factories exploiting the waterpower of local streams.

Despite technological sophistication of some of the village's factories, manufacturing in Poughkeepsie grew by fits and starts. According to the 1833 federal report on manufactures, three firms in Poughkeepsie together employed 99 men, women, and children in woolen manufacture, but by 1850 only one firm, employing fewer than 25 persons survived. Three cotton factories employed 120 persons in 1840, but the last of these closed up in the early fifties. Of three carpet factories, only one survived into the fifties. The Poughkeepsie Silk Company erected an elaborate plant during the silk worm craze of the thirties, only to fail soon after in the Panic. Three other silk factories were launched before 1885; however, none of them survived more than a few years.[11]

The city never developed a successful specialization such as upstate Troy did in stove manufacture with numerous firms and auxiliary enterprises. The largest employers by 1850 did not cluster in one or a few industries. A blast furnace and a chair factory founded in the forties joined the soon-to-be defunct cotton factory, one carpet factory, the older dyewood mill, and Matthew Vassar's brewery as the village's largest manufacturers.

Poughkeepsie's location on the Hudson River meant that its economy from the beginning was dependent on extralocal markets which provided the impetus for growth, and at the same time made the economic well-being of the city a function of events over which local entrepreneurs had little if any control. By the fifties a number of the city's cooperages, carriage shops, and foundries depended heavily upon the soon-to-be-ruined southern trade. Orders for large castings were filled for places as distant as Cincinnati and the Crystal Palace in England. Contractors organized local tailors and tailoresses to make ready-made garments for New York City and Philadelphia houses.[12] Thus, the immigrant invasion at mid-century entered a diversified economy with a history of manufacturing for a national market. Judged by the crude measure of the ratio of manufacturing workers-artisans as well as factory operatives to the total labor force, Poughkeepsie ranked twentieth out of the fifty largest urban places in the Northeast in 1860 in commitment to manufacturing, but only thirty-fifth in population.[13]

The ratio of manufacturing workers to total labor force does not take into account scale of enterprise. By that measure Poughkeepsie already lagged behind upstate manufacturing centers like Troy and Albany by 1860.[14] When exact comparison of scale beyond that date becomes possible, it

[11] The sections devoted to manufacturing in Edmund Platt's *Eagle's History of Poughkeepsie* (Poughkeepsie, N.Y., 1905) chart this uneven progress.

[12] *Daily Press* (Poughkeepsie), Jan. 10, 1852; *Telegraph and Democrat* (Poughkeepsie), June 15, 1857. Unless otherwise noted, all newspapers were published in Poughkeepsie, N.Y.

[13] Jeffrey G. Williamson and Joseph A. Swanson, "The Growth of Cities in the American Northeast, 1820–1870," *Explorations in Entrepreneurial History* 2d ser. 4, no. 1 (1966): 78–79 (Table A.2.3).

[14] Ehrlich, "Development of Manufactures," pp. 85–86.

undoubtedly will show Poughkeepsie lagging farther behind. The city had no factories with more than one hundred workers on the eve of civil war; it counted six with more than fifty employees—a blast furnace, mower and reaper works, chair factory, cooperage, brewery and dyewood mill—and eighteen with twenty to fifty, with each of the latter two categories comprising about 15 percent of the male labor force in 1860. By 1880 the percentages of males employed in manufacturing firms in the over fifty and twenty to fifty groups remained almost identical. However, two enterprises, the mower works and a new shoe factory opened in 1870, now had two hundred or more employees each. Two new garment factories had more than one hundred workers each, but they were mostly women. Two blast furnaces, the brewery, dyewood mill, and a new glass factory had more than fifty workers each, but no cooperage or chair factory had that large a work force any longer.

In some lines of manufacturing, especially where custom work and hand methods continued to prevail, the median size of firms actually decreased during the middle decades. One- or two-man shops were frequent among immigrants, but, regardless of nativity, large tailoring shops and shops making shoes, cabinets, carriages, and harnesses became less common in Poughkeepsie as national and regional competition increased. The invasion of goods manufactured elsewhere limited may firms to local customers and increasingly in some lines to a repairing business. Whereas two shoe merchants employed fourteen workers each, and another two employed twelve each to make shoes in 1850—one-third of them women—only one firm in 1860 reported as many as eleven workers, and the rest had six or less.

The small scale of much of Poughkeepsie's manufacturing did not mean that native artisans avoided the division of labor spreading throughout the Northeast in the antebellum decades. Separation of tasks outside the factory seems to have been common by the time of the immigrant influx, judging by such symptoms as the employment of women in shoemaking. Local shops even hired boys to perform the simpler operations in some crafts and industries. The son of one Poughkeepsie shoemaker recalled that whenever he was not in school during the forties he worked at anything he could find to do; among other jobs, he stripped tobacco for a local cigar manufacturer, worked in the wallpaper factory, "pricked tile" in the Vassar brewery, primed signs for a boss painter, and "closed uppers and fitted boots on the shoe bench with my father."[15]

Census enumerations between 1850 and 1880 do not reveal the full extent of this division of labor, usually reporting skilled workers by the

[15] A. S. Pease, *Selections of His Poems with an Autobiography and Geneaology* [*sic*] *of His Descendants* (Privately printed, 1915), p. 76.

name of their trade without any specification of the tasks they actually performed at their current places of employment. The frequent designation of bottomers, caners, painters, and varnishers in the chair factories was the exception in Poughkeepsie, not the rule. Thus, although judged by the proportion of all workers with professional, proprietorial, clerical, skilled, semi-skilled, and unskilled occupational designations, the structure of Poughkeepsie's labor force altered very little during these years, the breakdown of the craft system was evident even before the Civil War. The most revealing sign of specialization appears outside of manufacturing, the concern of this essay, in the increase of clerical and sales workers from 5 percent to 11 percent of the total and in greater specificity in their designations.

A sudden jump in semiskilled designations from 10 percent in 1870 to 16 percent in 1880 does represent a genuine expansion in the factory population; however, the expansion seems less dramatic after discovery that somewhere between one-fourth and one-third of the unspecified laborers reported in previous censuses probably were employed in factories. Such laborers always comprised at least one-sixth of the total labor force. Fortunately, city and county directories specified place of employment often enough to permit identification of much of the factory population in the mid-forties and fifties and again in the late seventies. Information in other sources on their tasks is spotty, so that the attempt to reconstruct the work process in individual factories must depend partially upon inference from accounts of the industry in other cities or in the nation at that time.

Native workers predominated in some of the village's factories in the forties, notably in chair making (see Table 36). On the other hand, British weavers formed a distinct enclave. The 1850 census recorded fifty-five weavers, four-fifths of them born in England and Scotland. These weavers comprised 14 percent of all male workers of those nationalities in that year. But the textile industry had begun to dwindle even before the floodtide of Irish immigration; by 1860 the number of weavers had been cut in half. As the industry contracted, so did the representation of the English and Scottish. Never again would the British in Poughkeepsie concentrate so heavily in one industry.

The pattern of employment among the earliest Irish and German immigrants anticipated their subsequent concentration. Obvious Irish names comprised less than 4 percent of the total male listings in the 1845 city directory; more than two-thirds of these appear with no occupation or with the designation "laborer," an even higher proportion at unskilled work than at the height of the famine migration. Three men reported themselves as working in foundries and another as following the molder's

*Table 36.* Ethnic composition of factory work forces

| | | % of factory work forces | | | | | | | |
|---|---|---|---|---|---|---|---|---|---|
| Factory | Year | Native-born, native parent | Irish | Native-born, Irish parent | German | Native-born, German parent | British | Native-born, British parent | Total no. of cases |
| Furnace | 1856 | 31.5% | 34.0% | – | 28.9% | – | 2.6% | 2.6% | 38 |
| | 1879 | 8.3 | 56.3 | 6.3 | 19.8 | 9.4 | – | – | 96 |
| Dyewood | 1879 | 31.0 | 44.8 | 13.8 | 3.4 | 3.4 | – | – | 29 |
| Chair | 1850 | 78.8 | 6.3 | – | 3.8 | – | 3.8 | – | 80 |
| | 1860 | 49.4 | 11.2 | 2.2 | 15.7 | 4.5 | 7.9 | 1.1 | 89 |
| | 1880 | 71.1 | – | 10.5 | 2.6 | 10.5 | 2.6 | – | 38 |
| Mower | 1879 | 60.2 | 11.0 | 5.1 | 8.5 | 5.1 | 3.4 | 2.5 | 118 |
| Skilled only | | 65.3 | 10.7 | 2.7 | 8.0 | 4.0 | 5.3 | 4.0 | 75 |
| Unskilled only | | 51.2 | 11.6 | 9.3 | 9.3 | 7.0 | – | – | 43 |
| Shoe | 1880 | 49.1 | 14.5 | 18.2 | 1.8 | 10.0 | 2.7 | 2.7 | 220 |
| Glass | 1880 | 35.4 | 7.3 | 31.7 | 2.4 | 4.9 | 18.3 | – | 82 |
| Skilled only | | 46.2 | 2.6 | 10.3 | 2.6 | – | 38.5 | – | 39 |
| Unskilled only | | 25.6 | 11.6 | 51.2 | 2.3 | 9.3 | – | – | 43 |

trade; only three listed themselves at other crafts. By contrast, four-fifths of the German names—less than 2 percent of all listings—are identified with the crafts of shoemaking, tailoring, butchering, brewing, and cigar making and with the one small factory owned by Germans since 1842, a pottery.

German and Irish newcomers together comprised one-third of Poughkeepsie's male labor force by 1860; native-born workers still accounted for three-fifths, a higher proportion than in many Northeastern cities. The Germans concentrated immediately in handicrafts where small-shop manufacture prevailed, but a substantial minority—perhaps as much as one-fourth—did find employment in the city's factories. Despite the out-migration during the fifties of many of the Irish who built the railroad, only one-sixth of the remainder appeared at skilled trade designations by 1860 compared to more than two-fifths at unspecified labor. Factory employment accordingly was more important to their economic progress in Poughkeepsie.

German and Irish immigrants predominated in three of Poughkeepsie's largest manufacturing enterprises in the fifties, the brewery, dyewood mill, and furnace. True to stereotype, these enterprises employed more unskilled than skilled labor and offered the unskilled tasks that were unusually heavy, dirty, or hot—and sometimes all three. Yet economic necessity alone does not adequately explain the relation of immigrants to these industries. The sharp contrast in stability of employment between the furnace and dyewood mill suggests that loyalties could be created—as they apparently were at the furnace—by a coincidence of better pay, nepotism, and a sense that the work itself did not demean, that its very difficulty had dignity.

The blast furnace, which opened in 1848 and was enlarged in 1852, provided the largest number of relatively permanent jobs in manufacturing for Catholics, German as well as Irish. A pastor of the German parish recalled that some of these Catholics "were trained iron mongers from outside and therefore they were very welcome here."[16] Although whites of native parentage as late as 1856 comprised nearly one-third of the thirty-eight identifiable furnace employees, they moved away from the city or changed jobs within it far more frequently than the immigrants. The Germans and Irish, each about one-third of the total, shared a common religion, a higher frequency of relatives also at the furnace, and greater stability in employment there. These newcomers anticipated the general tendency of their countrymen to settle down in Poughkeepsie in occupations where they became preeminent or, at the very least, a large minority.

The German Adamses, Stouts, and Millers remained furnacemen from the fifties to the eighties, some of them moving to the stacks near the upper landing in the sixties and others remaining at the older lower furnace. Germans became foremen and yard bosses at both. Burnses provided continuity for the Irish, one of them becoming a foundryman at the lower furnace in the sixties. The Irish steadily increased their numbers until by 1879 they comprised nearly two-thirds of the ninety-six identifiable furnace workers compared to more than one-fourth for the Germans and less than one-tenth for whites of native parentage. Three-fifths of this work force had been employed in Poughkeepsie for a decade or more, a degree of stability unmatched in most manufacturing enterprises. The lower furnace closed during the eighties, but two-fifths of the 1879 upper furnace workers still worked there in 1890, or nearly two-thirds of those who remained in Poughkeepsie at that date (see Table 37).

[16] *Jubilee Year Book of the Church of the Nativity* (Poughkeepsie, N.Y., 1897), p. 9.

*Table 37.* Occupation by 1890: comparison of 1879 dyewood mill and Fallkill Iron Co. workers

| | % of workers | | | | Total no. of workers in 1890 |
|---|---|---|---|---|---|
| | Same job as 1879 | Unspecified laborer | Skilled | Proprietor | |
| Dywood mill | 14.3 | 81.0 | — | 4.8 | 21 |
| Fallkill Iron Co. | 65.7 | 28.6 | 2.9 | 5.7 | 35 |

NOTE: Of the 29 dyewood-mill workers of 1879, seven had died or left Poughkeepsie by 1890. Fifteen of the 53 Fallkill workers of 1879 had disappeared by 1890. One probable additional case of persistence among the former and three among the latter have been excluded from the table because the linkage is inconclusive.

This stability of immigrants at the furnaces does not lend itself to easy explanation by any notion of superior opportunity. The reward for laborers there remained better than for casual labor, but improvements in the construction of blast furnaces increased productivity without increasing the skill required of workers.[17] Children did not go on to better occupations usually. The number of sons working in the city at skilled metal trades was negligible; the vast majority appear at laboring or no designated occupation. More of the employed daughters appear as servants than as dressmakers.

The furnaces seem like a working-class world apart. The work there remained hotter, dirtier, heavier, and more dangerous than in most of the city's manufacturing. Nevertheless, fragmentary evidence suggests a sense of camaraderie among furnacemen, the toughness of the work enhancing the sense of its manliness. The ironworks had a rhythm of their own; as one Poughkeepsian observed, "during a blast, which lasts from two to three years, the engines are stopped about half an hour only out of every twelve, while all the rest of the works go right ahead, day and night, Sundays, Fourth of Julys and all. . . . The flames from the furnaces in the night time illuminate the horizon."[18]

At the dyewood mill, neighbor to the upper furnace on the river front, machines cut and ground woods imported primarily from the West Indies. But the woods had to be unloaded at the river front and moved through the phases of manufacture, heavy but not especially dangerous work. The mill stood at the other extreme in continuity of work force; a mere one-fourth of its identifiable workers in 1879 had been employed in the

[17] "A Big Iron Plant, *Sunday Courier* (Hudson Valley), June 10, 1894; Eric J. Hobsbawm, *Industry and Empire: The Making of Modern English Society* (New York, 1968), p. 95.

[18] *Daily Eagle*, May 7, 1866.

city a decade earlier. The Irish comprised two-thirds of that factory by 1856 and only slightly less in 1879; they provided what little continuity in work force existed. Patrick Hannan still walked the mile or so down the river slope from his house on Bridge Street, his oldest son now joining him at the mill. But Hannan was the exception even among his countrymen. Native workers in the mill appear even more frequently to be drifters from job to job. Massachusetts-born Edwin Stearns had reported himself previously as a molder, then a saloon keeper; twenty-four-year-old William Robinson had been a painter and would later work on the railroad; his father had reported himself successively as laborer, boatman, and shoemaker.

Unlike the furnaces, which evidently valued experience and loyalty, the dyewood mill depended primarily upon younger and relatively transient workers. Few men spent their working lives in the mill; sons rarely followed their fathers there. Tracing subsequent occupational careers indicates that mill employment did not prepare men for better opportunities. Overwhelmingly they remained in less skilled manual jobs, and so did their children. The three younger sons of Patrick Hannan started at the shoe factory and two of them later became ironers in a laundry. His compatriots' children found employment as servants, workers in other factories, and laborers on the railroad, the new railroad bridge across the Hudson begun in the seventies, or other occasional tasks.

Irish and German workers did not comprise a majority of the work force in any other industry in Poughkeepsie, which was dominated by large shops or factories. In the manufacture of agricultural implements and—except from the mid-fifties to the early sixties—of chairs, two-thirds of the wage earners remained men of native parentage. The proportion of newcomers increased in factories opened during the seventies, but by then the second generation benefited more than immigrants. In the new Whitehouse shoe factory founded in 1870, men of native parentage accounted for about half of the total, or the same as they did in the labor force as a whole. The native-born of foreign—especially Irish—parentage made up nearly one-third and the foreign-born, one-fifth. The same tendency to greater representation of the second generation than of immigrants appears in the garment factories founded during the depression and in the glass factory opened in 1880. Younger workers predominated in the new enterprises of the seventies. Although the foreign-born remained half again more numerous than the second generation in the male labor force as a whole, the second generation already was nearly five times more numerous among workers less than thirty years old.

The continuing predominance of men of native parentage in so many of the city's factories poses two questions. First, did these factories offer much more highly skilled or remunerative work than the furnaces, dyewood mill, and brewery? Second, within these factories did men of native parentage hold the more highly skilled jobs? Comparing the two factories where native advantage remained greatest, the answer to the first question is yes—but the proportion of native-born persons in any given job is far from an infallible predictor of the level of skill required.

The Buckeye Mower Works had the highest proportion of skilled craftsmen; machinists, molders, and blacksmiths comprised a majority of its work force, not including more specialized workers, such as grinders and file cutters.[19] These craftsmen had more freedom in pursuing their work than operatives in most factories. They identified with their trades more than with their place of employment or the product they made; two-thirds of the workers ever designated as skilled reported themselves by their trades throughout their working careers in Poughkeepsie. If less skilled first jobs are eliminated, then the proportion so reporting themselves rises to more than three-fourths.

By contrast, the greater subdivision of labor at the chair factories required less skill of most workers. By 1860 these factories reported an array of specialized woodworking machinery, including boring, morticing, tenoning, dowling, turning, and planing machines. These machines made possible the employment of greener hands. Unlike skilled workers at Buckeye who reported themselves at their trades, almost all these workers reported themselves as "chair maker" or at the "chair factory." Moreover, of the seventy-three men so designated in the 1860 census who also remained employed in the city for at least a decade, little more than half reported themselves again at those designations or at closely related trades like those of cabinetmaker, turner, carpenter, or painter. Wages correspondingly were lower than at Buckeye. Whereas the rate for skilled labor at the mower works exceeded the going rate in most firms, the pay for supposedly skilled labor in the chair factories by 1880 was no more than the average for ordinary labor in the city.

Yet even though the chair factories were less remunerative and less skill-oriented, Buckeye in the long run proved to be more hospitable to the employment of immigrants. By 1880 men of native parentage comprised seventy-one percent of the chair factory workers compared to sixty-one percent at Buckeye. For the few years before and after 1860 when chairmaking boomed in Poughkeepsie, half of the work force became

[19] Older men with long residence in Poughkeepsie comprised more of the work force at Buckeye than of any other large plant. Among the 66 skilled workers in 1879 whose ages can be determined, half were at least 40 years old and more than one-fourth were over 50. Nearly two-fifths had been employed in Poughkeepsie for 20 years or more and nearly three-fourths for at least 10 years.

foreign-born. But as the industry declined, so did the proportion of German and Irish workers.

This decline did not result from the foreign-born persisting less often in the factories but rather from an increase in men of native parentage in new hiring in the industry. Whether this increase owes more to employer preference for native workers or the willingness of the natives to work for less cannot be determined; but certainly these new recruits had no apparent advantage over immigrant chairmakers who left the factories for other employment. All of the foreign-born who shifted out as chairmaking waned took up skilled work or vending. Several Germans worked only briefly in the factories before opening shops in unrelated lines like shoemaking and groceries, suggesting that they may have chosen factory employment as a stopgap until they could find opportunities to practice as journeymen the skills they brought with them or to find capital for self-employment.

The possibility remains that the immigrants who found employment at Buckeye or other factories with more highly skilled work forces were confined to unskilled jobs and that their children also fared less well than the children of skilled native workers. At one extreme, a clear stratification of workers by ethnic origin did occur in the glassworks; native-born workers of Irish parentage comprised one-half of the ordinary labor there but less than one-tenth of the skilled blowers, nearly half of whom were native and nearly two-fifths British. Even at Buckeye, which did employ first- and second-generation immigrants at its skilled trades, men of native parentage still accounted for nearly two-thirds of employees designated with skilled trades compared to one-half of those designated "works Buckeye." Furthermore, Buckeye may have been less willing to train first- and second-generation Americans in skills which they did not already possess, but the evidence here is statistically insignificant. Only two of the fifteen machinists of foreign birth or parentage had been enumerated previously at unskilled labor compared to eight of the twenty-five machinists of native parentage.

Neither possible native advantage in hiring and on-the-job training nor the underrepresentation of men of foreign birth and parentage among Buckeye's craftsmen, however, predicts the opportunities for children of the mower works' immigrant employees. For the children of Buckeye workers show little difference in occupational achievement, whether fathers were skilled or unskilled or had native or foreign parents. A minority of the sons and daughters of both found white-collar employment, mostly minor in character; a smaller minority appeared at other factory, service, or unskilled jobs; and the remainder, a bare majority, listed themselves at skilled jobs with metal trades predominating.

In a majority of cases where children's jobs can be identified, at least two of these three levels were represented by different children in the same family or appear in the career of an individual child. Native-born Albert Wilson had one son who became a draughtsman, but another labored at the glassworks. The son of Irish-born machinist James Morrow worked for some years in a machine shop before becoming a letter carrier. A son of German-born Joseph Heidel ran a saloon, and his daughters appear as a shoe factory operative and a tailoress.

Unskilled workers at Buckeye do not seem to have been at any disadvantage compared to the skilled in persuading Buckeye's foremen to train their boys as machinists and molders. Charles Rodgers's oldest boy started at the silk factory but then became a molder at Buckeye, later working at that trade for the separator factory; another son also learned molding. The son of Danish-born Henry Hansen became a machinist. In this way Buckeye helped narrow the difference in opportunity one might expect between the children of the factory's skilled and its unskilled workers.[20]

Furthermore, skilled apprenticeships for sons of unskilled workers at Buckeye constitute only one, if a rather special, instance of an apparently general tendency of Poughkeepsie's factories in this period to level those differences that could be anticipated in occupational careers within and between generations and ethnic groups. Increase in the scale and specialization of manufacturing progressively undermined the previously sharp distinction between artisan and laborer for men of every nativity who remained at manual work. Greater similarity in occupational mobility did not mean greater homogeneity of economic reward among manual occupations, however. Division of tasks increased remuneration for some workers while decreasing it for others; the upper and lower extremes of the hierarchy in wages for manual workers apparently widened a little between 1860 and 1890.[21] We do not have adequate studies yet of how much this continuing difference in incentive—and during the closing decades of the century, improvement in standard of living through rise in real wages—eased adjustment of the more highly skilled workers to a world where they no longer had as frequent access through occupational mobility to the prosperous middle class.

[20] There are a few instances where a worker designated as machinist or molder at Buckeye appears subsequently as a laborer, suggesting that he may have performed only very limited tasks related to those trades but had not undergone any apprenticeship. Men designated as grinders clearly belonged in this category at Buckeye; all of them previously appeared in Poughkeepsie as laborers; one did subsequently and another reported himself at one census as a machinist.

[21] Clarence D. Long, *Wages and Earnings in the United States, 1860–1890* (Princeton, 1960), pp. 94–104.

The most striking instance of leveling in the career patterns of manual workers appears in the coming together of sons of Irish laborers and sons of native skilled workers in the Whitehouse shoe factory, the largest single employer in Poughkeepsie during the seventies. Because Irish in the immigrant generation concentrated so heavily in casual labor whereas manual workers of native parentage much more often reported trades, this conjunction was likely wherever their children found common employment. The improvement for the Irish was substantial, if only because the minimum shoe factory wages were better than the going rates for ordinary labor. Any gain for the sons of native artisans seems dubious; the very youthfulness of the Whitehouse work force—nearly two-fifths of the male workers being less than twenty years old and more than two-thirds less than thirty in 1880—suggests that most of its tasks required little training or experience.

Lack of specification of tasks and responsibilities at Whitehouse makes it impossible to determine how much advantage the sons of native artisans had within the factory, but comparison by ethnicity of fathers' occupations with sons' occupations ten years after their listing at Whitehouse suggests that a narrowing of differences may have occurred at the factory. The occupational distribution of operatives of native parentage had not improved upon that of their fathers; but the proportion of native sons of Irish parentage at white-collar jobs was significantly higher and the proportion at unskilled labor lower than among their parents.

Immigrants and their children who entered Poughkeepsie's factories shared with native operatives common patterns of upward and downward occupational mobility. So long as factories did not differ too greatly in the range and distribution of skills required, strong similarities appear regardless of variations in the ethnic composition of their work forces. Operatives in the chair, mower, and shoe factories resemble one another in the skill levels of their fathers and in their own skill levels before and after listing at those plants (see Table 38.) About one-tenth of the fathers had been white-collar workers; a similar proportion of the operatives themselves had started at that level and would achieve it subsequently. The proportion of sons subsequently at unskilled work was less than the proportion of fathers at this level. The most striking difference, however, suggests limitations in the significance of commonly employed measures of upward and downward mobility. A higher proportion of Buckeye workers and their fathers appear at skilled trades in all listings; they also appear slightly less often in white-collar work. These most highly skilled and rewarded factory workers less often became clerks, grocers, saloon keepers, cigar and variety store owners perhaps for the good reason that much of

*Table 38.* Father's occupation and prior and subsequent occupations of members of three factory work forces

| | % of factories' work forces | | | | | |
|---|---|---|---|---|---|---|
| | Unskilled | Service | Factory | Skilled | Professional, proprietorial, and clerical | Total no. of workers |
| **Father's occupation** | | | | | | |
| Chair factory | 25.0 | 5.0 | 17.5 | 40.0 | 12.5 | 40 |
| Mower works | 17.1 | 17.1 | – | 60.0 | 5.7 | 35 |
| Shoe factory | 23.9 | 21.7 | 4.3 | 35.9 | 13.1 | 92 |
| **Prior occupation** | | | | | | |
| Chair factory | 36.8 | – | 10.5 | 42.1 | 10.5 | 19 |
| Mower works | 39.2 | 1.4 | 1.4 | 52.7 | 5.4 | 74 |
| Shoe factory | 38.5 | 7.7 | 7.7 | 30.8 | 15.4 | 13 |
| **Subsequent occupation** | | | | | | |
| Chair factory | 14.3 | 5.7 | 28.6 | 34.3 | 17.1 | 70 |
| Mower works | 17.6 | 5.4 | 20.3 | 52.7 | 4.1 | 74 |
| Shoe factory | 18.5 | 5.6 | 44.4 | 17.7 | 13.7 | 124 |

NOTE: The men described in this table were employed in the mower works and the shoe factory in 1880 and in the chair factory at any census from 1850 to 1880. Only prior and subsequent occupations in Poughkeepsie separated from this employment by a decade or more are tabulated here. Where several shifts in occupation occurred only the earliest and latest have been tabulated.

such apparent upward mobility among former operatives did not bring more security or reward usually than Buckeye workers already had.

A few plant superintendents and shop foremen rose well above their skilled beginnings and passed their advantage on to their children. However, the majority of factory supervisory workers who can be identified show the same range of employment as other skilled workers and many of their children remained at manual work. Men of native and British parentage monopolized the top positions throughout the middle decades, but workers of German and Irish birth or parentage frequently appear as foremen. The exceptional success was James Carroll, an Irish boss molder, who used his savings from the foundry to open a meat market; his five children became lawyers, professional nurses, and a clerk. More typically, one of the sons of German-born Charles Crugher, yard boss at the lower furnace, became a brakeman and then a conductor on the railroad;

the other son, Henry, became an engineer, first at Buckeye and then at the glassworks. One of Henry's sons joined him there by 1900; another found employment in the separator factory.

With the exception of native-born George Hine, who set up his own shoe factory after leaving Whitehouse, foremen in Poughkeepsie had no more success than other skilled workers in entering the city's entrepreneurial class after 1850. Craftsmen did not become major manufacturers as they did in the machine industry of Paterson, N.J.[22] In smaller enterprises partnerships of artisans who provided the skill and merchants who supplied the capital were not unusual, but none of them grew to any size in Poughkeepsie during this period, and almost all of the participants were native-born.

Recent immigrants were as rare as former artisans among factory owners. The apparent exception, the pottery works acquired by the Caire family from Bavaria in 1842, rarely employed more than twenty workers. Like other factory owners and many immigrant employers in craft shops, the Caires hired workers of different nationalities. Only the balance of nationalities varied from firm to firm.

The most important generalization to be drawn from the record of immigrants in Poughkeepsie's larger manufacturing enterprises is a negative one. The newcomers did not dominate factory labor, although workers of Irish birth or parentage did account for a disproportionate share of the work force in firms where heavier or dirtier tasks prevailed, and men of native parentage had a disproportionate share of the more attractive employments. Newcomers shared the skilled as well as unskilled work with men of native parentage and seem to have benefited as much from it. They also shared the vertical occupational mobility of factory workers generally and the limitations of that mobility.

In an age of increasing scale and specialization the usual ceiling for the occupational mobility of skilled workers lowered as that for less skilled workers lifted somewhat; increasingly both came to share a common working-class status, natives as well as newcomers. Artisans who became shopowners early in the nineteenth century had a better chance of becoming members of the city's comfortable middle class than did the minority of factory operatives who after 1860 now succeeded in joining the growing ranks of clerical and sales workers or became the operators of petty retail and service ventures.

Moreover, the majority of men employed in manufacturing in

[22] Herbert G. Gutman, "The Reality of the Rags-to-Riches 'Myth': The Case of the Paterson, New Jersey, Locomotive, Iron, and Machinery Manufacturers, 1830–1880," in Stephan Thernstrom and Richard Sennett, eds., *Nineteenth-Century Cities* (New Haven, 1969), pp. 98–124.

Poughkeepsie did not work in factories, not even in shops of as many as twenty workers. Throughout the middle decades artisan manufacture on a small scale continued to predominate in many industries and to be important in most. In the manufacturing census of 1860, firms employing less than ten men each included all of the twenty-nine boot and shoeshops, ten meat markets, ten blacksmith shops, five saddlers and harness makers, four turners and sawyers, three jewelers, and three soap manufacturers, all but two of eight cigar manufacturers, seven bakeries and confectionaries, six machine and toolshops, five cooperages, and all but four of twenty-one merchant tailors and clothiers. The manufacturing census of 1880 was much less inclusive but suggests a similar proportion in most of these industries.

Immigrant even more than native skilled workers concentrated in smaller shops. In some industries they may have even delayed mechanization a little, if not the subdivision of tasks. So long as machines did not yield a superior or much cheaper product, especially in specialties with limited markets, the presence of foreign craftsmen willing to work for low wages made it easier for employers to put off investment in fixed capital. In coopering, where some shops were much larger and absorbed more immigrants than any other skilled trade during the fifties, machine work in the biggest factory was confined as late as 1866 to dressing the staves and headings. As the *Eagle* reported, "Each man then takes a certain portion of them [staves and headings] and proceeds to the construction of barrels by piece work, the article not leaving his hands until finished."[23] But the evidence for delay in mechanization is mixed. In the clothing industry, where immigrants comprised the majority of wage earners, introduction of sewing machines proceeded fairly rapidly during the fifties, although the scale of firms remained small and most had only one machine.

Whether the perpetuation of small-shop manufacture ever resulted in more than marginal economic returns remains in question and so, therefore, does its significance in immigrant adaptation to an industrializing economy. If it offered a better opportunity than factory employment—even in the short run—then the apparent native advantage in hiring in the more attractive factory employments appears in a different light. For British and German artisans opened their own shops more often than skilled workers of native parentage (see Table 39).

The Germans pose this question most sharply in Poughkeepsie and in many other American cities at mid-century. Germans dominated many handicraft trades, displacing native workers; their achievement of self-employment in these trades was phenomenal. By 1880 men of German

[23] *Daily Eagle*, Apr. 24, 1866.

*Table 39.* Occupational mobility of workers starting at skilled jobs by decade and nativity

| Nativity | Decade | No. of cases | % of workers: Remain skilled | Rise to white collar | Fall to low manual |
|---|---|---|---|---|---|
| Native-born, native parent | 1850–60 | 260 | 68.8 | 23.1 | 8.1 |
| | 1860–70 | 328 | 72.0 | 21.6 | 6.4 |
| | 1870–80 | 420 | 73.6 | 15.0 | 11.4 |
| British | 1850–60 | 37 | 73.0 | 27.0 | — |
| | 1860–70 | 49 | 73.5 | 20.4 | 6.1 |
| | 1870–80 | 42 | 73.8 | 19.0 | 7.1 |
| Native-born, British parent | 1870–80 | 43 | 74.4 | 18.6 | 7.0 |
| German | 1850–60 | 34 | 55.9 | 35.3 | 8.8 |
| | 1860–70 | 110 | 52.7 | 41.8 | 5.5 |
| | 1870–80 | 116 | 69.8 | 23.3 | 6.9 |
| Native-born, German parent | 1870–80 | 62 | 62.9 | 27.4 | 9.7 |
| Irish | 1850–60 | 46 | 67.4 | 23.9 | 8.7 |
| | 1860–70 | 93 | 71.0 | 12.9 | 16.1 |
| | 1870–80 | 106 | 83.0 | 3.8 | 13.2 |
| Native-born, Irish parent | 1870–80 | 60 | 66.7 | 18.3 | 15.0 |

birth or parentage in Poughkeepsie accounted for one-sixth of the city's labor force but comprised half or more of all workers in shoemaking (excluding the shoe factory), tailoring, baking, butchering, brewing, and cigar making and well over half of the shop owners in these trades. Rates of persistence in the city and within these trades for Germans consistently exceeded the rates for other ethnic groups.[24] In woodworking trades, such as coopering and cabinetmaking, but not in sash and blind manufacture, Germans became the largest minority.

[24] See my "Workers Divided: The Effect of Craft and Ethnic Differences in Poughkeepsie, New York, 1850–1880," in Thernstrom and Sennett, *Nineteenth-Century Cities*, pp. 49–96, especially pp. 76–80.

The success of German artisans in displacing natives and other immigrants in so many trades seems to have depended upon special circumstances prevailing at mid-century, primarily the deteriorating situation of handicraft workers in the German states and the limited progress as yet of specialization and mechanization in those crafts in the United States. The organization of German crafts and the competition within them prepared emigrants to capitalize upon the uneven pace of industrialization in their new home, and especially upon the lag between the time ready-to-wear goods began to be mass-produced and the time they took to dominate local markets outside the biggest cities. By 1880 there is evidence that the initial prosperity of German artisans in Poughkeepsie and their upward mobility as shop owners was not so solid as it seemed in the fifties and sixties. Native, Irish, and British handicraftsmen suffered equally from declining prosperity in these trades, but the Germans have been chosen for illustration because their economic progress as a group depended so heavily upon the handicrafts.

The German artisans who emigrated to America during the thirties and forties, and to a lesser extent during the fifties, stood at the opposite pole in mentality from the proverbially inventive Yankee, ever in search of new ways of making his fortune. They were refugees from change, specifically, from the overpopulation and the extension of economic freedom within the German states, which threatened not only their individual prosperity but also the stability and the cherished old ways of the small home towns from which they so overwhelmingly came. The guild system integrated the political, social, and economic life of their town so as to insure the virtue and livelihood of its citizens and exclude alien, disrupting elements of every kind. The process of achieving membership in a craft epitomized this parochial and protective outlook. A journeyman could not marry or become a citizen until he had been made a master worker. This involved close consideration in which his morality and respectability as well as the economic impact of his prospective business upon the prosperity of other masters loomed as large or larger than the quality of his masterwork.

Morality, respectability, prosperity, and the status of family man and citizen inhered in proper initiation into and practice of one's craft. Dominant in practice during the eighteenth century, that ideal continued to motivate the losing battle artisans fought in the German states during the first half of the nineteenth century to perpetuate guild regulation against the progressive encroachments of economic liberalism. Such an ideal hardly encouraged a pragmatic, opportunistic approach to occupational adaptation in the New World. The continuing identification of so many German-Americans even in the second generation with handicrafts which no longer offered prosperity may reflect the enduring potency of the ideal. At the same time, the facts of an evident surplus of artisans in Germany by the 1840s and increasingly ruinous competition among them taught new lessons about the tactics necessary for survival, presuming a continued identification with craft manufacture.

The beginnings of these lessons had occurred during the Napoleonic occupation and had been extended by the uneven progress in the various states of legislation curbing the powers of the guilds. Once the restrictions on the number of masters permitted in each trade in a town were lifted, shops multiplied. The result was competition so intense that few artisans could prosper. Even in Baden, where the obligation to join a guild in order to practice a trade was not abolished until 1862, masters soon outnumbered journeymen. In the larger towns and cities many masters lost their independence for all practical purposes when merchants and dealers were given the legal right to accept orders for custom work and repairing as well as to sell finished goods. Small shop owners soon found it necessary to supplement their direct orders from individual customers with orders they filled at lower rates for merchants or else to become wage earners working in their own homes.

The very marginality of the shops to which so many German handworkers were accustomed better prepared them as immigrants for a close struggle for survival. American artisans could not easily compete with them in habits, standard of living, and expectations. The 1860 report of the New York Association for the Improvement of the Condition of the Poor described the impact of the Germans "who settle in our large towns, where they almost always monopolize certain branches of trade and industry. They can work for less wages than Americans, and live where an Irishman would starve. As they limit their wants to their necessities, and rarely spend all they earn, they generally become prosperous money-making citizens."[25]

Within the limits of the handicraft tradition, Germans in America showed as much adaptability as men of native parentage. Indeed, as the guild system broke down, impatience with the traditional apprenticeship mounted within the German States themselves. Young men shortened their training and also switched trades when opportunity beckoned.

Among the twenty-five relatively successful German immigrants in Poughkeepsie for whom detailed biographies exist, the father's occupation

[25] Abbott, *Documents*, p. 833. For the deterioration of the guild system, I have relied primarily upon J. H. Clapham, *The Economic Development of France and Germany, 1815–1914* (Cambridge, Eng., 1936) and Theodore S. Hamerow, *Restoration, Revolution, Reaction: Economics and Politics in Germany, 1815–1871* (Princeton, 1958). For the description of the guild system at its height, I am indebted to the analysis of German home towns by Mack Walker, *German Home Towns: Community, State, and General Estate* (Ithaca, N.Y., 1971).

in Germany is specified for twelve sons. Only five of these sons first apprenticed in their father's trade or profession, and only two, a butcher and a shoemaker, pursued it for life. Only ten of the twenty-five subjects followed the trade they themselves started in. Louis Fierabend finished an apprenticeship as a comb maker in Wimpfen, Hesse, and then spent two years learning butchering before coming to America. Jacob Schraut apprenticed as a cooper at Kreuznach in the Rhine province, but began learning the baker's trade as soon as he arrived in New York City. Change of trade was not confined to the period of apprenticeship. Philip Klady, son of a Bavarian carriage manufacturer, practiced coopering as a journeyman for eleven years in Poughkeepsie, part of that time in the employ of the Vassar brewery; in 1857 Klady entered the brewing business for himself and became one of the city's more prosperous Germans.

The careers of the most successful Germans do mislead in one important respect. While these proprietors made money initially within their trades at a time when older methods of manufacture still prevailed, their increase in fortunes primarily reflected shrewd investment. Peter Thielman, the shoemaker-turned-shoe-merchant, Jacob Bahret, the merchant tailor, and Jacob Blankenhorn, the butcher, became money lenders and landlords to their countrymen who emigrated later. Charles Kirchner, the butcher, speculated so successfully in local real estate that he became the richest German in the city. Only clothier Mark Schwartz, the next richest German, depended primarily upon his trade for his fortune. He organized the manufacture of ready-made garments on a scale not seen before in Poughkeepsie, employing sixty tailors by 1880.[26]

Most German artisans achieved more modest prosperity. While their record in achieving independence, in going into business for themselves, and advertising in the city's business directory far exceeds the performance of any other ethnic group, their careers in business tended to be easier and more successful in the fifties and sixties than in the seventies and eighties. A comparison of Germans assessed in the tax lists of 1880 and 1890 is symptomatic. Fortunes made earlier may have grown larger by 1890, but there are hardly any names added to the ranks of those with property assessed at more than $10,000.

[26] See the credit reports for Thielman on p. 84, Bahret on pp. 3, 415, Blankhorn on pp. 338, 590, Kirchner on pp. 338, 426, 650, and Schwartz on pp. 135, 141, 331, 363, 517, 579, of volumes 73 and 74 of the Mercantile Agency ledgers, Dun and Bradstreet Collection, Manuscript Division, Baker Library, Harvard Business School, Cambridge, Mass. The credit ledgers contain reports on more than one thousand five hundred businesses begun in Poughkeepsie between 1847 and 1880. The generalizations here are based upon analysis of all these reports. The detailed biographies for the 25 Germans are found in *Commemorative Biographical Record of Dutchess County, New York* (Chicago, 1897).

The causes of this apparent failure of later German immigrants and of the native-born of German parentage to equal the record of the earlier immigrants unfold in the credit reports of R. G. Dun and Company. Until the mid-sixties German artisans with their own shops often are reported as doing a "snug" business and "making more than a living" in trades like tailoring and shoemaking by combining custom work with a limited stock of ready-made goods. The more successful proprietors increasingly emphasized retailing, keeping custom work and repair as a sideline. Henry Roth, formerly a cutter for a merchant tailor of native parentage, began in custom work for himself but by 1870 also "keeps small stock of gentlemen's furnishings" and by 1878 was reported as owning a "house worth $3,500, nice stock and snug business."[27]

By the early seventies a growing number of reports state that the artisan had no shop or had a very small shop with a poorly assorted stock of ready-made goods, that he worked at his bench at home jobbing for local stores, or that he did a "repairing business," and that he barely made a living. In 1868 Andrew Oberst kept a "shop for making and repairing boots almost exclusively"; by 1876 he "does a little cobbling, carries no stock" and by the end of the decade found employment in the shirt factory while his wife sold groceries at home.[28] The depression of the seventies reduced many shop owners who previously had prospered modestly from good credit risks to being listed as "worthless" or "C.O.D.," although they continued in business for themselves.

Anthony Barth, who kept a small shoeshop near the main business street until after the turn of the century, was one of those who struggled on, shifting from custom work to repairing. A reporter in 1883 described him as doing "a cobbling business which keeps him pegging away all the time in order to take care of his family which consists of a wife and thirteen children." Reminiscing about the trade in 1908, Barth observed that "now girls are working in the factories and hundreds of good shoemakers are looking for something to eat. Over half of the shoemakers who formerly worked in the shops are working at other lines of business and making more money."[29]

Barth contrasted this sad state with "thirty years ago when all shoes were made by hand, [and] the shoemaker earned a fair salary from $12 to $16 a week. Every shoeshop had from five to ten shoemakers working." Like so much twentieth-century nostalgia about artisan manufacture, nostalgia which misled sociologists like W. Lloyd Warner and the Lynds

[27] Dun and Bradstreet Collection, pp. 119, 331, 345, 419.

[28] Dun and Bradstreet Collection, p. 203.

[29] "Old Lasts Tell Story," *Sunday Courier* (Hudson Valley), Feb. 12, 1908; Dun and Bradstreet Collection, p. 313.

about how distant the golden age of craftsmanship was, Barth's reminiscence not only romanticizes the "good old days" somewhat but makes them seem more recent than they were. In Poughkeepsie those days were closer to fifty rather than to thirty years past. On the eve of the Civil War, when Barth was a twenty-year-old journeyman only recently arrived from Württemberg, many shops were already more marginal and paid lower wages than he suggests. As early as 1863 the city's *Daily Press* described the revolution in shoemaking in the nation: "Work has been scattered, but new machinery coming into use—pegging and stitching machines, one of them doing the work of ten, twenty or thirty men and these set up in factories—soon will have only factory shoes. Shoemakers must adjust as they'll soon have to follow the business to places where the factories are located."[30] Seven years later the biggest factory in Poughkeepsie was J. O. Whitehouse's newly opened shoe factory, which employed more women and girls and boys in their teens than adult men, and of the men very few had apprenticed as shoemakers.

Germans did continue to prosper in those crafts, notably in food, where manufacturing remained smaller in scale or less mechanized. Partly by capitalizing on the growing taste for ice cream and developing a regional trade in it, the Schrauts built their baking and confectionery business into one of the city's showpieces by the turn of the century.[31] Several German cigar makers capitalized on their countrymen's proficiency in that handicraft to become the region's leading wholesalers, displacing native tobacco merchants, who previously dominated the business. In 1850 there seems to have been relatively little local manufacture of cigars, and the first surge of the industry during the fifties gave Germans only slight preeminence over journeymen of native parentage. By 1880 the thirty-nine cigar makers of 1860 had become fifty-eight, all of the increase accounted for by Germans.

The most successful organizer of the business, John Schwartz, by 1870 already "manufactures quite extensively and makes large sales to county dealers." Smaller firms in the trade also often did well. Even by 1886 John Baumann, who "makes a few cigars" and "employs one man as helper, makes money." A credit report in 1870 commented that Philip Lampert had "been here a number of years—manufactures some little and sells over the counter"; a report twelve years later said Lampert "began without anything, has made money."[32]

Wages for journeymen in the craft remained somewhat better than for

[30] *Daily Press*, Oct. 28, 1863.

[31] Platt, *Eagle's History*, pp. 195–96.

[32] Dun and Bradstreet Collection, pp. 118, 356, 505, 649 for Schwartz, p. D for Baumann, and pp. 247, 317, 472 for Lampert.

shoemakers in the late sixties, although cigar making remained only partially organized in Poughkeepsie. Less than half belonged to the union when Schwartz's men struck in 1868. Schwartz fired union members and went to New York City to get replacements. By the late eighties, however, all cigar makers in Poughkeepsie belonged to the union, which "thus far found no difficulty with our employer, save one, who has grossly violated the apprentice law."[33] After the turn of the century hand methods would become as obsolete in cigar manufacturing as they had decades earlier in shoemaking.

In the short run, German artisans adapted to Poughkeepsie's economy with impressive results, dominating the food and apparel trades and prospering at least modestly by so doing. But in the longer run this very concentration in handicrafts proved to be no advantage. The early careers of the second generation forecast the future. In 1880 the native-born of German parentage number more clerks—although some of these were employed by their fathers—but also more factory operatives than the immigrant generation. Furthermore, skilled workers in the second generation showed more tendency to cluster in trades like cigar making and butchering, where the pay was less than in trades like machinist, molder, carpenter, and mason.

By 1896 German and Irish names on the directory were a little more common among the city's machinists and engineers, about one-fourth of the total. But men of native and British parentage clearly still predominated. Three-fifths of the molders of 1870 had been of Irish and German birth or parentage; names identified with those nationalities comprised only half of the 1896 total. These three metal trades grew faster than the city's population, as they did everywhere in the nation; but Poughkeepsie in the late nineteenth century did not experience the rapid and sustained expansion of producer-goods manufacturing that occurred in so many industrial centers. Such expanion might have widened opportunities for the native-born of Irish and German parentage who already by 1880 had become three-fourths as numerous in the city's labor force as the immigrant generation.

The second generation did find employment in the new consumer-goods factories of the seventies. For the first time, teen-age boys and girls and women outnumbered adult males within some of the city's biggest enterprises. Although the shoe factory had opened in 1870, the shirt and skirt factories were not launched until the depression was several years old. Native workers continued to predominate, being represented in these

[33] *Daily Eagle*, Jan. 6, 1868; New York, *Sixth Annual Report of the Bureau of Statistics of Labor of the State of New York for the Year 1888* (Albany, 1889), p. 606.

factories in about the same proportion as they were in the labor force as a whole; workers of Irish birth and especially parentage were over-represented.

Considering only male workers who were less than thirty years old in the 1880 census, fourteen percent of those of native and German parentage were enumerated as factory operatives contrasted with twenty-one percent of those of Irish parentage. The importance of factory employment as a leveling upward for the children of the "old" immigration is suggested by the fact that in 1880 only nine percent of the young men with native fathers, seven percent of those with German fathers, and twenty-eight percent of those with Irish fathers appear at unspecified labor compared to eleven percent of the native, twenty-four percent of the German, and fifty-five percent of the Irish males in the 1850 census.

The increase in factory employment and decrease in ordinary labor among the native-born of Irish and German parentage is the only significant evidence of leveling upward between generations in Poughkeepsie's manufacturing during the last half of the century. The immigrant generation set the pattern of self-employment in almost all of the manufacturing and also the construction trades, where their children had much success as shop owners or bosses. Because of their early achievement in custom manufacture, the German-born seem to have prospered as often as the second generation would by the turn of the century and to have done so in a wider range of industries. Where success depended upon manual skills, upward mobility in occupation and property preceded assimilation. Only in the world of the professions, finance, and larger commercial enterprise, where ease with the language, manners, customs, and business practices of Americans counted for more than it did in manufacturing would the more assimilated second generation be the first to find frequent employment.

In summation, tracing occupational careers in one small city, and especially the specific avenues of mobility within and between generations, suggests five important qualifications of traditonal interpretations of the relationship between immigration and industrialization in the mid-nineteeth century. First, in many localities immigrants trained in handicrafts may have delayed rather than hastened the destruction of artisan manufacture by the factory system in their industries. Second, the concentration of immigrants in handicrafts in smaller cities, at least during the fifties and sixties, often resulted in modest and sometimes substantial prosperity for the newcomers, but increasingly became a dead end in the seventies and eighties. Third, where this concentration persisted, the expected difference in mobility between the first and second generation in

America may not appear. Thus, German immigrants in Poughkeepsie at mid-century achieved self-employment more often than their native-born children. Fourth, artisans in the traditional handicrafts, regardless of national origin, rarely entered factories, but their children often did. The transition from artisan manufacture to factory employment fell between generations rather than within careers. Fifth, judging by subsequent occupational mobility only, factory employment had a leveling effect. The subsequent career patterns of the increasing number of both artisans and laborers who took factory jobs are very similar, further blurring previously distinct spheres within manual work. For the children of the Irish, who so often worked at ordinary labor in the first generation, the factory was an important avenue of mobility. Whether most northeastern cities at mid-century—even small ones with similarly diversified economies—resemble Poughkeepsie in these tendencies is yet to be determined.

# Summary
## *John Modell*

It is a lonely task to be asked to wrap up something that is in the process of unraveling. I think it is a beautiful kind of unraveling that has been happening in the last, somewhat contentious hour or hour and a half; and I think there has been, in fact, a heightening sense of tension and disagreement and intellectual involvement throughout the conference. That is a very good sign. I wonder whether we can sustain a basic consensus among ourselves for very much longer and whether we will not proceed to argue—about what we are trying to do as pedagogues, what we are trying to do as historians, and what we are trying to do as sociologists. I don't refute any of these labels, and I think each raises questions of a somewhat different kind.

This is another matter again. What we have in common here, it struck me, is that everyone seems to think that ethnicity is important in some sense. I suppose that is not surprising, given the nature of the gathering, but I am not sure that this is a very good idea. There are people in the world, and there are scholars in the United States, who think that ethnicity is not a particularly important category. I wonder whether it would not have been a good idea to include among ourselves some of these people, people like those ecologists and other wicked people who want to banish ethnicity from our active independent variables. No one has really tried to raise that kind of challenge among us, though I think, in a sense, that the Hershberg and the Glasco papers, among others, sort of partialed it out and asked, "Well, how important in fact was ethnicity?"

Many of the comments from the audience in each of the sessions really took up that point, but there was no one on the program to take it up really consistently and in a not inoffensive manner. Rich Juliani simply raised the question, and Mike Gordon said, "I work a lot on faith." Well, we all work a lot on faith, and perhaps we need to institutionalize among us someone to challenge that kind of faith, someone who works with the opposite faith.

Maybe we are too exclusively historians here. In fact, maybe we are too concerned with the historian's problems in dealing with ethnicity, since others are no less concerned, but in different ways. Maybe it would have been better for us to have been a more mixed group.

It seems to me that essentially three different approaches to ethnicity have been presented here. These are somewhat mushy distinctions, but I would throw them out for what they are worth. One of the approaches essentially maintains that *ethnicity endures*, it sticks around, and is an interesting, and a meaningful thing. Fine! Another approach shows that *ethnicity adapts*: an immigrant culture takes what is present here in this country and in its own inimitable way creates something new, which is an adaptation.

The third approach, which excites me, is that *ethnicity interacts* with what is here. That is, the institutions, the environment that these immigrants and their children face in the United States, are also malleable, changeable. The fact of ethnicity and the fact of immigration do something to alter the environment. Tamara Hareven's paper was very suggestive along these lines, as was David Montgomery's. All three approaches have the great virtue of linking European industrial history and American industrial history. I think that a remark of Hansen was mentioned, but Brinley Thomas was never mentioned here as the person who tried to do this very systematically. Well, maybe it is true and we ought to go along in the direction that Brinley Thomas suggests, perhaps with more concern with culture than he demonstrates, and try to treat the Atlantic World as a single system in which the United States, for example, is resource-rich and population-poor, by contrast with the various European countries. Resource-rich, population-poor, and institutionally and culturally malleable: just look at the Jersey City police.

Something I notice quite generally in the papers presented here, which I myself share, is a real savoring of detail. We are historians, after all, and we love to hear about the successes in Hamilton, Ontario, for example, or something about Mr. Griffin's particular people, or about the distribution of occupations among Irishwomen in the Sixth Ward of New York City. For me these numbers represent people, and I savor these things along with the participants here. Pursuit of such details and their packaging in some kind of attractive form seems to me to be an important task for historians, and I am very happy to see so much of it here. And many details of ethnic life have been linked—if unconsciously—with other institutions of society, though too often still we hear of ethnicity as a quality apart from all others.

Ethnicity, the family, and the factory seem to be interrelated questions, which, in the papers presented here, gain from examination together. Ethnicity and the nature of work is a promising theme; white ethnicity and nativism come out again and again. There was no effort, however, and it may be the size of the temptations allowed or the particular phase that we are in in the development of the new ethnic history, to comprehend an ethnic culture in toto, as a whole. There is no real ethnographic effort, that I see. The new history is all very piecemeal. In this respect it may be that the older ethnic historians have something very important to tell us. We don't know how all these things fit together, or, perhaps, how to *present* them together. There was here no effort to show us how all these things fit together for any particular ethnic group, with the unfortunate cost, I think, that we have a new version of the "old immigrant traits transplanted" idea. We are looking at traits, generally not totally in isolation, thank goodness, but they are traits nonetheless, and we are not seeing the totality of an ethnic culture in transit.

It is significant that we are still messing around with the assimilation-acculturation paradigm, mostly knocking away at it. But even so, almost every paper here has been organized around that particular straw man. I did not see it really treated seriously, though, formally, many of the contributions to this conference seem to have been organized to test the paradigm. It may have a lot more to offer us than that. And maybe we don't need it as a straw man at all.

But do we need a synthetic approach? Do we need a synthesis to replace the assimilation-acculturation paradigm? Do we need some general theme or process to tie together the various studies that we have heard, the various approaches that we have seen to ethnicity? Or can we truthfully go without? Well, of course, that is a question about research strategy for our discipline as a whole and for the other disciplines that follow along in our wake and are interested in the past.

I think that the whole question of the sociology of historiography would be worthwhile for us to think over quite seriously. At the moment forums like ours are the basis for informing one another of where we are going. But this is necessarily a small kind of forum, and even if we can be working fruitfully, working out our own informal understandings in place of formal synthesis, perhaps those people not included among us suffer for our talking in private without putting forth any kind of synthesis to tie the work together. Or perhaps you feel that what we are doing doesn't tie together even in our own heads? I think we, for the most part, do hear something approaching a synthesis orchestrating our efforts, but it's not written into the score, and in the end it is the score that is played.

I myself think that the sophisticated filiopietism that I hear in some of the works here is a good thing, a necessary thing. In part it is a goad to do the work that we are doing. In part, I think, the new filiopietism is a meaningful phenomenon in its own right, having to do with changes in our society. But we really have to begin to ask—I guess we really are asking, for it has come out in criticism of the new filiopietistic works—whether this is the best way to translate the assimilation-acculturation paradigm into testable hypotheses. Are we not setting up total disorder, on one hand, as a straw man, and saying, "No, no there wasn't disorder, there was some kind of order"? Are we not taking very much the easiest way out? Are we, or are we not, just saying that gemeinschaft has been replaced by gesellschaft, but with interludes of ethnicity, some of these of long duration? And if we are, is what we're saying to the sociologists much more than that we choose to look *closer* than they do?

Maybe we ought to be taking on the paradigm as a whole. We have a problem in that our research techniques, as displayed here, seem not to be very well suited to dealing with long-run changes: gemeinschaft to gesellschaft, or assimilation-accommodation-acculturation. It will be perhaps useful to organize our ethnic case studies, as presented here, so that they will fit into a time perspective that will allow us to ask, over a long period of time, whether in fact the hypothesized linear trends—assimilation, acculturation, mobility-to-white-collar, family nuclearization, and rationalization of life in general have taken place.

You can't deal with that kind of question, I think, in a thirty-year period or a fifty-year period, as most of these papers do. So I don't know if we have been giving a fair trial to the classical synthesis. We have to ask whether ethnicity is something that only creates a sort of lumpiness, stickiness, and unevenness in essentially linear processes or whether, indeed, there are no linear processes. We haven't, I think, adopted the long-time perspective that will permit us to do that.

We have made other methodological errors that came out in the papers that I heard, which make it even more difficult to examine the meaning of ethnicity in history over a long period of time. Specifically, we have a particular concern with ethnic and poor people, but they are not all the people there are. The processes that we are talking about, if we are talking about any of these hypothesized linear processes, are societal processes. They don't occur to particular groups, they only occur in a society or a subgroup as a whole. If we take just people who consider themselves members of an ethnic group in 1973, or whatever, or if we deal only with factory laborers, we ignore the whole membership of these groups objectively defined in terms of genealogy. If we do not treat *all* the immigrants and *all* their children—again we are not permitting adequate test. We have a bias toward the poor and the downtrodden which may come from our being in reaction to elite history, but this may be a problem when it comes to actually testing the synthetic view we often claim to be testing.

It seems to me that in this meeting we spent a relatively great amount of time discussing and defining *ethnic,* and a relatively lesser amount of time defining and discussing the other term of the conference, *industrial* or *industrialization.* I, myself, even in a conference whose participants are especially concerned with ethnicity, would have brought the points out the other way around. Perhaps this is my own prejudice, but it seems to me that of the two phenomena, industrialization is the more widespread, the more nearly universal process, the more international. It is the larger process in which perhaps ethnicity and the changes that have taken place in the meaning of ethnicity and immigrant groups have taken place. We should look at the context first, it seems to me, and in this respect I very much admire what is going on at the Philadelphia Social History Project. Studies of Philadelphia's whole population are being prosecuted, and the process of industrial change is examined first, with ethnicity following second. This seems to me to be the best way to elicit the meaning of ethnicity in the context of industrialization.

We have heard remarkably little talk, at any rate, about what industrialization means. "The bottom up" may explain this, but besides the bottom, there are a lot of other things that must be examined in industrialization, things which have a lot to do with ethnicity.

We ought to talk more about the white-collar classes. I guess some of this came out in David Montgomery's paper on how workers were treated, studied, coerced, and led by their employers. But we need to know who these employers and their managers and supervisors and foremen were; we need to know what their ideas were, and we need to know how their lives fitted into the hypothesized shift to modern social relations. We need to know, too, about capital and capital-intensiveness. We heard a little about this when we talked about machinery, but the questions of entrepreneurial behavior—about whether to put in a lot of labor, or put in new machines; whether to try to drive the laborers hard, or whether to just let them come and go—must be faced. These questions bear directly upon skills, machines, capital-intensiveness, the organization of labor, and so forth. And they have to do again with productivity, productivity per capita, wages, and poverty.

I think all these things, all these facts of our industrial history, have to be studied together with the question of what happened to ethnic groups and immigrants. To my mind the concept that surfaced again and again but was not formally articulated is the most important linkage concept: the labor force. What jobs were there; what did these jobs entail; who worked at them? It seems to me this concept gets us down from the industrialization level to the level of what the workers see, to the structure of opportunity. We must look very, very carefully at both the systemic and the individual translations of this notion. In the papers here we see them only sporadically.

Through the structure of opportunity, through the changing labor force, the paths we want to trace are called careers, and that study has begun in some of these papers, but again I think we could systematize it a little more. As I see it, to the labor force and to the structure of opportunity, ethnicity makes a great deal of difference, and this difference is, in the end, political. We have learned, if we have learned anything, that all groups have not had the same kind of access to the labor force. They have separate structures of opportunity. We have now a somewhat segregated labor force, as we had a somewhat segregated labor force in the past. This is a matter of politics, in the broader sense, and we talked about these politics, again, sporadically, here in this meeting. We talked about the police and strikebreaking and a little bit about unions, and that's politics in the sense that I mean. Professor Montgomery's sociological departments seem to me a significant aspect of politics in the broader sense, for such corporate efforts speak to how employers' perceptions were changed about workers' predilections, rights, and obstinacies. We talked very slightly about immigration policy and immigration restriction. But what more important political-economic decisions could be made? And how crucial in understanding the changing structure of opportunities to understand how immigration policy fit into economic policy?

Maybe I should close by coming out on the side of the efficiency expert whose fall from a catwalk into a cauldron of molten metal evoked from Pat Lannigan the exclamation "three cheers for efficiency." I will defy Pat and all my soul-felt feeling for him by reminding you that whatever we think about the blessings of long-range change, catwalks *have* become safer. In fact, efficiency experts have become a little bit more efficient. Our appreciation of the ethnic must not mislead us into accepting an image of a static industrial America, nor our appreciation for the resiliency of the underdog to blind us to the degree to which a context only somewhat of his making affected his world, his career, and his horizons.

# Contributors

GEORGE ALTER is associated with the Philadelphia Society History Project sponsored by the University of Pennsylvania.

LAURENCE GLASCO, Associate Professor of History, University of Pittsburgh. Author of "The Life Cycles and Household Structure of American Ethnic Groups: Irish, Germans, and Native-born Whites in Buffalo, N.Y., 1855," *Journal of Urban History* (May 1975).

CAROLINE GOLAB, Assistant Professor of History and City Planning, University of Pennsylvania. Professor Golab is currently working on a book tentatively titled *Philadelphia's Immigrants, 1870–1920: A Study in Geographic History*.

MICHAEL GORDON received his Ph.D. in history from the University of Rochester in 1976.

CLYDE GRIFFEN, Lucy Maynard Salmon Professor of American History, Vassar College. Coauthor with Sally Griffen of *Natives and Newcomers: The Ordering of Opportunity in Mid-Nineteenth-Century Poughkeepsie, New York,* Harvard University Press, forthcoming.

CAROL GRONEMAN, Research Associate, New York Council for the Humanities and Assistant Professor of History, John Jay College, CUNY. Professor Groneman has served as a member of the faculty of the Sarah Lawrence Summer Institute on Women's History and is cochairman of the Columbia University Seminar on the History of the Working Class. She is working on a study of the Five Points slum in nineteenth-century New York City.

TAMARA K. HAREVEN, Professor of History and Director of the History of the Family Project, Clark University. Professor Hareven is a Fellow at the Harvard Center for Population Studies, editor of the *Journal of Family History*, and associate editor of *Children and Youth in America: A Documentary History*. She is author of *Family and Kin in American Industrial Communities* as well as numerous articles dealing with the history of the family.

THEODORE HERSHBERG, Associate Professor of History and Director of the Philadelphia Social History Project, University of Pennsylvania. Author of many articles appearing in the *Journal of Interdisciplinary History, Journal of Social History,* and *Journal of Family History* and guest editor of "A Special Issue: The Philadelphia Social History Project," *Historical Methods Newsletter* (1976). Professor Hershberg is editor of *Industrialization and Urbanization in Nineteenth-Century Philadelphia: Work, Space, and Group Experience*, Oxford University Press, forthcoming.

BRUCE LAURIE, Assistant Professor, University of Massachusetts at Amherst. Author of several articles on nineteenth-century working-class culture and coeditor with Milton Cantor of *Class, Sex, and the Woman Worker*, Greenwood Press, forthcoming.

DAVID MONTGOMERY, Professor of History, University of Pittsburgh. Author of *Beyond Equality: Labor and the Radical Republicans, 1862–1872* and "The 'New Unionism' and the Transformation of Workers' Consciousness in America, 1909–1922," *Journal of Social History* (1974). Professor Montgomery is currently writing a book on the transformation of work relations and workers' control struggles in industrial America between the 1860s and 1920s.

DOUGLAS V. SHAW, Assistant Professor of Urban Studies and History. Author of "The Politics of Nativism: Jersey City's 1871 Commission Charter," in William Wright, ed., *Urban New Jersey since 1870* and "Immigrants, Politics, and the Tensions of Urban Growth," In Joel Schwartz and Daniel Prosser, eds., *Cities of the Garden State*, Kendall/Hunt, forthcoming.

VIRGINIA YANS-MCLAUGHLIN, Professor of History, Sarah Lawrence College. Author of *Family and Community: Italian Immigrants in Buffalo, 1880–1930* and several articles on immigration and family history.

# Index